Venturing Offshore

The World of Offshore Investing

REPUBLIC OF IRELAND

ISLE OF MAN

LUXEMBOURG

LIECHTENSTEIN

GUERNSEY

JERSEY

SWITZERLAND

ANDORRA

MONACO

GIBRALTAR

CYPRUS

MADEIRA

MALTA

HONG KONG

SEYCHELLES

0   3000   6000 km

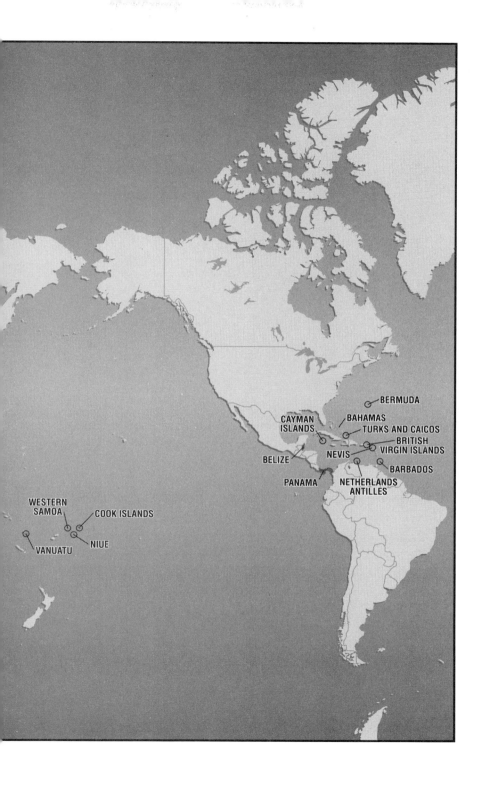

Venturing Offshore

A Guide to Offshore Investing for Canadians

Sunny Handa
Danielle Miller
Richard Smith

Published in 2000 by Stoddart Publishing Co. Limited
34 Lesmill Road, Toronto, Canada M3B 2T6
180 Varick Street, 9th Floor, New York, New York 10014

Distributed in Canada by:
General Distribution Services Ltd.
325 Humber College Blvd., Toronto, Ontario M9W 7C3
Tel. (416) 213-1919   Fax (416) 213-1917
Email cservice@genpub.com

Distributed in the United States by:
General Distribution Services Inc.
85 River Rock Drive, Suite 202, Buffalo, New York 14207
Toll-free Tel. 1-800-805-1083   Toll-free Fax 1-800-481-6207
Email gdsinc@genpub.com

04 03 02 01 00   1 2 3 4 5

Canadian Cataloguing in Publication Data

Handa, Sunny
Venturing offshore: a guide to offshore investing for Canadians

Includes bibliographical references and index.
ISBN 0-7737-6063-6

1. Investments, Canadian.   I. Miller, Danielle, 1970– .
II. Smith, Richard, 1972– .   III. Title.

HG4538.H362 2000   332.67'371   C99-932672-4

Cover design: Kinetics Design & Illustration
Text design: Kinetics Design & Illustration

Printed and bound in Canada

THE CANADA COUNCIL | LE CONSEIL DES ARTS
FOR THE ARTS | DU CANADA
SINCE 1957 | DEPUIS 1957

*We acknowledge for their financial support of our publishing
program the Canada Council, the Ontario Arts Council, and
the Government of Canada through the Book Publishing
Industry Development Program (BPIDP).*

*To our families, for their
love, encouragement, and support,
and to T.B.*

Contents

Preface

*T*his book was a collaborative effort, each author contributing time, energy, and experience. It began as an idea conceived by Sunny Handa and Danielle Miller in Brussels during the summer of 1997. Richard Smith was brought on board in early 1998. The first draft was written largely during the summer, fall, and winter months of 1998–99. We each brought very different backgrounds to this project, and we each learned from the others. It must be said that there is nothing more enjoyable than working with good friends on a project of this nature.

As with many such undertakings, there are a number of people to thank, each of whom helped us along with this project by contributing either time and effort or words of encouragement. We would like to thank the law firm of Fasken Martineau, and more particularly Marc-André Fabien, who provided us with the financial support and resources necessary to bring this project to completion. We would also like to thank Carole Essiembre of Fasken

Martineau for her hard work and good nature as she assembled the research and various drafts of what seemed like a never-ending mountain of paper. Peter Villani graciously reviewed an early draft of this manuscript and provided us with his comments. To Don Bastian of Stoddart Publishing, who believed in and backed this project from beginning to end, and Janice Weaver, who meticulously edited this manuscript, we would like to extend our deepest appreciation.

We would also like to thank Professor Patrick Healy of the Faculty of Law, McGill University, for his suggestions on the chapter on investment scams; Yves Roussell of the RCMP, who gave generously of his time for the same chapter; Leo Kolivakis, who was prepared to meet with and talk to a perfect stranger about offshore financial structures; and of course, Professor Tom Naylor of McGill University, who not only shared much valuable information but also was a source of tremendous support and encouragement. Sunny Handa would like to extend a special thanks to Ronald Fon, a long-time friend whose early interest in offshore investing proved most infectious. Richard Smith also wishes to extend a special thanks to Céline for her extraordinary patience and support during the dog-days of researching and writing this manuscript.

Finally, we would each like to thank our families for their love, encouragement, and support.

Introduction

The idea that we live in a global village has never seemed more true. Recent advances in communications and computer technology, coupled with international harmonization in the world of trade and financial investment, have reduced the importance of national borders. Large multinational businesses have been roaming the globe for years, choosing to set up elements of their operations in whatever jurisdiction best suits them. Today, however, the ability to set up businesses, parts of businesses, or investments in jurisdictions foreign to one's own is accessible to players of all sizes, including individuals with limited investment resources.

Unfortunately, obtaining the education and information necessary to proceed offshore continues to be an obstacle for many smaller players. The offshore world existed, for a long time, in relative secrecy. Advice has traditionally been costly and hard to come by. Offshore books and guides were generally expensive, highly technical texts made accessible mainly to accountants and lawyers.

There is a further problem that has kept offshore investing out of the hands of smaller players. Traditionally, this type of planning has had a reputation associated with tax evasion and crime. This reputation, though possibly deserved in a few cases, is generally without foundation. Offshore planning is not per se illegal, nor is it morally reprehensible. There are rules, both in an investor's home country and in the offshore jurisdiction, that must be followed. The benefits of offshore planning (i.e., asset protection, tax reduction, lax regulations, better investment opportunities) make good economic sense and can be realized without doing anything illegal. However, investing offshore also presents the opportunity to engage in illicit activities and to exploit trans-jurisdictional problems in law enforcement and information-sharing. In sum, offshore investing can be approached either as sensible, aboveboard business and investment planning or as a vehicle to avoid laws.

That said, if you are reading about offshore planning for the first time, you have likely picked up this book thinking that tax reduction or elimination is what offshore investing is all about. While this was true in the past, much has changed in recent years. The Canadian government has, over the past decade, made a concerted effort to eliminate the tax savings used by Canadians investing offshore. Most notably, the government made amendments to the Income Tax Act in 1994. Other rules have also been added, some of which came into force as recently as April 1999. Furthermore, Paul Martin's 1999 budget targeted offshore trusts and investment funds.

The government will investigate these areas carefully to ensure that the tax rules associated with such investment vehicles do not yield any differential tax benefits. In other words, investing offshore for tax reasons is becoming increasingly difficult and requires the use of highly complex and expensive legal structures. We have devoted a considerable portion of this book to discussing the operations of the tax regime that governs Canadian investment offshore and, where possible, have tried to highlight the limited tax benefits that continue to exist. There are certainly still some advantages to offshore planning from a tax-savings point of view, but today it is increasingly about other benefits, such as diversifying your portfolio, protecting assets, and maintaining secrecy.

A number of financial planners and business advisers are moving their operations offshore and are advising clients to do the same with their investments. Often, these clients do not understand the complex rules that apply to them. Texts available on the subject, and these are increasing in number, frequently provide high-level strategies or information without answering the investors' most basic questions. Often novice investors proceed based on misinformation culled through discussions with friends and acquaintances.

The purpose of this book is to provide beginners with an accessible, inexpensive, and readable guide to offshore planning. It has been written and formatted in a friendly style that is suitable for non-expert readers interested in learning about offshore investing. This book is a guide that will consolidate, demystify, and explain offshore concepts. It is *not* a substitute for professional advice from a financial or tax planner, an accountant, or a lawyer. It will, however, prepare you to have an intelligent conversation about the suitability of offshore investing with any of these professionals by introducing you to the main concepts and players.

This guide will be useful to

~ ageing middle- to upper-middle-class individuals with substantial savings or investments who reside in a country that taxes ancillary income and who seek tax-planning opportunities;

~ business people who are seeking to structure all or part of their operations offshore;

~ those who obtain income from jurisdictions other than their country of origin and wish to shelter this money;

~ snowbirds (those who move to warmer climates for significant periods of time each year);

~ corporate executives who are residing outside their country of origin and are seeking tax-planning opportunities in the country where they are working; and

~ others wishing to understand basic offshore legal structures and mechanisms.

The book is divided into four general parts. The first demystifies offshore concepts, informs readers of their options and opportunities when investing offshore, and describes the initial steps that must be taken prior to venturing offshore. Next, we have included several chapters that treat some of the more important tax laws affecting individuals in Canada. The third part profiles several typical offshore investors, alerts you to some common investment-related scams, and tells you how to pull all the concepts together.

The final part of the book provides profile information about a number of countries that are attractive to offshore investors. Information provided includes the pricing of offshore structures (i.e., incorporation costs), filing requirements, corporate requirements (i.e., number of directors, their place of residence), the availability of shelf companies, and so on. Part Four includes this information in both long form and summary form, for ease of reference. It should be noted that the list of countries chosen is not exhaustive; other countries have been omitted because of space considerations.

Although the information provided in this book is a result of hours of tireless research, it is nonetheless a compilation that is fixed at a point in time. The offshore world is ever-changing. While we hope our efforts will give you a glimpse into what goes on in the offshore world, nothing in this book serves as a substitute for obtaining competent professional advice from lawyers, accountants, financial planners, and others specializing in offshore-planning techniques. Offshore planning is so complex that to proceed without such advice is foolhardy at best.

PART ONE

Offshore Basics

Venturing
Offshore

In this chapter, you will learn:
~ Why you should consider offshore planning

All of us have heard about offshore investing. To many, moving money offshore is something affordable to only the rich. We occasionally read about Canada's wealthier families setting up offshore trusts and benefiting from their associated tax advantages. We also read about international finance in the latest best-selling novels. Yet surprisingly little is known by the general public about offshore investing. This, however, is about to change. As recently as twenty years ago, mutual funds were a mystery to many. They were used only by savvy investors and professionals, and the typical fund client was wealthy. Today, even the most inexperienced investor likely holds some form of mutual-fund investment in his portfolio. More important, that same investor likely understands something about how mutual funds work.

Access to mutual funds has opened up to the middle class. You need invest only a few hundred dollars to get started. Why the change? Falling interest rates put pressure on financial institutions to devise alternative products for the middle class. Similarly, the move to cheap information technology and data processing has lowered the transaction costs involved in dealing with smaller investors. The information and advertising campaigns conducted by mutual-fund companies and financial institutions such as banks have been enormous in scope. This has resulted in a slew of books and newspaper and magazine articles that have served to educate the public.

Offshore investing may be following a similar pattern. To date, it has remained within the purview of only the wealthy and knowledgeable investor. But high domestic taxes, creditor risk, improved lower-cost telecommunications, and the Internet have begun to change the face of offshore investing. More financial advisers are starting to recommend offshore products, and often these are as simple as mutual funds investing in foreign companies or bonds. It is our prediction that over the next twenty years, there will be a boom in offshore investing. It will become increasingly organized and institutionalized. Today, although it is no longer shrouded in secrecy and myth as it once was, the offshore-investment industry nevertheless remains relatively fragmented.

Before proceeding any further, it is important that we define, in more precise terms, what is meant by offshore planning. Once that is done, we will discuss the reasons for moving your investments offshore. The chapters that follow address, among other things, various types of offshore structures that can be used to channel these investments. These include offshore corporations, trusts, and bank accounts. Other structures and investments (e.g., mutual funds) will also be discussed throughout the text, although they will not be given any detailed treatment. There are many books on the market and Web sites on the Internet that discuss specific investment opportunities. The purpose of this book is to familiarize you with certain types of offshore structures and techniques, so that you may better evaluate specific investment and planning strategies.

What Is Offshore Planning?

Simply put, offshore planning means placing your money or other negotiable valuables for a given purpose (i.e., growth, income, asset protection from creditors) in a legal jurisdiction other than your own. While this sounds simple enough as a concept, investors of all types know surprisingly little about the many instruments and financial structures that become available to them when they expand their investment horizons beyond their national borders. Most Canadian investors have engaged in limited offshore investing, though they've typically done this without realizing it. International mutual funds are one example of an offshore investment. Investing in U.S. capital markets (for example, buying Microsoft stock listed on the NASDAQ) is another. Indeed, any Canadian holding U.S. equities or bonds is an offshore investor.

Ironically, the term "offshore" has an associated stigma. It evokes visions of slippery financial advisers playing fast and loose with tax rules and other laws. Yet when we think of an offshore investor as any Canadian holding U.S. equities, this negative view quickly dissipates.

Why Go Offshore?

There are many good reasons to invest or place your assets offshore. But before we consider these, it is important to understand that each is effectively related to jurisdictional differences. Moving offshore allows you, for the most part, to leave your home country's legal system for that of another. In many cases, these other countries want to attract foreign investment, and thus will present foreigners with more favourable investment-related rules than are available in their home jurisdictions. Most countries, including Canada and the U.S., provide foreign investors with certain tax and other advantages when they invest their money. Different jurisdictions have targeted different segments of the foreign investment market, with different degrees of aggressiveness.

Those jurisdictions that have been popularly called tax havens have typically provided foreigners with an opportunity to create tax-free legal structures such as companies and trusts that are resident in the haven jurisdiction. For some smaller countries, the service industry that facilitates foreign investment (i.e., lawyers, accountants, banks, trust companies) is a significant, if not the most significant, aspect of their economy.

Of course, when foreigners invest in another country, they are effectively moving money, and therefore potential tax revenues, out of their own country. If you don't have a strong moral position on supporting your domestic social structure, there may be nothing preventing you from moving offshore. There are often, however, complicated and onerous tax rules in place to try to prevent or discourage the flight of capital from a country. For example, a domestic government may tax an offshore trust held by a resident if the resident exercises effective control over the trust's assets. You may also be deemed to sell your assets to yourself, thus triggering a capital gain (or loss), before moving your investments offshore. Another effective way for a government to discourage the flight of capital is to perpetuate the myth that offshore investing is associated with criminal activity and is therefore morally reprehensible. In truth, most offshore investing is above-board and does not violate any laws. Rather, it takes note of the differences between legal systems and investment opportunities, and attempts to exploit those differences.

We turn now to the most oft-cited reasons for investing offshore. Although this list is not exhaustive, it gives a good sense of the flexible nature of and motivations behind investing offshore.

Taxes
Tax Avoidance/Evasion/Planning
With the exception of portfolio diversification (largely through the purchase of global mutual funds), the most popular reason for wanting to invest offshore is to reduce or eliminate taxes. Tax reduction/elimination has traditionally been labelled as either tax avoidance or tax evasion. The former involves operating within the boundaries of the law with the purpose of reducing, deferring, or eliminating taxes payable. Tax evasion, by contrast, is a crime. It involves deceiving the tax authorities about income earned or

other information so that they cannot levy the required amount of tax. Moving your money to an offshore bank account and not declaring the interest earned is a form of tax evasion because, in Canada, a resident is taxed on his or her worldwide income.

Recently a third term, "tax planning," has come into popular use. It serves as a replacement for the term "tax avoidance." Tax legislation in many Western countries, including Canada, now contains general anti-avoidance rules. These rules stipulate that financial structures whose *primary purpose* is to help you avoid the payment of taxes will not, notwithstanding their legality, insulate you. In order to avoid the anti-avoidance rules, you must have some other valid reason for setting up these structures.

As a result of these new anti-avoidance rules, the term "tax avoidance" has been contaminated. Fortunately, tax planning, as a concept, currently exists without any such stigma; it represents the structuring of your financial affairs so as to reduce or even eliminate taxes in a manner that will not offend tax rules, including anti-avoidance provisions. The techniques we'll discuss that affect one's level of taxation can be characterized as tax-planning tips. Of course, you should consult a tax professional skilled in offshore-planning techniques before following any of these tips.

Canadian Tax Rules

It is important to note at the outset that the Canadian tax regime is very strict and imposes a complex set of obligations on Canadians who use offshore investment structures. The purpose of these rules is to eliminate any tax benefit you may have by moving your assets offshore. You will encounter, later in this book, the notion of foreign accrual property income (FAPI) rules. These rules, along with others, force Canadians to disclose income earned offshore and report it as part of their taxable income. Under the FAPI regime, the use of offshore corporations or trusts may not protect any income earned from being taxed in the hands of the individual behind the corporation or trust. New rules, which came into force in April 1999, also require Canadians to report investments held offshore when they total an amount greater than $100,000. In sum, offshore planning for strict tax reduction/elimination is very complex and costly. It is not typically affordable by investors with a middle-class income. Rather, offshore planning should be considered for a combination of reasons (listed below), with tax savings and benefits becoming increasingly less relevant.

Estate Planning

The term "estate planning" broadly refers to the manner in which you set up the components of your estate in order to manipulate the income derived from it. A simple example would be to invest in a Canadian company whose shares have a dividend, as opposed to investing in an interest-bearing instrument such as a savings bond. Under Canadian law, savings bonds are taxed at a higher rate than are dividends of Canadian corporations. Another example would be to shift common shares of a closely held Canadian private corporation, which might reasonably accumulate value in the future, to members of your family who can benefit from an unused capital gains exemption. (Of course, you will have to pay capital gains taxes on the initial transfer of these shares.) This will allow you to limit your future income and thus reduce taxes if you are in a relatively high tax bracket.

Estate planning therefore takes many forms. While there are common techniques used, no specific method is applicable to all. Each person will want to plan his estate based on his situation and preferences (including his acceptance of risk in investing). Offshore planning expands your options in estate planning by presenting a wider range of investment opportunities and structures. Estate planning is intricately related to tax planning, mentioned above, but it also takes into account considerations such as those set out below, including asset protection and secrecy. The term "estate planning" is generally a catch-all.

Threat of Estate/Wealth/Death Taxes

Although Canada no longer imposes death taxes (you are, however, deemed to sell your assets and thus pay capital gains taxes on death unless you can benefit from a rollover provision — for example, on transfers to your spouse) in the Income Tax Act, the topic seems to reappear every few years. For example, Ontario's

NDP government, in power in the early 1990s, was considering introducing a tax payable by an estate on death. The use of a trust mechanism, whether resident offshore or not, may help you avoid the payment of such taxes should they ever be introduced. Of course, the trust, depending on its jurisdiction of residence, may itself be subject to some form of tax.

Avoiding Forced Inheritance Provisions

Offshore planning allows you to avoid forced inheritance provisions in the law. Many jurisdictions have very specific laws relating to successions. In Canada, succession law falls within the jurisdiction of the provinces. When a testator dies, the testator's spouse generally has the right to make an election under the law. This election allows the spouse to override the testator's will and claim a portion of his or her estate. A testator who wishes to circumvent this legal mechanism may use a trust, created during his lifetime for the benefit of another (the testator may even be one of the beneficiaries), to hold his or her assets. By setting up the trust in certain offshore jurisdictions, such as the Isle of Man, a testator (now the settlor of the trust) can avoid these forced inheritance provisions (in the case of the Isle of Man, the Trusts Act of 1995 makes this possible).

Asset Protection

After tax reduction/elimination, asset protection is probably the most popular reason for offshore planning. Asset protection involves placing your assets in a financial structure (such as a trust, a bank, or a corporation) to keep them out of the hands of potential creditors or claimants (i.e., those who have a court-based claim). Asset protection is increasingly popular with professionals based in the U.S. who are exposed to malpractice risk (for example, doctors or directors of companies).

There are various degrees of security that you will obtain when placing your assets offshore. The degree of security will depend on the types of structures used. Typically, an asset-protection trust is used. This structure involves transferring the legal title (as opposed to the beneficial title) of your assets into the hands of a trustee, thus effectively protecting the assets from future creditors who may have a legal claim. The trust acts as a separate legal person capable of holding title to property.

Other structures can also be used to ensure asset protection. For example, certain offshore banking centres have very strong laws in place to ensure secrecy. If creditors cannot find your assets, they may be less likely to take action. Of course, if a court in your domestic jurisdiction orders you to pay an amount, and that amount is hidden in an offshore bank account, you must still, by law, make the payment. It is for this reason that proper asset protection will involve a combination of offshore structures, including an asset-protection trust, an offshore bank account, and even an offshore corporation. A proper asset-protection set-up will ensure that you are legally secure against creditors and even the courts (which are limited to ordering a transfer of your own assets, and not of those held by a bona fide trust). Corporations, trusts, and offshore banking are explained in detail in the chapters that follow.

Divorce Protection

Although it is not the purpose of this book to promote fraudulent transactions or even those that skirt the law (in fact, it is the purpose of this book to show how you can better plan your investments *within* the boundaries of the law), we would be remiss in failing to mention the widespread use of offshore investing to protect assets in cases of divorce. Many jurisdictions, including all provinces in Canada, provide for a form of asset splitting upon divorce. In some cases, a prenuptial agreement may be used to limit the splitting of these assets, but in others not even a prenuptial agreement will suffice. (The law may prohibit the operation of such agreements with respect to certain assets. This is typically the case with a matrimonial home and its furnishings.) If you do not have a prenuptial agreement or cannot benefit from the use of one, offshore investing presents an opportunity to place your movable assets offshore and out of the reach of your spouse. Note that this does not always mean that you are hiding your assets so they cannot be found or claimed. By using a trust structure, for example, you may legally avoid asset splitting upon divorce, as the assets would be held in the name of the trustee for the beneficiaries of the trust and not in your own name. As you can well imagine, having a measure of secrecy attached to the trust provides a double layer of protection; your spouse cannot break open a trust if he or she is not aware of it. Of course, in all cases you will have to consult with an attorney to ensure, in a divorce situation, that you are acting within the bounds of the law.

Anonymity and Secrecy

Intimately related to asset protection is the use of offshore structures to maintain secrecy about your holdings. Secrecy, however, is only one component of asset protection. Strong asset protection will continue to guard your assets even when secrecy has been compromised. Conversely, the goal of maintaining secrecy is not always pursued for reasons of protecting assets from potential creditors or claimants. Some individuals simply value their privacy.

Certain offshore jurisdictions have laws that ensure the concealment of investors' financial holdings. Severe penalties, including jail terms, will be levied against those who compromise an investor's privacy. Some jurisdictions will guarantee absolute secrecy in every situation (of course, there can never be a guarantee of 100 percent secrecy — there are stories of workers at financial institutions being bribed by foreign taxation agents seeking information about investors). Other jurisdictions, including Switzerland, which is renowned for maintaining confidentiality in financial transactions, will share information with foreign governments in certain situations. Typically, these situations include investigations of activities that would constitute a crime in the offshore jurisdiction as well (for example, money laundering). Tax evasion, it should be noted, is typically not considered a situation where information would be shared.

If maintaining secrecy is your goal, you should carefully investigate and assess the rules of the jurisdiction being considered. Of course, you must not forget that tax evasion is a crime in Canada. It is also important to note that Canadian law was recently changed to include a requirement that if you have more than $100,000 invested offshore, you must report to the government the nature of your investments. This rule, which has come under fire (and whose implementation had been delayed) for many years, will militate against Canadians attempting to maintain anonymity and secrecy in their investment planning. It is not clear how this new rule will operate or how effective it will be in terms of deterring offshore planning. It is likely that the outcry from taxpayers will continue unabated, and that the government will be persuaded to lessen the effects of the rule. Already, public pressure has forced the government to implement the rule in such a way that the reporting of investments is to be done on a categorized, as opposed to a specific, basis.

Investment Opportunities/Higher Rates of Return

At its simplest level, offshore investing is about discovering new investment opportunities and earning higher rates of return. Although tax planning, secrecy, and other goals have traditionally attracted the sophisticated offshore investor, the amateur is increasingly being presented with new opportunities for investment. Simple investments such as development bonds (i.e., bonds issued by governments of developing countries) offer investors excellent rates of return at comparatively low levels of risk. Because the flow of money out of Western countries has been so limited in past years, developing countries have had to offer high rates of return at relatively low levels of risk in order to attract investment. Furthermore, such investments may typically be made in Western currencies (i.e., U.S. dollars or British pounds) and do not have to be made in the developing country's currency, which may be susceptible to fluctuation in value. Other examples of offshore opportunities include investing in interest-bearing instruments in other currencies, which guards against fluctuations in your domestic currency, and investing in equities on foreign exchanges, which opens up the number of available companies in which to invest and guards against country-specific risk. (Domestic companies typically trade their stock on local exchanges, which exposes investors to country-specific risks in addition to company-specific risks. Diversifying your equity portfolio across several countries vastly reduces country-specific risk.)

In short, offshore investing presents you with a number of investment opportunities that can be tailored to suit your particular financial situation and preferences. Having a greater number of investment opportunities allows you to diversify your portfolio, eliminating certain forms of risk. Furthermore, owing to the newness of offshore investing, there are still bargains to be had in certain jurisdictions. An awareness of these bargains allows you to earn a higher rate of return. In sum, some form of offshore investment makes good sense for every investor.

Work Done Abroad

If you work in a jurisdiction other than your home jurisdiction, you may want to keep the money abroad. There are several reasons for doing this, including the desire to minimize taxes. You may wish to incorporate in a third jurisdiction a company that would bill for the work done. The amounts paid to the company would then remain with the company paying taxes, if any, in the offshore jurisdiction. The money could then be repatriated to your home country by way of dividends or another tax-favourable manner, and in annual sums that suit your particular situation (i.e., so as not to push you into the highest bracket). Of course, there are many other more effective structures that may be used. The tax rules associated with Canadians working abroad are extremely complicated. We treat them in some detail in the chapters that deal with taxation.

Relaxed Regulation

Investing offshore allows you to benefit from investment instruments that may not be available in your home country owing to regulatory requirements. Of course, these requirements are often imposed for good reason, such as the protection of small investors. However, in some cases the regulations are overly rigid and do not permit flexibility in developing financial products. Offshore jurisdictions with lax regulations may present excellent investment opportunities. But you must realize that the comfort associated with knowing that a financial institution is being carefully scrutinized by regulators will be gone. *Caveat emptor* (buyer beware) is an important rule to remember.

Political and Economic Stability

It seems counterintuitive to argue that a reason for investing off-shore is to take advantage of political stability. After all, offshore jurisdictions have the reputation of being small islands with frequent coups. This is more myth than reality, however. Consider, for example, offshore centres such as Switzerland and its tradition of banking. Conversely, consider Canada and its difficulties with Quebec, a province that is perpetually engaged in a struggle to separate. Should such a separation ever occur, the political and economic consequences will likely be severe. Quebec and Canada have been living with this uncertainty for some twenty years. For Canadians, investing assets in a country such as Switzerland may, in fact, act as a shield against domestic political and economic instability.

Currency Stability

A related reason for investing offshore is to shield your money from fluctuations in currency-exchange rates. Throughout 1998, many of the world's currencies began to readjust (lose) their value. Of course, when a currency loses its value, it is losing it vis-à-vis another currency — typically, the U.S. dollar. There are many other currencies that are also considered safe harbours in times of crisis, such as the Swiss franc.

Currency Controls

Another related concern is the potential for currency controls (exchange restrictions). Arguably, this risk has traditionally been low for Canadians, as the Canadian economy is heavily dependent on international trade. Nevertheless, with increasing instability in currency-exchange rates (recall the drops in the value of the Canadian dollar in 1998), the risk of currency restrictions, though still low, is now greater than it has traditionally been.

Snowbirds

"Snowbirds" is a term used to refer to individuals who choose to spend their winters in warmer, sunnier climates. Given the harshness of the Canadian winter, it is not surprising that there are many Canadian snowbirds. For example, many Quebecers and Ontarians, especially those at or near retirement age, spend their winters in Florida and their summers in Canada. There are several reasons to retain links with your home country, as opposed to moving to the warmer climate year-round. There are nationalist reasons, family reasons, and in the case of a Canada-U.S. comparison, issues such as publicly funded health care (insurance can be prohibitively expensive for older Canadians who move to the U.S.).

For snowbirds, it is often desirable to maintain investments in the offshore jurisdiction (i.e., the place where they have their winter home). Keeping offshore accounts is convenient, offers increased diversification in investment products and opportunities, and helps hedge against currency risks. The information in this book, especially that concerning the operation of Canadian offshore tax rules, will assist snowbirds in assessing their financial position.

Accumulation of Income Prior to Retirement
Another reason to consider investing offshore is to set up a retirement position in another jurisdiction to be used sometime in the future. By setting up a retirement trust for yourself or your spouse, you can accumulate income in the hands of the trust. It will be taxed at the foreign tax rate. Of course, as will be discussed, this type of set-up is subject to Canadian taxation-attribution rules. To be effective, the trust must be set up in such a way as to satisfy a myriad of Canadian tax rules.

Expansion of Business Abroad
In addition to improving personal financial-planning situations, offshore planning is often used to expand domestic business operations abroad (or to begin new businesses abroad). Canadian companies wishing to do business in a foreign country have available many opportunities to structure their offshore operations in a financially beneficial manner. For example, a business wishing to expand to India may consider setting up a company in Mauritius. Mauritius and India have a tax treaty whereby Mauritian companies operating in India do not have to pay Indian company taxes.

The Mauritian taxes payable are, by contrast, extremely low for companies operating abroad. If a Canadian firm sets up directly in India, taxes will have to be paid at the higher Indian rate.

Offshore Insurance

Although it's beyond the scope and intended complexity of this book, some mention should be made of the practice of offshore insurance, as you will likely encounter it in your travels through the offshore financial world. Simply put, offshore insurance involves setting up an offshore corporation that can serve to insure your onshore risks. In many offshore jurisdictions, setting up an insurance company may help you avoid many regulatory hurdles; you will therefore be liable for lower transaction costs. This is especially the case when an offshore insurance company is in the business of insuring a risk that is not located in the offshore jurisdiction (and that has equity holdings held by persons resident outside of the jurisdiction). Offshore insurance companies are typically set up by large domestic businesses that need to be insured. Consequently, it is likely that you will not need to know about setting up your own such company.

Conclusion

In truth, most people choose the offshore alternative for many of the reasons listed above. Two of the most popular have traditionally been tax reduction and asset protection. Because the financial structures used will differ with the goal being sought, offshore financial planning can become quite complex. It is therefore not unusual to see trusts, international business (or exempt) corporations, and banking arrangements used in conjunction with one another. It is also not unusual to see each of these structures maintained in separate jurisdictions. That said, there is no single "magic formula" for these arrangements — they will vary with the rules of the jurisdictions and the risk tolerance of the persons involved. For example, a complex structure would not make sense to someone wishing to invest $20,000 offshore. If you do not have a significant sum to invest, you should consider more modest offshore products, including mutual funds, bonds (state-sponsored bonds and corporate bonds), equity investments, and even offshore bank accounts (which may pay high rates of interest).

Once you have set up your offshore investment, it is simply a matter of adding to it as you go. Over ten years, you will find that the amounts can grow to very large sums. Of course, if you have not implemented a proper tax-planning strategy, you risk having to pay high taxes in the jurisdiction in which you are resident (i.e., Canada). We discuss these tax rules in detail in the chapters that follow. But implementing a proper tax-planning strategy, in light of Canadian tax rules, can be a very expensive and difficult task. For many modest investors, it is best to avoid becoming obsessed with tax reduction and elimination. While it is important that you consider the tax implications of your investment strategy, you will often find that with modest investments, there is little you can do. (You may, for example, choose to invest in foreign equities instead of interest-bearing instruments in order to take advantage of the reduced tax payable for capital gains.) Nevertheless, offshore planning for such investors should still be considered for the other reasons mentioned (such as diversification and better investment opportunities). Even if you cannot employ expensive tax-reduction strategies, you will have more net after-tax income.

Offshore Corporations

In this chapter, you will learn:
~ *The basic rules associated with owning and operating a corporation*
~ *The differences between onshore and offshore corporations*
~ *The basic uses of offshore corporations*

*T*here are many types of mechanisms or structures that can be used to plan your offshore investments. These structures are creations of legislation in the offshore jurisdiction. Additional offshore structures are continually being designed by those jurisdictions that cater to foreign investment so they can meet new needs and remain competitive. After all, being able to attract foreign investment means big business to a country.

In this chapter, we examine a number of these investment structures, beginning with the three that are most frequently used: the corporation, the trust, and the bank account. Each of these is a fundamental vehicle upon which other structures can be built. Furthermore, offshore structures can be combined with one another to form new investment structures that present altogether new benefits. While this may sound vague and complicated at this point, it will become quite clear as you read on.

The Corporation

Everyone is familiar with the term "corporation." We deal with corporations on a daily basis, whether we're paying our phone bill to the phone company (a corporation) or doing our shopping at the grocery store (typically a corporation). Most people, when asked to define a corporation, will reply, "It's a company." This is only half right. A company is a business entity that may be a sole proprietorship, a partnership, or a corporation. Each of these structures is treated differently under the law. Sole proprietorships mean that one individual is owner, director, and manager of the company. The sole proprietor is liable for all the debts of the company, and also collects all of the revenues. A child who mows lawns in his neighbourhood is running a sole proprietorship. Typically, you need register with a government authority only to use a name other than your own (for example, XYZ Lawn Mowers) and to collect sales taxes (i.e., GST and PST) if your revenues exceed a certain amount (at the time of this writing, $30,000 a year).

Partnerships are similar to sole proprietorships, except that several persons own the company. Each co-owner is personally jointly and severally liable for the debts of the partnership, with the exception of limited partners (whose participation must be disclosed to third parties). Income earned via the partnership is divided up between the partners and forms part of each partner's personal income for tax purposes. Partnerships may have to be registered with a governmental authority, depending on the jurisdiction.

Both sole proprietorships and partnerships are essentially extensions of an individual's capacity to conduct business as a person (this concept will become clearer as you read on). Each individual, at the end of the day, is personally responsible for the business's fortunes and failures.

This brings us to the third type of company structure: the

corporation. A corporation is different from sole proprietorships and partnerships in that, under the law, a corporation is a "person" in its own right. Corporations are owned by other persons (shareholders, who may be either individuals or corporations), controlled by directors, and managed by officers. Each corporation has a residence in its own right, which has nothing to do with the residence of its owners. A corporation may earn profits or it may lose money. Such gains and losses affect the net worth of the corporation, and in turn the value of the shares held by shareholders. However, the corporation's profits and losses do not directly affect the earnings of the shareholders. Each corporation files its own tax returns, which are separate and apart from those of its shareholders. Typically, shareholders will account for their dealings with a corporation only when they are paid dividends on shares, or when they sell the shares and incur either a capital gain or a capital loss.

Corporations are creations of law. Consequently, the exact details as to the rights, obligations, method of constitution, filing requirements, fees and taxes payable, as well as all other aspects of corporate existence, may differ among jurisdictions. These differences can become very important when choosing a jurisdiction within which to incorporate.

As mentioned, the rights of ownership and power over management of a corporation are separate. Each year (the time period may vary from jurisdiction to jurisdiction), shareholders collectively vote in the corporation's board of directors. The board, once elected, is responsible for carrying out the business of the corporation in the best interests of the corporation and of its shareholders as a whole. The board of directors is responsible for strategic planning and direction, and will often meet to address important issues concerning the business of the corporation. The actual daily running and operations of the corporation are the responsibility of the corporation's officers (i.e., the president, the vice-presidents, and the other managers). Large corporations will often be set up in a hierarchical form, with many layers of management. Finally, there are the corporation's employees, who produce the products and generate the services that bring the corporation its revenues (technically speaking, officers are also employees). Of course, smaller corporations may have only a single individual in all of the roles mentioned: shareholder, director, and officer.

At this point, the benefits of incorporation may still be unclear. While there are many advantages to owning a corporation (for example, limiting your personal liability), we will use a simple tax-saving example to illustrate one group of benefits. Individuals in Canada pay taxes on an exponentially increasing scale. As an employee of a company, an individual must pay taxes on the amount he draws as a salary. Let's assume such an individual also runs a business out of his home after hours. Each dollar he earns as a sole proprietor of this business is added to his annual income. He must therefore pay taxes on this money at a relatively high tax rate. If, however, he incorporates this home business, the corporation will be earning the money, not the individual. The corporation must still pay taxes, but the corporate tax rate, depending on the individual's particular circumstances, may be lower than his personal tax rate.

As a shareholder of a corporation, an individual will not have immediate rights to the money earned by the corporation. He will have to employ a mechanism to withdraw these funds. Three such mechanisms are to declare dividends on the shares, to take the money out as an employee or contractor, and to allow the money to accrue in the corporation and sell it to another. All three methods can be used individually or be combined to maximize the tax savings for the individual.

The Offshore Corporation

Apart from legal differences based on the jurisdiction chosen, the offshore corporation operates in much the same way as a domestic corporation. The benefit of keeping the corporation offshore is that the corporation's residence — and thus the laws it must obey — is of a different jurisdiction from that of the individual. The ability to situate your wealth in a different jurisdiction allows you, in effect, to "shop around" for the legal system that best suits your purposes. Choosing a different tax system is but one benefit of this. A more favourable regulatory system for governing financial securities (e.g., for those wishing to run their own mutual funds) would be an example of another benefit.

Incorporating a company offshore allows you to create an artificial person whom you control; this person has a different residence and operates under different laws. This is a fundamental principle of offshore investing; it's that simple. This book will build on this concept of splitting your financial personality, and will discuss why and how offshore structures, such as the corporation, can be used to benefit a host of individuals with different socio-economic backgrounds.

Next, we will discuss the three most typical forms of incorporation available to the offshore investor: the regular corporation, the exempt corporation, and the international business corporation (IBC). Of course, not every jurisdiction will support all of these corporations, and the definitions that follow are generalizations only. Be sure to investigate the corporate forms offered in each jurisdiction and study their features. Each will be different, even if only slightly.

The Regular Corporation

The regular, or domestic, corporation is just that: it is the traditional corporate entity used by local persons to conduct business primarily within the jurisdiction of incorporation. Many jurisdictions — including Canada, for example — support only a single type of corporation (while it is true that in Canada you may incorporate provincially or federally, both types of corporations are generally treated similarly under the law). International business corporations and exempt corporations are the brainchildren of jurisdictions seeking to become offshore centres. Thus when you speak of a regular corporation in an offshore context, you are referring to a type of corporation generally not available to foreigners who wish to reside offshore and not involve themselves directly in the daily business of the jurisdiction of incorporation. Regular corporations are generally taxed relatively highly compared with their international business and exempt counterparts, with the expectation that they will use the resources and services of the jurisdiction.

The Exempt Corporation

Exempt, or non-resident, corporations are vehicles designed to attract foreign investment. They represent a halfway point between regular and international business corporations. In fact, the decision to allow exempt corporations is for many jurisdictions a first step to becoming an offshore centre. The international business corporation, often a later creation, makes use of modernized corporate features to attract additional business.

The International Business Corporation

The term "international business corporation" is typically used by Caribbean offshore havens. Jurisdictions that do not offer incorporation under this specific term may nonetheless offer similar structures under different names. For the purposes of this book, we use the term broadly to refer to similarly structured corporations, whether they are called international business corporations (IBCs) or not.

As corporate animals, international business corporations have evolved to suit the needs of and to attract foreign investors. IBCs are often restricted to operating outside the offshore jurisdiction in which they are incorporated. In other words, they cannot transact business within that jurisdiction.

If you set up an international business corporation, you will obtain the benefits of using a corporation as a basic investment structure (as discussed earlier in this section), as well as the benefits of specific differences in legal rules in the offshore jurisdiction being considered. We turn now to a list of these benefits.

Choosing a Jurisdiction

As every offshore jurisdiction will offer different benefits to international business corporations, it is important to have some idea of what features may be available and how they will affect your investment needs. In this section, we set out some, though by no means all, of the features that merit careful consideration when choosing an offshore jurisdiction in which to incorporate.

Because the most important consideration is typically the

reduction or elimination of taxes payable, it is important to choose a jurisdiction with a low or non-existent corporate tax rate. It is also worth considering whether the jurisdiction has a double-tax treaty with your home country or with the jurisdiction to which you wish to repatriate funds. Having a company situated in a tax-treaty jurisdiction will allow you to minimize or eliminate withholding taxes when repatriating funds through the payment of dividends or royalties (if those funds are repatriated to a treaty state). Non-treaty jurisdictions typically charge little or no corporate tax (though they may charge an annual company fee) and do not have any taxation treaties with any other countries. These jurisdictions often market themselves in this fashion. Furthermore, such jurisdictions often have strict secrecy legislation preventing the sharing of information with tax authorities or others who may be investigating the affairs of shareholders of an offshore company.

In deciding whether to set up your corporation in a treaty or non-treaty jurisdiction, you must consider the nature of your investment or business in that jurisdiction. When it comes to investing and keeping money offshore, a non-treaty state is often instinctively preferred by novice offshore investors. This is also true when an investor wants to use the offshore jurisdiction as a launching point for his or her business. But given Canadian taxation rules, this may not be the wisest choice — unless you wish to engage in tax evasion. Setting up in a double-taxation treaty country allows you to do things above-board, and to benefit from the typically lower treaty tax rate. For example, if you plan to use your offshore corporation as a conduit for the import or export of goods, you may wish to choose a nation that has tax treaties with the key jurisdictions with which you are doing business. Using a tax-treaty state may also be beneficial if you hold intellectual property as part of an ongoing domestic business. In such a case, it might be wise to set up an offshore holding company, which would hold the intellectual property and license it to others. The royalties could then be kept offshore and brought back onshore with only minimal withholding taxes payable in the offshore jurisdiction. Domestic taxes would likely be substantially reduced if the right jurisdiction is chosen.

Another feature worth considering when choosing where to incorporate is the offshore jurisdiction's companies' law. Many jurisdictions seeking to entice the use of their international business corporations offer the following benefits:

~ high degrees of secrecy;

~ limited set-up and annual fees;

~ limited reporting requirements (or sometimes none);

~ the ability to issue bearer shares, whereby no shareholder is identified or registered with the company or with the regulatory authority that governs companies;

~ no employment rules with respect to resident corporations;

~ no residence rules for shareholders or directors of the company (this means you will be able to remain abroad);

~ no requirement for a registered office within the jurisdiction;

~ no taxes on income earned through investment or other business dealings;

~ directors' and shareholders' meetings that can be held anywhere;

~ no taxes on income earned or capital held;

~ tax treaties with key jurisdictions;

~ no exchange controls;

~ no minimum capital requirements;

~ no annual audits; and

~ nominee directors and shareholders.

We have deliberately omitted explanations for items in the above list, as they are self-explanatory. This list can act as a detailed checklist for evaluating a jurisdiction in which you are considering incorporating a company. But it is important to note that the above is essentially a wish list. You should not expect to find all of these elements in one jurisdiction. Rather, you will have to prioritize and rank those characteristics that best fit your needs, and then examine whether they are present in the jurisdiction you are considering.

Uses of Offshore Corporations

There are many important and beneficial uses of international business corporations. Although the subject of personal offshore planning is treated more carefully in the tenth chapter, "Profiles," which lays out examples of personal offshore-planning techniques and how they may apply to different individual situations, here we limit ourselves to uses of offshore corporations in both a personal investment and an operational business context. We do not treat trusts, bank accounts, or other offshore structures here and mention only some popular methods of using international business corporations.

We have already discussed the possible taxation benefits that come with using offshore corporations, but there are many other benefits. An important reason for incorporating offshore is to limit your liability (this is also an important consideration when setting up a domestic corporation). By creating a fictive legal person, the company's owner (shareholder) is shielding himself from liability. (If you also serve as a director, there are a few cases where you cannot be shielded, such as with criminal offences and environmental abuses, but these will depend on the jurisdiction in which the corporation resides and/or operates.) Additionally, setting up an offshore corporation gives you an international profile. This may be an important factor in convincing clients or other investors that you are a sophisticated business person. There are, of course, many other compelling reasons to set up offshore companies. We will now deal with some of the more important of these, organized according to the type of activity for which you wish to plan.

Investment Companies

With both business and personal investing, it is common to use the international business corporation to hold your investment portfolio. As a legal person, a corporation is capable of holding personal property, including currency, mutual funds, stocks, and bonds. Tax rates paid by corporations, especially those in certain offshore jurisdictions, may be significantly lower than your onshore personal tax rates. But as you will see in the chapters that follow, the use of offshore corporations in this way may trigger tax-ation-attribution rules, thus nullifying these benefits. Avoiding these rules requires a complex and expensive tax-planning strategy, which is not generally accessible to middle-income investors.

In some cases, the corporation may be set up in a jurisdiction that has a double-taxation treaty with the controlling shareholder's home country. In such a case, any funds repatriated to the home country may be eligible for a tax credit, providing taxes have been paid in the corporation's jurisdiction.

Other important benefits include confidentiality, as well as the opportunity to invest in financial products that would not other-wise be available to an individual (for example, U.S. citizens are barred from investing in certain countries or financial instruments).

International Trading (Import/Export Companies)

For those involved in international trading (i.e., the import/export business), an international business corporation can provide many benefits. Its simplest use is as an intermediary conduit between the exporting and the importing jurisdictions. In other words, if you wish to buy shirts in country A and import them for sale into country B, the establishment of an intermediary international business corporation in country C may allow you to reduce taxes payable. The country C company would purchase the shirts from country A and sell them at a higher rate to the final destination, country B. In other words, the profits would accumulate with the international business corporation in country C, which would pre-sumably be a low- or no-tax jurisdiction. As the purchase price in country B would be high, the profit made on the retail sale would be relatively low and would therefore not attract a great amount of taxes payable.

Of course, as is generally the case with Canadian taxation rules, nothing is ever that simple. Under the foreign accrual property income (FAPI) rules, as amended in 1994 (Section 95(2)(a.1) of the Canadian Income Tax Act), the company in country C, in this example, would be considered to be a controlled foreign affiliate, and marking up goods in this way would result in a tax payable by

the Canadian owner of the corporation. However, when the foreign corporation (the company in country C) adds to the value of
the good (for example, by processing some part of it), the FAPI
rules can be avoided. If the good is originally manufactured in the
jurisdiction in which the offshore company is located, you may
also avoid the FAPI rules. In other words, using an offshore structure for importing goods can be effective from a taxation point of
view, providing that careful attention is paid to onshore taxation
rules. A competent taxation adviser/financial planner who is conversant in offshore-planning techniques should be able to guide
you through the establishment and execution of such a structure.

Intellectual Property Holding Company

Increasingly, investors are using offshore vehicles to become
involved in the licensing of intellectual property. "Intellectual
property" refers to informational products and includes ideas and
their expression, trademarks, trade names, goodwill, and other
intangible creations. Intellectual property does not occupy physical space, but rather is made up of organized information or data
(a computer program would be an example of a piece of intellectual property).

A numbers of laws protect forms of intellectual property
(though not all forms of intellectual property are necessarily protected). Examples of these laws include copyright laws, trademark
laws, patent laws, trade secret laws, and laws protecting semi-
conductor chips. Intellectual property laws operate on a national,
as opposed to international, basis. This means that intellectual
property that is protected in one jurisdiction may not be protected
(or may be protected differently) in another jurisdiction. There are
international treaties that attempt to harmonize these rules, but
protection is nonetheless the responsibility of each national government. As Western economies move towards a greater reliance on
information and intellectual property products, offshore-planning
tools are becoming an increasingly popular aspect of their licensing.

The simplest and most common method of using an offshore
company to benefit a seller or licensor of intellectual property is to
establish one in a low-tax jurisdiction and assign all intellectual

property rights to it. An assignment is simply a conveyance, or transfer, of those rights and is generally in the form of a written assignment agreement. Once the offshore company is in possession of the intellectual property, it can license it back to licensees in various jurisdictions. The licence fees or royalties that are paid back to the offshore company can then be accumulated at low- or no-tax rates, depending on the jurisdiction in which you are incorporated and the double-taxation treaties available. Repatriating these funds to the original assignor of the intellectual property is also an important part of deciding which jurisdiction is best. Those with good double-taxation treaties with your home jurisdiction will allow you to repatriate the monies and pay considerably less in taxes than would be the case in a jurisdiction where this structure is not used.

Property Ownership

Offshore companies can also be used to own property in foreign jurisdictions, and thus reduce taxes payable in that jurisdiction (especially capital gains and property transfer taxes). For example, a Canadian who owns a corporation that is based in an offshore jurisdiction, and that in turn owns property in another country, could, depending on the jurisdiction, avoid capital gains taxes when selling the property. The United Kingdom would be an example of a jurisdiction where a capital gain would not be taxed. By contrast, owning property and selling it in Canada would trigger a capital gains tax payable by the property owner (either a corporation or an individual). Of course, in both examples, Canadian tax rules may still potentially apply to the investor owning the corporation, but the point is that you would not pay taxes on the initial capital gain in the offshore jurisdiction.

Specialty Regulated Industries

Certain industries, such as the film industry, often have protectionist measures associated with them. In those cases, a film company may have to be resident in a particular jurisdiction in order to comply with regulatory requirements or to otherwise benefit from local laws. For example, in the fields of telecommunications and broadcasting in Canada, there are restrictions on who may conduct certain types of businesses (e.g., a Canadian telecommunications carrier must be a Canadian corporation). If you wish to conduct certain types of business in foreign jurisdictions, it may be necessary to incorporate in that jurisdiction. Remember, every jurisdiction but your own is an offshore jurisdiction.

Shipping Companies

Those of you who are interested in buying a boat or ship would be well served to use an offshore corporation to do so. Certain offshore jurisdictions (including the Isle of Man, Jersey, Cyprus, and the Bahamas) have extremely low registration fees and provide exemptions for income derived from shipping activities. Registration of the craft in certain British protectorates will also enable you to fly the British flag, as well as to obtain other prestigious benefits associated with such a registration. All of this is possible by incorporating an offshore company that will own the craft.

Using Double-Taxation Treaties to Your Advantage

Canada has entered into a number of double-taxation treaties with various countries. If you run a business in an offshore jurisdiction that has entered into one of these double-taxation treaties, you will be able to pay taxes (generally lower than those in Canada) in the offshore jurisdiction and then repatriate the funds to Canada as dividends. For larger companies, where it makes good business sense to break up functions such as marketing, data processing, warehousing, and so on, setting up various subsidiaries in such jurisdictions may prove quite lucrative.

Forming offshore corporations with a view to benefiting from double-taxation treaties does not apply only to links with Canada. Setting up a company in a low-tax offshore jurisdiction that has a beneficial tax treaty with a third jurisdiction may also prove quite lucrative. An example would be setting up a Mauritian corporation that invests in India. Obtaining a certificate of tax residence in Mauritius will permit you to take full advantages of the Indo-Mauritian Double Taxation Agreement. When a Mauritian company owns an Indian subsidiary, the subsidiary may repatriate funds to the Mauritian parent at a very low tax rate. In this way, you can set up a series of international offshore corporations that, through the payment of dividends, capital gains, or interest from one to the other, may result in tax savings.

Canadian Immigrant Trusts

Although the examples in this section deal with corporations, it is important to mention the Canadian immigrant trust. We thought it would make better sense to place it here, among examples of other offshore-planning advantages, than anywhere else in the book. Immigrants coming to Canada have at their disposal the opportunity to set up a Canadian immigrant trust under the Income Tax Act. These discretionary trusts may be set up in offshore jurisdictions. They are eligible to earn tax-free income and tax-free capital gains for up to five years. On the first day of January of the fifth year, this tax-free period terminates. It is often recommended that if you are considering immigrating to Canada, you do so as close to January 1 within a new year as possible. This type of trust is designed to encourage immigration to Canada by those who have substantial assets but fear high Canadian tax rates. In the 1999 budget, Finance Minister Paul Martin recommended that this five-year exception for new immigrants continue to apply, notwithstanding other recommended changes, to non-resident trust taxation rules.

Offshore Trusts

In this chapter, you will learn:
~ *A brief history of trusts*
~ *Basic trust concepts*
~ *Ways to constitute and deal with a trust*

*T*his chapter deals with trusts. Although the term "trust" is generally well known (we have trust companies, etc.), little is known about how trusts function. There are many forms of trusts — the concept is a fluid one and is not tightly fixed in law. The word "trust," when used in everyday conversation, refers to two types of trusts: *inter vivos* and testamentary. A testamentary trust is one that is created on the death of a settlor. For the purposes of offshore investing, the *inter vivos* trust, created during the lifetime of the settlor, is of greater interest.

Both testamentary and *inter vivos* trusts are known as express trusts. They are created at the express will of the settlor. Other types of trusts may be created implicitly, by operation of law (in Canada these are either constructive or resulting trusts). We will consider only the two forms of express trusts.

At their most basic level, trusts represent a legal relationship among three parties: the settlor, the beneficiaries, and the trustee(s). A trust involves a division of ownership rights to a piece of property between the trustee and the beneficiaries. A settlor is the person who constitutes (creates) the trust and transfers property to it. Once the trust is constituted, legal title to the property passes to the trustee and beneficial (also known as equitable) title to the beneficiaries.

Splitting the legal title and the beneficial title is the action at the core of the trust concept. Legal title allows the trustee to deal with and control the property at law. For example, a trustee who has legal title over funds may deposit them into and withdraw them from a bank. But a trustee's legal title comes with one important caveat: a trustee must exercise it for the benefit of the beneficiaries of the trust. Trusts may be constituted with specific terms or may give the trustees discretionary rights. In either case, the trustee must always act in accordance with the terms of the trust for the beneficiaries of the trust. If a trustee fails to act in such a manner, he or she will be in breach of trust, and may be sued by the beneficiaries.

History

The modern trust has its origins in the office of the chancellor in England (today known as the Courts of Chancery or Courts of Equity). The chancellor, a representative of the king, could issue decisions granting relief to those who had been unable to find justice before the common-law courts. A citizen could turn to the chancellor if the common-law courts either had been bound by precedent cases in such a way that the judgement was unfair or had been unfairly influenced by the other party in the case (often a wealthy landowner). The chancellor's decisions were made on a case-by-case basis; they were not to form part of the common law. Nevertheless, as these situations increased in frequency, certain trends in the chancellor's decisions became evident. This parallel system of justice became known as the law of equity.

It is with the law of equity, and not the common law or statute, that trusts had their beginnings. Specifically, it was equity as applied to the law of uses. In England, under feudal law, an heir to a property who had not reached the age of majority would have to pay a tax to the feudal lord. To spare their beneficiaries from this tax, testators would transfer the land to persons who had reached the age of majority (known as feoffees), though it would remain for the use of the true heirs. While the scheme generally worked beautifully, in some cases the feoffee would ignore the testator's wishes and would not act in the interests of the true heirs. The common-law courts were powerless to compel the feoffee, as the legal title to the land was his. As a result, the minor heirs turned to the chancellor in equity. The chancellor, not wanting to conflict with the system of legal entitlement as established in the common law, chose instead to impose on the feoffee a set of obligations requiring that his legal entitlement to the property be exercised only for the benefit of the true heirs. The chancellor had split the concept of ownership into legal and beneficial ownership. Gradually, as case after case came before the chancellor, a body of law began to develop. This represented the beginnings of the law of trusts in common-law jurisdictions. But what about trusts in civil-law jurisdictions?

The term "civil-law jurisdiction" (also known as a civilian legal system) is often confused with the term "civil law" (which is the law governing the relations between persons). Civilian legal systems are to be contrasted with common-law legal systems. The common law draws its laws from past legal decisions; civilian systems of law, in theory, impose their legal principles from a civil code. The civilian system of law dates back to Roman times; its modern roots are in the French Napoleonic code. Civil-law systems are in force throughout most countries of the world, including France, Switzerland, Liechtenstein, Luxembourg, Guernsey, Jersey, and Scotland, as well as in the state of Louisiana and the province of Quebec. Common-law jurisdictions include much of Canada, the United States, Australia, New Zealand, and England (as well as all former British colonies). Offshore jurisdictions, therefore, may be either common-law or civil-law jurisdictions.

The concept of the trust as formed through the law of equity is, owing to its roots, foreign to civil-law systems. Nevertheless, countries with civil-law systems often have similar arrangements, though with a different historical basis and legal grounding (and sometimes a different vocabulary of terms). Some jurisdictions, such as Quebec, support the concept of a trust that operates in more or less the same manner as a trust in a common-law jurisdiction. Another civil-law jurisdiction, Austria, supports the *Anstalt,* a cousin of the trust. To prevent the law from diverging too much from place to place, many civil-law jurisdictions have signed the 1984 Convention on Law Applicable to Trusts (adopted by the Hague Conference on Private International Law, also known as the Hague Convention, a convention that standardizes international trust rules). Among other things, the Hague Convention defines both trust and trustee as legal entities, as well as setting out a trustee's powers and obligations, the rights of third parties to break a trust, and the applicable choice of law for a trust. Although the Hague Convention provides some measure of comfort in those civil-law jurisdictions that have adopted it, it is generally better for an investor seeking to structure his affairs using a trust to use a common-law jurisdiction, at least for the creation and legal residence of the trust. That said, those jurisdictions that have gained notoriety as tax havens all have sophisticated trust mechanisms in place. Their courts are also quite sophisticated when it comes to the treatment of trusts. The aforementioned warning, then, applies only for investors seeking to structure their investments in civil-law jurisdictions not typically considered to be tax havens.

Differences between an Offshore Trust and a Domestic Trust

There are no readily identifiable differences between an offshore trust and a domestic trust. Both structures allow you to transfer property to them for the benefit of someone else. As mentioned throughout this chapter, different trust laws will apply in different jurisdictions. In Canada, the United States, and other Western countries, trust law focuses on tax considerations and on preventing fraudulent conveyances. In these countries, the trust is not viewed as a structure with which to minimize taxes, and it has a more limited role in terms of creditor protection. In the offshore world, trust rules apply somewhat differently. Generally, there are no (or very limited) taxes payable by a trust, making it an ideal shelter for investments. Furthermore, many offshore jurisdictions, although keen to limit the use of their trusts when there are fraudulent conveyances, understand your need for certainty in planning your financial affairs. In other words, they usually enforce very strict limitation periods, but after that creditors may not attack a trust even if the conveyance was fraudulent in the home jurisdiction. Of course, rules for setting up and maintaining trusts vary from jurisdiction to jurisdiction, although those that apply generally are discussed in this chapter. It is essential, before setting up a trust, that you verify the rules with a professional in the jurisdiction you're considering.

Creating the Trust

Generally, trusts may be created for any purpose that does not offend public policy. There is no real magic to creating a trust, although certain jurisdictions may have formalities that have to be observed (for example, the trust may have to be represented by a trust deed that is in writing and signed). Aside from these special restrictions, a trust is created when a person (the settlor) transfers title in his property to a trustee for the benefit of another. This may, if there is no specific legal requirement, be done orally or in writing. When dealing in the offshore world, it is a good idea to put such documents in writing and to sign them, preferably in front of witnesses. (Witnesses establish proof that the trust was indeed constituted on the day noted in the deed. This may be important to tax authorities should they ever question the existence or dating of the trust. On the other hand, witnesses effectively weaken the secrecy of the trust, which may be desired. Each situation will be different and each settlor will have to decide what is more important.) As would be expected, testamentary trusts are typically created through the execution of a will (i.e., upon a testator/settlor's death). You should note that, unlike a simple *inter vivos* trust, a will often has very strict formal requirements. You should contact a lawyer or a notary if you are considering drafting or changing a will.

Before creating a trust, a settlor will want to plan out the exact manner in which the trust should operate. For the remainder of this section, we consider various issues that should be addressed in each existing trust or considered prior to creating a trust. These include issues pertaining to the beneficiaries, the trustees, the residence of the trust, the protector, discretionary and irrevocable trusts, asset-protection trusts, purpose trusts, the differences between an offshore trust and a domestic trust, and secrecy.

Beneficiaries

Once you have determined that a trust vehicle is suitable for your needs, the next step is to identify your beneficiaries. Beneficiaries can be individuals, legal persons (such as corporations), or even purposes (for example, wildlife preservation). They can be one in number or can consist of a class of persons. The settlor may, in some cases, also be a beneficiary of the trust.

Remember that the beneficiaries do not immediately get legal title to the trust property; rather, they are vested with beneficial title. In other words, the trust is created for their benefit, but distributions to them are controlled by the terms of the trust and possibly also by the trustees (who may or may not be given discretionary powers over distributions). Notwithstanding their lack of legal title, beneficiaries of a trust are not altogether without legal powers with respect to their entitlement under the trust. First, beneficiaries have a right to expect that the trustee will discharge his or her duties for their benefit. A trustee who fails to do so is in breach of trust, and may be removed as trustee and/or sued by the trust for damages. Typically, a jurisdiction will confer powers of removal of trustees on a court. In many cases, beneficiaries may apply to the court to remove a trustee who is failing to act properly with respect to the trust property.

Beneficiaries may also avail themselves of a special right to terminate a trust and thus vest the beneficial interest. In Canada, one such rule is known as the rule in *Saunders v. Vautier*[1] (named after the case in which the court established the rule). According to the rule in *Saunders v. Vautier,* a beneficiary who is an adult and of full capacity, and who is absolutely entitled to property contained in a trust (i.e., there must be no discretion or other factor that could vary the amount of the beneficial interest), may apply to the court to "bust the trust." Interestingly, many jurisdictions rely on a similar rule in deeming a beneficiary's income from a trust. A beneficiary who has an absolute entitlement over an ascertainable piece of property held in a trust may be deemed to control and therefore receive the property as income, even when the income continues to be held in trust. As you will see in the chapter that deals with the taxation of a trust, an absolute entitlement may also subject a beneficiary to tax liability.

Fortunately, there are some simple solutions to this problem. Creating a contingency on which the trust will operate is one. For example, a settlor may state that he will leave his property in trust for his son, who shall receive it when he attains the age of eighteen, failing which the property will go to a specified homeless shelter. This covers the possibility that the son may not live to eighteen. He therefore does not have an absolute entitlement to the trust property. Another solution is to create a discretionary class of beneficiaries and to give the trustee discretion over the distributions. No one beneficiary can then be said to have an absolute entitlement to any property.

Trustees

Choosing the trustees is one of the most difficult aspects of creating a trust. As a settlor you may serve as trustee, although in the case of an offshore trust (in order to minimize your tax exposure in Canada), you should not be the only trustee; instead, you should serve as a co-trustee. Serving as a co-trustee will give you some measure of direct control over the trust property. This is important in terms of reducing both administration costs (in time and energy) and the risk of allowing someone else to manage your property (although many trustees are honest and professional).

There is, however, a downside to remaining as co-trustee. As will be discussed in the chapter dealing with the taxation of trusts, the Canadian revenue authorities (and this applies in most other jurisdictions as well) will deem a trust to be a Canadian resident if there is effective control of that trust in Canada. Therefore, in the case of an offshore trust, it is essential that the trustees remain resident in the offshore jurisdiction. Furthermore, if a settlor is the sole trustee, and in some cases even if he is a co-trustee, the revenue authorities may deem the trust's income to be that of the settlor for the purposes of taxation.

There's another reason for not remaining as co-trustee, and it has to do with the asset-protection qualities of the trust. As mentioned in the last chapter, one of the principal benefits of moving your investments and assets offshore using a trust mechanism is that it keeps them out of the hands of creditors and those seeking to enforce judgements against you. With an asset-protection trust, a settlor divests himself of his assets by placing them in a trust. Since legal title passes to the trust, the assets are out of the reach of anyone with a claim against the settlor. By remaining a co-trustee, however, the settlor increases the risk of a court not recognizing the trust mechanism; a court may deem the settlor to hold legal title to the assets. Of course, because the assets remain in a foreign jurisdiction, enforcement of a domestic court order seizing the assets may be difficult or even impossible, thus providing an added layer of protection. Nevertheless, the domestic court may consider you to be in contempt if you do not comply with an order to deliver up the assets to the winning side in a lawsuit. By creating a trust that is under the full control of an arm's-length trustee, you dramatically decrease the risk of such court action.

Generally, it is a good idea to divest yourself of legal title to the property as much as possible, keeping in mind your confidence in the trustees.

Who Should Be Your Trustee?

This brings us to the matter of who you should appoint as a trustee. There are a number of possibilities: large institutions such as banks or trust companies; small companies specializing in offshore-trust management; lawyer(s) in the offshore jurisdiction; friends or relatives; or even yourself (i.e., the settlor). No single one of these is best for all situations, but there are some commonsense considerations on which you can base your decision.

First, you should know that a trustee can be a legal person (such as a corporation), an individual, or a combination of persons and individuals (there is no limit on the number). In the case of multiple trustees, decisions regarding the trust will be based on the agreement of a majority of the trustees. (For the remainder of this text, the singular term "trustee" shall be used. Note that this is for convenience only and assumes the potential use of multiple trustees.)

Although the list of trustees given above shows that you have a number of options to choose from, it is generally preferable for an investor moving offshore to use an institutional trustee with a solid track record. Institutional trustees have the experience and the wherewithal to effect transactions efficiently and in the necessary legal form. Although your familiarity with an institutional trustee may not be as strong as your familiarity with a family member, for example, there are likely to be fewer difficulties over the long run with the institutional trustee. Furthermore, the knowledge and savvy of the institutional trustee is likely to be lacking with a family member. That said, it is possible to use a combination of both institutional and other trustees to administer the offshore trust. However, this may make decisions more difficult to coordinate. There are other roles, such as that of protector, for family members and close personal friends to play (see the section on protectors, which follows).

The Trustee's Powers

A trustee's powers are governed by the trust deed, which is drafted by the settlor. The trustee's powers over the trust property may be either narrowly or broadly construed.

In most offshore situations, where tax planning is a motivation for the creation of the trust, it is important to grant the trustee discretionary power. Granting this power allows the link between the settlor and the assets pledged to the trust to be broken. This is vital to convincing domestic tax authorities that the settlor has created a bona fide trust and does not control the assets. If the settlor does not give the trustee discretion over the trust's distributions, the tax authorities may deem the trust's income to belong to the settlor. Examples of discretionary power include the power to invest the trust property as the trustee sees fit, the ability to change the beneficiaries of the trust, the ability to distribute both the income and the capital (*corpus*) of the trust, the ability to refuse such distributions, the ability to change the residence of the trust, or some combination of these powers.

Some settlors may feel awkward or uncomfortable granting the trustee such broad powers. It is therefore important that trustees be chosen very carefully. Mechanisms such as the use of a protector and a letter of wishes (discussed later in this chapter) will further serve to control and influence the trustee's actions. A settlor may also appoint him- or herself as a trustee. This strategy, as mentioned, is dangerous in light of tax-attribution rules that may deem the settlor to be in control of, and therefore liable for, tax on the income earned by the trust. If, as a settlor, you feel it necessary to remain as a co-trustee, then you must ensure that you are in a minority position and that a majority of the trustees reside in offshore jurisdictions. This will serve to keep the trust offshore. (It is also prudent to ensure that at least one offshore jurisdiction is home to a majority of trustees, thus establishing the residence of the trust in that jurisdiction.)

Residence of the Trust

The residence of a trust is the same as the residence of the person(s) controlling the trust. Typically, this would be the trustee. However, in some cases the settlor may exercise certain powers (such as veto power over distributions of income or capital, or the ability to fire and appoint trustees) that will cause the residence of the trust to change to that of the settlor. The same may be true of the protector(s) of the trust, should they be used (see following). If more than one person serves as trustee, the residence of the trust will be held to be the residence where de facto control is exercised. Why is the residence of a trust important? It will define what legal system and rules apply. The point of moving your assets into an offshore trust is to benefit from both the trust structure and the rules of the offshore jurisdiction. Therefore it is very important that the residence of the trust be carefully maintained.

The Canadian revenue authorities will do their best to show that an offshore trust is controlled in Canada if, for example, they suspect that it was set up to avoid the payment of taxes. If they succeed, then the income of the trust may be attributed to the settlor and taxed in his or her hands. If the authorities can show Canadian control but cannot show that the settlor established the trust solely to avoid the payment of taxes, then its income will be taxed in Canada but not attributed to the settlor (i.e., the trust will be liable).

Taxation of the Trust

Taxation of trusts is discussed in detail in a later chapter that deals with taxation issues generally. However, there are a few issues worth noting at this point in the discussion. First, a trust, if properly constituted and controlled by an offshore resident (i.e., a trustee), will be taxed in its country of residence. As mentioned, it is absolutely vital that proper and effective control of the trust occur from the offshore jurisdiction. If not, the trust will be considered to be resident in the jurisdiction where control is being exercised.

A settlor seeking to transfer cash to an offshore trust can do so without direct tax consequences. However, a settlor cannot move other assets to a trust in such an easy manner. Property, whether real (such as land) or personal (a car, stocks, etc.), will have to be transferred at its fair market value. In other words, a settlor will be deemed to dispose of his assets before transferring them. If the asset has gained in value, this deemed disposition will trigger the payment of Canadian capital gains taxes. The Income Tax Act does contain a rollover provision that will defer the payment of capital gains taxes if the trust is set up for the sole benefit of the settlor's spouse. In this case, no deemed disposition would occur when setting up the trust.

Once a trust is properly set up, it is taxed on income as a person in its own right. Many offshore jurisdictions seeking to attract foreign investors do not tax trusts settled by, and for the benefit of, foreigners.

Protector

Although it was suggested earlier that it is a good idea for a settlor to relinquish control of a trust to the trustees wherever possible, it will often be the case that a settlor cannot stomach such a loss of control over his or her assets. The concept of a protector of the trust evolved to assuage such fears. A protector's function is simply to keep watch over the trustee to ensure that he or she is performing his or her duties properly. Not all jurisdictions have provided in their trust law for the appointment of a protector; others will support differing duties and powers for a protector. For example, both Bermuda and Jersey support the view that a protector owes a fiduciary duty to the beneficiaries.[2] Notwithstanding legal technicalities and differences between jurisdictions, it is important to consider appointing a protector, especially if you are uncertain of or worried about the competence and honesty of the trustees.

It is, of course, important that you appoint a protector you can trust. A relative or a close friend is often a good choice. The protector does not have to deal with the day-to-day operation of the trust — this is the trustee's job. Rather, the protector must simply monitor the trustee (the degree of monitoring needed will depend on the situation).

Generally speaking, a settlor has discretion over the powers he may grant a protector. Two of the more common are the authority to remove and appoint a trustee and the authority to require that a trustee give notice before exercising his discretionary powers or a certain subset of those powers.

A protector's duties and powers are typically defined by the trust document, and not by statute. Protectors may also be granted the ability to appoint and remove trustees, the ability to change the terms of the trust, veto power over the exercise of the trustee's discretion, the authority to change the residence of the trust, and the power to change the choice of law applicable to the trust. Because the protector's role is so flexible, it is not surprising that the residence of the trust may be deemed, by relevant revenue authorities, to be that of the protector. If the protector's role is effectively to be the mind and will behind the trust, there is a strong risk that the residence of the trust will be that of the protector and not the trustee. A settlor who wishes to be a protector of his own trust should be aware of this dilemma. If he maintains enough control over the trust to make himself comfortable, it is possible that tax authorities will deem the trust to be located in the jurisdiction where the settlor resides. If, on the other hand, the settlor wishes the trust to remain offshore, then his role as protector will be marginal and relatively weak.

Discretionary and Irrevocable Trusts

Two further concepts should be considered before setting up a trust offshore: trustee discretion and the revocability of the trust. To avoid having the income earned by the trust deemed to be that of the beneficiary, it is often essential to give the trustee discretionary power over distribution of income and/or capital. Thus it is not clear which beneficiary or class of beneficiaries will be entitled to the income until it is actually paid out. This will often serve to frustrate domestic tax rules that will deem trust income to be the beneficiaries' if their entitlement is not in doubt. Note that in Canada the rules for deeming income to a beneficiary of a trust are highly complex. These are discussed in the chapter dealing with taxation of trusts.

The settlor should also think about the revocability of the trust. A revocable trust is one that the settlor may wind up in order to have the trust property returned. Related to revocable trusts are reversionary trusts (where the trust document provides that trust property will revert to the settlor) and trusts where the settlor is able to direct or restrict the distribution of property held therein. In each of these cases, Canadian tax rules will treat the trust property as belonging to the settlor. In other words, even if a trust has been created, the tax authorities will ignore the trust mechanism. Again, more detailed explanations will follow.

Letter of Wishes

If a discretionary trust is created, a settlor may influence the discretion of the trustee through a document known as a letter of wishes. As its name implies, a letter of wishes is simply a letter outlining the settlor's wishes with respect to the trust. A letter of wishes is not a binding legal document, and the trustee is free to ignore it if he feels that a better course of action is warranted. Nevertheless, a letter of wishes can be a very effective means of signalling to a trustee how the trust should be administered. The fact that it has no binding legal status can impact positively on the tax situation of the settlor. As a letter of wishes does not tie the trustee's hands, the settlor will not be deemed to be controlling the trust, and tax-attribution rules will not come into play.

Asset-Protection Trusts

After tax planning, asset protection is probably the next strongest motive for the establishment of offshore trusts. An asset-protection trust has different residency requirements from those associated with trusts set up for tax-planning purposes. In fact, a domestic trust (as opposed to an offshore trust) may provide effective asset protection, though it will offer a settlor relatively weak tax-planning protection. Moving an asset-protection trust offshore provides an added measure of secrecy by shielding assets from the view of creditors. Asset-protection trusts are also a useful means of protecting your assets against personal liability claims (such as professional malpractice claims or claims against corporate directors), as well as divorce or separation claims.

Offshore asset-protection trusts are nothing more than trusts resident in an offshore jurisdiction with the specific purpose of asset protection. Many jurisdictions, including the Bahamas, the Cayman Islands, the Cook Islands, Cyprus, Gibraltar, Mauritius, and the Turks and Caicos, have enacted specific legislation designed to guard asset-protection trusts from the claims of creditors or others who wish to set the trust aside. To benefit from such protection, you simply need to make the trust resident in one of these jurisdictions. Of course, each jurisdiction's laws are slightly different. Consulting a lawyer who is knowledgeable in offshore-trust arrangements will help ensure an effective set-up.

It is important to understand that asset-protection trusts, as well as the other offshore structures discussed in this book, are not illegal or "shady." Properly executed asset-protection trusts should conform to Canadian federal and provincial legislation. Once this is done, Canadian law will respect the parameters of the trust and the offshore rules that govern it. Applicable Canadian legislation includes laws relating to fraudulent conveyances, common-law rules, the Criminal Code, the Bankruptcy and Insolvency Act, as well as laws relating to assignments and conveyances. Although a comprehensive review of these laws is well beyond the scope of this text, we must point out that they all restrict the creation of a trust (by restricting the transfer of assets) where the purpose is to avoid a current debt or to defraud existing creditors. The prohibitions apply to existing situations and to situations where a settlor knows, or ought reasonably to have known, that the transfer will adversely affect an interested party. These rules do not apply if you are simply being prudent in anticipating a potential threat. In other words, the rules do not restrict sensible offshore planning. Once you are caught in a situation where your assets are threatened, it is often too late.

Transferring Assets to an Asset-Protection Trust

Generally, you are free to transfer whatever assets you want to a trust, providing that you have ownership of the assets and that you do not violate specific laws that govern the transfer of assets (including laws governing fraudulent conveyances and bankruptcy). In transferring an asset to a trust, your goal will be to ensure that the transaction will not subsequently be voidable. If an asset is transferred to a trust in such a way that it does not offend these rules, then the asset will belong to the trust and cannot be attacked by your creditors.

Although the laws that can render transactions voidable will vary from jurisdiction to jurisdiction, there are some commonalities. Generally, for a creditor to successfully attack the transfer of property to a trust, he must show that

- ~ he has been defrauded by virtue of the transfer of the property;
- ~ the transfer of the property was made by you with knowledge that the creditor was in the process of making a claim;
- ~ the transferred property renders you insolvent, and there are

outstanding creditors (if the transferee is a bona fide purchaser for value, the transaction may survive, although this does not apply to trusts where the beneficiaries are members of your family).

Many common-law jurisdictions rely on the principles established in an English statute known as the Statute of Elizabeth (although this statute no longer applies in England itself). One of the notable features of the Statute of Elizabeth is that it does not have any time limitations. This means that future transfers are always potentially voidable. Fortunately, certain common-law jurisdictions, especially those frequently used for the establishment of asset-protection trusts, have repealed or modified their statutes to provide for short limitation periods, usually less than five years, after which the trust cannot be voided.

In sum, transfers to a trust by a settlor who has knowledge that he or she is defrauding creditors may be set aside by courts in both the onshore and the offshore jurisdictions. However, creditors may have to enforce this claim within relatively short time periods, especially if the transfers have been made to a trust in a commonly used offshore jurisdiction. Of course, a creditor may bring the claim in Canada, but since the assets will likely already have been transferred to the offshore trust, the Canadian court's judgement will probably be difficult to enforce. Another natural barrier to creditors seeking to enforce claims is that they must first find the jurisdiction in which the trust has been constituted. This is not always an easy task, as secrecy is often highly valued in such transactions. The creditors must also find the actual trustees and the actual assets. Finally, they must bring an action in this faraway jurisdiction, which will entail finding appropriate legal counsel and often travelling to and from the jurisdiction. These transaction costs often militate against such claims being pursued.

Secrecy

In addition to asset protection, one of the main benefits of using a trust as a vehicle to invest money offshore is the ability to maintain privacy or secrecy. *Trusts, unlike corporations, typically do not have to be registered with any central government authority.* Trusts may, however, be taxed in some jurisdictions, thereby leaving a record of their existence. But this record may not, depending on the jurisdiction, be detailed enough to allow for the identification of any of the parties other than the trustee. Furthermore, taxation information is not necessarily open for review by other governments or by private parties (i.e., your creditors). Typically, another government's right to request and access information will be embodied in a treaty (such as a tax treaty) and can be easily verified. The freedom of an offshore jurisdiction to share information about resident trusts, companies, and individuals will also be defined in the legislation of that jurisdiction. Jurisdictions that specialize in attracting offshore investment will frequently have legislation that prevents the sharing of information with others; it will often even be a criminal offence to reveal the investment information of another person. Such safeguards make these offshore jurisdictions more attractive to potential investors.

Purpose Trusts

Unlike the trusts described above, which are set up to benefit a person or group of persons, a purpose trust is established to carry out a particular purpose. A purpose trust might, for example, hold property and distribute the income from that property to groups that promote a political party, an agenda, or another issue. A purpose trust might also be used to hold the shares of a corporation and to vote for a given board of directors (with the votes exercised by the trustee). The effect of this technique is to remove the shares from the hands of individual shareholders, who may be subject to creditor claims. By placing the shares in the trust, the directors are assured of being re-elected (assuming that the trust holds a majority of the voting shares of the company).

It is important to note that purpose trusts do not exist in equity (i.e., at law) without specific legislation. The sole exception to this rule are trusts established for charitable purposes. Nevertheless, legislation supporting purpose trusts has been enacted in many offshore jurisdictions, including Barbados, Bermuda, Anguilla, the Cayman Islands, and the British Virgin Islands, to name a few.

If you wish to create a purpose trust, you should ensure that both the jurisdiction in which you reside and the jurisdiction in which the trust is to reside (generally the residence of a majority of the trustees) support the creation of purpose trusts.

FOUR

Offshore Banking

In this chapter, you will learn:
~ What to look for when choosing an offshore bank
~ How to set up an offshore account

While the use of an international business corporation or trust is purely optional when investing offshore, the use of offshore banking facilities or other, similar facilities is often required (except in the case of offshore vehicles such as foreign stocks or bonds). In this chapter, we review some of the issues and concerns you should consider when opening an offshore bank account.

First you must decide if you wish to open an offshore bank account in your name, or if you plan to use an intermediate financial structure such as a trust or a corporation instead. This trust or corporation, which often must be resident in the offshore jurisdiction, will then be used to open the bank account. Use of an intermediate structure may be required, depending on your offshore-planning goals. For example, an intermediate structure such as a trust should be used if asset protection is a concern. If tax reduction or elimination is the goal, a trust or a corporation may do. If you simply wish to benefit from offshore banking services and take advantage of higher rates of return or different currency deposits, then no intermediate structure is necessary.

Investing your assets in an offshore financial institution is a tricky business. These institutions come in many sizes and offer a host of products at differing rates of return and with different features. If secrecy is your goal, then it is essential that the bank used does not have branches or other holdings in your country of residence, or even in countries with which your country of residence has a tax-treaty relationship. An offshore bank with a branch in Canada, though convenient, may be open to scrutiny by Revenue Canada. Indeed, the tax agency could seize the bank's assets if it does not provide information that Revenue Canada seeks about a client, even if that person is a client only of the bank's affiliate in the offshore jurisdiction. Unfortunately, this eliminates some of the world's biggest banks as candidates for your investments. These banks typically have branches in many countries, including Canada and the U.S. Once the larger banks are eliminated, the selection becomes much more difficult; you will be operating in uncharted waters, faced with names that you have never encountered.

When assessing an offshore bank, consider the jurisdiction within which it is operating (find out, for example, if there is any strong form of regulation of the bank), the size of the bank (in terms of assets, capital, branches, and number of employees), the bank's reputation (this can be gleaned through discussions with offshore financial advisers and other professionals), and the quality of its management (you may be able to find this out in literature that is distributed by the bank itself).

As a safeguard, consider distributing your holdings among many banks. By spreading out your assets, you reduce the risk of losing it all should one bank fail. On the other hand, the risk of your offshore activities being disclosed also increases as you increase your number of banks. Each investor will have a different level of tolerance for these risks, and will have to balance each accordingly.

Bank Account Features

When choosing an offshore bank, carefully consider the account particulars. Each bank will offer a range of products. Some may be flexible and diverse, while others may be rigid and limited. The following list highlights a number of factors you should consider.

~ In which currencies will the bank allow accounts to be opened?

~ Does the bank offer credit cards and chequing accounts?

~ What are the bank's communication facilities?

~ Does the bank allow access to accounts via phone calls, faxes, or e-mails?

~ Is the bank a member of SWIFT (a transaction clearing mechanism)?

~ Does the bank offer competitive interest rates? (These should be tied to the foreign-exchange risk of the currency in which the account is held.)

~ Are debit cards on global ATM systems (such as the Plus or Cirrus system) available?

~ What are the rules governing the secrecy of the bank, and has the bank ever had an incident where it divulged information about a depositor?

Opening the Account

The process for opening an offshore bank account, as with all things in the offshore world, varies greatly depending on the bank and the jurisdiction. You may be able to open an offshore account simply by writing a letter to the bank requesting the necessary forms, which will be sent to you in the post. Once received, the forms are completed and remitted to the bank. Some banks will also require a letter of reference from an existing bank, financial institution, or lawyer. In more sophisticated banking jurisdictions, such as Switzerland, Liechtenstein, or even Britain, a personal interview may be required. This means that you will have to travel to the jurisdiction and make an appointment with the bank manager. With some of the more reputable banks, it will be impossible to obtain an interview without a reference from an existing bank or from a professional with whom the bank has had dealings. This mechanism is used by the banks to discourage individuals who are likely to use the bank to launder money. Banks that are consistently found to launder money and assist in other criminal activities are putting themselves at a great amount of risk with large Western jurisdictions, which will pressure local authorities to divulge information about account holders, and even to shut down the banks (by revoking their charters).

Getting the Money Offshore

Arguably, one of the most difficult tasks you will face in this type of investing is moving the money privately from an onshore account to an offshore one. Although the techniques described below have an air of illegality or immorality because of their clandestine nature, they should not. Moving money quietly and privately offshore is perfectly legal. There are laws in certain jurisdictions, such as the United States, that require you to report the movement of sums of money or other negotiable instruments above a certain threshold. But as long as you comply with these laws, there is no illegality in moving the money offshore. Canada has no such laws. The Income Tax Act requires that you report aggregate offshore holdings greater than $100,000, although the exact details of the investments are not required.

So why the need for secrecy? As discussed, certain individuals wish to keep their affairs private. This may be because an investor wants to shelter money from future creditors or others who may one day have a claim, or simply because he is uncomfortable with the knowledge that others are capable of tracking or finding out his net worth (for example, an investor may want to hide his net worth from criminals or others who may target well-to-do individuals). Whatever your reasons for wishing to maintain your privacy, it is not illegal to move money offshore secretly.

Moving your money offshore can be a difficult task. The simplest way to do it is to write a cheque on your onshore account and deposit it into your offshore account. This is also the least private method by which to move your money. Cheques drawn on onshore accounts are traceable; records and even photocopies of these cheques are kept on file and can be accessed by revenue authorities, as well as claimants who have a court order. This is also true of wire transfers and other similar means of transferring funds.

The most common means of transferring funds for first-time offshore investors is to travel to the jurisdiction with the funds. This has several benefits. It allows you to personally examine both the people and the place in which you are considering investing your money. (In many cases, a personal meeting with a representative of the financial institution may actually be required by the institution.) It also allows you to have a good vacation in what is often a warm and sunny country! Of course, there are downsides to travelling offshore with cash. It could be stolen, for example, and if you are searched at customs, you may be hard-pressed to explain why you are carrying large sums of money (the money may even be confiscated by customs officials, on the assumption that it was to be used in drug transactions).

Another way to get the money offshore is to use a money order or cashier's (certified) cheque made out to Cash. Note that in some jurisdictions, such as the United States, cashier's cheques and money orders cannot be made out to Cash for sums greater than a prescribed amount ($10,000 in the case of the U.S.). Money orders that exceed this threshold must be made out to specific parties and the details forwarded to customs officials in accordance with money-transfer laws. Thus it is important to find out how much you are entitled to take out of the country without making a report to customs. Also note that money orders should not include your name, as they are returned to the originating bank once they are cashed and therefore the transaction becomes traceable. Furthermore, you should not, when purchasing the money order, use funds directly from your own account. In other words, you should go to your bank, withdraw the funds, and then purchase a money order in cash at another branch or bank. This will break any ties between the money order and your account, thus rendering the transaction untraceable. If you are using money orders and do not wish to travel from your home, the most private way to send the money is via the post. If your money order gets lost in transit or somehow does not reach the bank, you have a receipt for it and can have the issue investigated by the bank where you purchased it. If all goes well, the money order will be successfully deposited into the offshore account, and there will be no link between the money and your onshore account (and therefore, no link to you).

Another option is to use a funds courier. These are organizations that will send a courier abroad with your money. Of course, the risk of losing your money to a con artist posing as a funds courier is great. Furthermore, the cost of sending a courier is only marginally less than the cost of travelling to the jurisdiction yourself.

As you can see, moving your money offshore is a complicated matter that requires some thought and planning. If it is done properly, you can maintain your privacy quite effectively. If it is not done properly, then you will have left a chink in your financial fortress.

Repatriating Your Offshore Funds

Although getting your money offshore is difficult, repatriating your funds is less complicated. You may freely draw on your bank account in the offshore jurisdiction using money orders and other such untraceable instruments.

Often, credit cards are used by the account holder. The card balance is then paid directly from the account. This form of repatriation of funds leaves a good deal of traceability, as all credit card transactions are recorded and archived by card companies. Wire transfers of cash cause similar problems, because they are also traceable. As with depositing funds, an actual visit to the bank and a cash withdrawal in person is probably the least traceable and most private means of repatriating your funds.

That said, it is always important to note that Canadian tax authorities require that Canadian residents pay tax on their worldwide income. Such income must be reported whether it is earnings from a business or interest on a bank account. While there is currently no requirement that a Canadian resident or citizen report specific *withdrawals* from a bank (regardless of its jurisdiction), there are requirements that Canadians report all *holdings* of assets in offshore jurisdictions. Such reporting will include money held in offshore bank accounts.

If your money is held by a trust or a corporation, you will have to report any withdrawals for personal, as opposed to business, use as a taxable benefit on your individual tax return, as the money does not formally belong to you. There is, however, a wrinkle with respect to trust money. Money drawn from income of the trust is taxable in the hands of the beneficiary; this does not apply, however, to money drawn from the *corpus,* or principal, of the trust. The tax-reporting rules for Canadian residents are extremely complicated, and therefore are treated in depth in the following part of the book. In particular, we would draw your attention to the foreign accrual property income (FAPI) rules, which effectively eliminate many of the potential tax savings available to Canadians who invest offshore.

Operating the Offshore Bank Account

Although it is very easy to describe setting up offshore structures such as corporations, trusts, and bank accounts, it is quite another thing to actually operate them. Operating an offshore bank account has traditionally been a tedious process, and thus is one of the weak links of offshore planning for the middle-income investor. Time differences, poor telecommunications systems, and unfamiliarity with jargon, products, and services have all stood in the way of the middle-income investor. Fortunately, as we move further into the Information Age, this is changing. Telecommunication systems have greatly improved in the past few years, and with the advent of the Internet (and sophisticated encryption techniques), other hurdles of distance and accessibility are gradually being conquered. It is now possible to access financial services such as bank accounts and other investment vehicles via your Web browser at any time of the day or night. Computer servers on the other end receive the order and either hold it for processing until the morning or, in some cases, process it immediately.

Internet facilities are gradually becoming more readily available in traditional offshore jurisdictions; financial institutions there have quickly realized that they can multiply their client base effectively and efficiently by using inexpensive computing technologies. When you're considering setting up a bank account, it is important that you inquire about the availability of Internet-banking services. If these are not available, then you should inquire about the availability of fax services and test out the quality of voice communication.

In some cases, you will need only limited access to your offshore banking facility. You may use your account simply to collect money, or you may avail yourself of direct-payment schemes such as ATM/debit cards, cheques, or credit cards that are paid directly out of your account. If this is the case, then rapid access to the bank's office may not be a concern, although you never know when your needs may change.

Owning Your Own Bank

Although it is beyond the scope of this book, we would be remiss in not mentioning something about owning your own bank. In many industrialized countries, such as Canada and the United States, the concept of an individual or a group of individuals owning a bank seems far-fetched. These jurisdictions control banking activities through strict laws and regulations, often citing consumer protection as the objective. As you move into the world of offshore investing, however, you will quickly realize that this concern may be overstated, and that other jurisdictions do not necessarily share these views. In some offshore jurisdictions, though by no means all, it is possible for an individual or group of individuals to own and operate a bank with relatively limited resources.

Investors seeking to own their own personal offshore bank may either start their own bank from the ground up or buy an existing bank. Both approaches have their advantages and disadvantages. Opening your own bank from scratch is a complicated process and is often more costly. However, it allows you to gain a solid understanding of the mechanics of offshore banking, and also provides you with some comfort that the institution is sound. Buying an existing bank can be done more quickly and at less cost, but you will need a good deal of professional assistance to navigate the complex waters that surround such transactions. There is also more risk when purchasing an existing bank with an unknown history. Some private banks have been, and still are, used to launder money.

Owning your own personal offshore bank allows you (as the bank) to invest your money (in exactly the same way Western banks do), as well as to collect deposits, which the bank may then invest. Personal offshore banks can also be used as a replacement for foreign banks when it comes to setting up various offshore structures. In this way, an offshore bank is simply another structure for financial planning, much like the trust and the international business corporation.

There are several benefits to using a bank structure. For example, confidentiality laws in offshore jurisdictions force banks to keep information about investors extremely private. This may add another layer to the privacy wall, if that is what you require. Other possible incentives include tax benefits in certain Western countries for nationals who own offshore banks. The United States, for example, provides certain tax advantages for American-owned offshore banks.

If you are interested in setting up a personal offshore bank, you will definitely need the assistance of professionals. Establishing a bank will, for one thing, be more costly than some of the other techniques and mechanisms mentioned thus far. Furthermore, offshore jurisdictions that do allow personal offshore banks tend to charge high initial and annual licensing fees. As always, law and accounting firms familiar with the jurisdiction in question are usually a good place to start your inquiries.

The offshore world presents many other business opportunities not mentioned thus far. Some of the other offshore instruments commonly used by investors include mutual funds, development bonds, insurance and re-insurance companies, corporate bonds, trust companies, and ship registrations. We will not examine any of these in any great depth in this book. You will, however, find a limited discussion of some of these items (such as mutual funds and development bonds) at various points in the text.

Taxation

Issues

FIVE

Canadian Taxation

In this chapter, you will learn:
~ *To distinguish between tax avoidance and tax evasion*
~ *To identify which persons are subject to Canadian taxes*
~ *How individuals are taxed according to their residency status*

*C*anadians enjoy a very high standard of living. Unfortunately, the fiscal cost associated with sustaining this collective wealth has risen steadily over the past fifty years. If you consider both direct and indirect forms of taxation, you will find that Canadian taxes rank among the highest in the world. With such a heavy tax burden, Canadians must take proper financial planning quite seriously.

One aspect of financial planning is the arrangement of your affairs in a manner that minimizes your tax burden while continuing to meet your financial needs and objectives. Proper financial planning (or tax avoidance) also minimizes your taxes while respecting existing rules and regulations. In contrast, tax evasion is a strategy founded on ignoring, circumventing, or violating known tax laws. At times, the differences between tax avoidance and tax evasion become quite tenuous. But these distinctions are even more significant when dealing with offshore jurisdictions, because many low- or no-tax jurisdictions bear the stigma of having been (or continuing to be) involved in money-laundering or tax-evasive activities. As a result, transactions with these jurisdictions undergo greater scrutiny from Canadian tax authorities.

Tax evasion in Canada is extremely risky and carries with it great costs. These can include legal sanctions, family disruptions, job loss, and irreparable damage to your reputation. While we hope that this is a stern warning against tax evasion, it must be noted that Canadian tax law is not always clearly established; some room for interpretation does exist. Also, Revenue Canada makes administrative decisions or rules to regulate the treatment of taxpayers, but these rules do not carry the force of law. The validity of such administrative decisions or rules can always be challenged in court (though often at some cost).

These chapters cannot possibly answer every question readers will have about Canadian taxes. Our objective is to provide you with the knowledge you need to make informed decisions. But remember, in virtually all situations, proper financial planning requires the assistance of a professional adviser. This requirement only increases when transactions in foreign jurisdictions are contemplated.

In this chapter, we will examine the taxation of individuals in Canada, particularly as our tax laws relate to persons deemed residents and part-year residents. As you will discover, the concept of residency is at the core of the Canadian tax system. In the chapters that follow, we will explore how corporations and trusts are taxed in Canada, how individuals can become non-residents of Canada, and how non-residents are taxed in Canada.

The Taxation of Individuals

Canadian taxes are assessed based on the residency of the taxpayer. If you are a resident of Canada, you must pay Canadian taxes regardless of your citizenship. Remember, there is an important distinction between residency and citizenship: becoming a non-resident does not mean you lose your Canadian citizenship or the benefits of that citizenship. In fact, as a Canadian, you can retain your citizenship no matter where you choose to reside (note, however, that in some countries, dual citizenship is not permitted).

Your status as a taxpayer (i.e., whether or not you must pay Canadian taxes) changes as your residential ties with Canada change. There are four broad categories of residents: factual residents, part-year residents, deemed residents, and non-residents. Most Canadians are considered factual residents because they work and reside primarily in Canada. Persons who have departed from or arrived in Canada during the year are considered part-year residents. Others, by virtue of special tax rules, are deemed to be residents of Canada. Finally, there are those who do not maintain significant residential ties with Canada, and who visit for only short periods of time; they are considered non-residents. To determine whether you are taxable in Canada, you must first determine your residency status. Residency rules also apply to corporations and trusts, and will be discussed in the chapters that follow.

Factual Residents

Factual residents of Canada must pay Canadian taxes on their *worldwide* income. That is, income earned in both Canada and abroad is taxable in Canada, and both kinds of income are assessed the same marginal tax rates (i.e., the tax rate charged on the last dollar earned). Foreign-source income must be included in your taxable income even if taxes were paid in the jurisdiction where it was earned. Tax credits may, however, be available to alleviate or eliminate the effects of double taxation. Since Canada's tax rates are higher than those of most other countries, a person with significant foreign-source income will prefer not to be regarded as a factual resident of Canada, particularly if no tax treaty exists between Canada and the country that is the source of his or her foreign income.

Canadian residency is a question of fact. Your residency status is based on the extent of the links you maintain with Canada. Revenue

Canada has compiled a list of factors that it considers relevant in assessing your residency status. These include the following:

~ where your immediate family is;

~ whether you maintain in Canada a dwelling-house that is available for use;

~ whether you maintain personal property, such as a car or a bank account, in Canada;

~ whether you maintain professional and social memberships in Canada; and

~ whether you retain provincial health coverage.

These criteria are administrative in nature; that is, they are not legally binding. They can be challenged and other factors can be introduced that could better establish your residency status, and by corollary, your tax status. Typically, the greater the ties you maintain with Canada, the more likely you are to be considered a resident and thus taxed on your worldwide income.

There are some residents of Canada who are generally not subject to Canadian taxes, although they live and work in this country. These include officials of foreign governments and members of their families; servants to officials of foreign governments; visiting armed forces personnel; and some visiting foreign teachers and professors.

Deemed Residents

Certain persons, although not factually residing in Canada, are deemed to be residents for tax purposes. These people are subject to Canadian taxes on their worldwide income, very much as factual residents are, and are required to file a special annual tax return called the T1 General for Non-Residents and Deemed Residents. There are some minor differences in how factual and deemed residents are taxed: deemed residents are more likely to receive tax-free allowances, and they may deduct certain foreign payments, such as moving, childcare, and attendant-care expenses, which are not deductible by factual residents.

There are two categories of deemed residents: sojourners in Canada and Canadian officials working abroad.

Sojourners in Canada

If you sojourn (i.e., physically remain) in Canada for 183 days or more in a year, you will be deemed a resident for the *entire year,* regardless of your citizenship. You need not have earned any income in Canada for this rule to apply. For example, if you are an American citizen who normally resides in California, but you spent 200 days in a single calendar year travelling throughout Canada, you would be deemed a resident and taxed on your *worldwide* income for the entire year (not just the 200 days). As a result, you would be liable for both Canadian and U.S. taxes on the income you earned during that year. (Note that a sojourner's tax status may change from year to year.)

Sojourners are treated as residents of Canada but not as residents of a particular province. Consequently, they are not required to file any provincial forms with their tax return and must pay a federal surtax in lieu of provincial taxes. This rule has two important exceptions. First, persons who sojourn in Quebec for 183 days or more are deemed residents of Quebec and must file a separate Quebec tax return. Second, persons carrying on business through a permanent establishment in Canada must allocate their business income among the different provinces and file provincial forms. These people may also claim provincial tax credits.

Canadian Officials Working Abroad

Because Canadian taxes are assessed according to one's residency status, many members of the foreign service and the Canadian armed forces, who actually reside in a different country, would escape paying them. To address this, the Income Tax Act deems such persons, their spouses, and their dependent children to be residents of Canada, and thus taxable in Canada on their worldwide income. People deemed in this way to be residents of Canada include

a) members of the Canadian armed forces;

b) ambassadors, ministers, high commissioners, officers, or servants of a federal or provincial Crown corporation or agency;

c) persons working in a foreign country for the Canadian International Development Agency (CIDA), so long as they resided in Canada at some time during the three months that preceded their assignment;

d) members of the overseas Canadian armed forces school staff who elect to be treated as deemed residents;

e) the spouse of any of the individuals listed above, so long as he or she was a Canadian resident in the past and the couple continues to live together; and

f) dependent children of any of the persons listed above — with the exception of dependent children belonging only to those individuals listed in (e) — if their income does not exceed $6,794.

As is the case with sojourners, Canadian officials working abroad are not deemed to be residents of a particular province. They too must pay a federal surtax in lieu of provincial taxes. Please also note that Revenue Quebec may, in certain circumstances, deem an individual to be a resident of Quebec and require that individual to file a separate provincial tax return.

Part-Year Residents

You are a part-year resident if you arrived in or left Canada during the year. More specifically, you are a part-year resident if, during the taxation year, you

~ gave up your Canadian residence and established residence in another country; or

~ established permanent residence in Canada.

Note that you are not a part-year resident if you sojourned in Canada for 183 days or more prior to establishing permanent residence in Canada. As has already been discussed, you would then be deemed a resident of Canada for the entire year and would be taxable on your worldwide income.

Part-year residents can divide the calendar year into two periods: a period of residence and a second period of non-residence. They must pay tax on the worldwide income they earned during their period of residence. For their period of non-residence, they are subject to the same tax rules that apply to typical non-residents, as is discussed later in this chapter. Part-year residents file only one tax return for the year of transition, and must adjust their income and deductions accordingly.

Deductions

In general, the same deductions that are available to factual residents in calculating taxable income are also available to part-year residents. These deductions, however, cannot exceed the deductions that would have been available had these people been resident for the entire year. Also, deductions that are applicable to both the period of residence and the period of non-residence must be adjusted to reflect the period of residence, typically by prorating the number of days of residence to the total number of days in the year.

Although loss carryovers are explained in more detail in the chapter on non-residents, it is important that you understand how they apply to part-year residents. In a broad sense, loss carryovers are either capital or non-capital in nature. Capital losses stem from the disposition of capital property. For example, if you bought shares of a public company for $1,000 and later sold those same shares for only $600, you would have incurred a capital loss of $400. Non-capital losses include business losses, losses from farming activities, and losses from employment (an example of a person suffering an employment loss would be a salesperson who earned less in commissions than he paid in non-refundable work expenses). Allowable business investment losses are special capital losses.

Unused non-capital and net capital losses incurred while you were a resident of Canada may be used to reduce your taxable income only for periods in which you were a full-time or part-year resident of Canada. In other words, you cannot use these losses to reduce your taxable income while you were a non-resident. There are, however, two important exceptions to this last rule. First, if you incurred business and farm losses in Canada while you were a resident, you may use these losses to reduce income earned from Canadian business or farming activities after you become a non-resident. Second, allowable business investment losses and allowable capital losses that you incurred while you were a non-resident may be used to reduce your taxable income for the current year if you earned capital gains from selling taxable Canadian property. Taxable Canadian property is defined in a later chapter.

If you return to Canada after a period of non-residence, you can apply any unused loss carryovers incurred during earlier years of residence. If you are establishing residence in Canada for the first time, however, you may deduct only business and employment losses that you incurred in Canada prior to becoming a resident. In both cases, only losses that have not expired may be used.

Personal Tax Credits

Personal tax credits can be divided into two categories. In the first category are tax credits that are available to residents and part-year residents alike, regardless of the number of days an individual resided in Canada. These tax credits include

- ~ charitable donations and gifts to Canada or a province;
- ~ personal tuition fees;
- ~ personal disability amount;
- ~ Canada Pension Plan or Quebec Pension Plan contributions; and
- ~ Employment Insurance contributions.

The second category of tax credits is available only if all or substantially all (90 percent in practice) of a claimant's worldwide income for the calendar year is subject to Canadian tax. These tax credits, if available, must be calculated by pro-rating the number of days that the claimant was a resident of Canada to the total number of days in the calendar year. For example, if a claimant was entitled to a credit worth $600 for the year, but he had resided in Canada for only nine months, the maximum amount he could claim would be $450. Tax credits that fall into this second category include

- ~ basic personal amount;
- ~ age amount;
- ~ married amount;
- ~ equivalent-to-spouse amount;
- ~ disability amount;

~ disability amount transferred from a relative;

~ unused spousal credits (pro-rated for your spouse's period of residence); and

~ unused tuition and education amounts transferred from a child.

The total amount of each personal tax credit cannot exceed the amount to which a claimant would have been entitled had he or she been a resident throughout the entire year. For tax credits that vary based on income levels, you must pro-rate the upper- or lower-income limits rather than pro-rating the total credit. Note, however, that the minimum expense limits for the medical expense tax credit are not adjusted.

SIX

The Taxation of Corporations

In this chapter, you will learn:
~ *To identify corporations that are subject to Canadian income taxes*
~ *How the foreign accrual property income (FAPI) rules operate in relation to corporations*
~ *How not to trigger the general anti-avoidance rule (GAAR) in your financial planning*

Sophisticated offshore-planning strategies usually involve the use of corporations and trusts. Consequently, it is important to understand how corporations and trusts are taxed in Canada. We will discuss issues related to the taxation of corporations in this chapter and issues related to the taxation of trusts in the following chapter. Both chapters should improve your ability to make informed decisions about offshore planning.

Corporations, like individuals, are taxed based on residency. Put simply, a corporation that resides in Canada must pay Canadian taxes on its worldwide income. Of course, the rules governing the computation of taxable income, deductions, and tax liability for corporations resident in Canada are extremely complex, and thus an examination of them exceeds the scope of this book. Instead, this chapter focuses on matters affecting the taxation of corporations only in the context of offshore planning. First, we examine the factors that determine whether a corporation is liable for Canadian taxes. Second, we consider the tax effect of non-resident corporations on their Canadian resident shareholders. Finally, we analyze the effect of the Canadian foreign accrual property income (FAPI) rules, which are of critical importance to any offshore investment plan.

Residency of a Corporation

As stated earlier, corporations resident in Canada are subject to taxes on their worldwide income. The term "residence" is not defined in the Income Tax Act, so we must look to the common law or to the various deeming provisions of the Income Tax Act. In addition, a corporation that does not reside in Canada may be subject to Canadian taxes if it carries on business through a permanent establishment in Canada, such as an office or a store.

Common Law

At common law, the residence of a corporation is the place where the central management and control occur. This rule has been interpreted as meaning the place where the corporate decisions are made or where the board of directors meets; however, it is not that narrow. While the board of directors may have de jure (legal) control, it is de facto (actual) control that is relevant to the determination of residency. In other words, it is where the corporation is effectively and in fact controlled that establishes its place of residence. This distinction is important to investors: they may not want to be named as directors of offshore corporations, because it may cause the corporation to be taxable in Canada. As an alternative to assuming the role of director, some offshore investors have retained a power of attorney over the corporation. Both approaches, however, could still lead a Canadian court to find that the investor effectively controls the corporation. And the obvious problem with not assuming a directorship role *or* retaining a power of attorney is that an investor effectively loses control of any assets transferred to the corporation.

Although all companies incorporated in Canada are residents of Canada, the place of incorporation is not necessarily relevant to the determination of residency for the purposes of taxation. For example, a company incorporated in South Africa could be liable for Canadian taxes on its worldwide income if the key management and control decisions were made in Canada. Tax treaties between Canada and the country of incorporation could eliminate or alleviate the effects of double taxation.

Deemed Residency

The Income Tax Act deems any company incorporated in Canada to be a resident of Canada. It is immaterial where the corporation operates or where its key management decisions are made. All that matters is that the company was incorporated in Canada.

Since all Canadian-incorporated companies are deemed to be residents of Canada, they are subject to Canadian tax based on their worldwide income. For this reason, it would be unwise for a non-resident to use a Canadian-incorporated company to hold foreign investments. For Canadians considering setting up an offshore business, it may also make more sense to avoid incorporating in Canada.

Foreign Accrual Property Income Rules

The foreign accrual property income (FAPI) rules were designed by Revenue Canada to discourage or prevent taxpayers from using offshore jurisdictions to shield their income from Canadian taxes. The rules are extremely complex and are structured to capture income earned in a foreign jurisdiction. The FAPI rules will generally attribute the foreign income to the Canadian resident who can be most logically linked to it. The FAPI rules affect personal planning structures that include corporations, trusts, or both. They have made offshore planning for tax-reduction purposes very difficult and very costly. You should also note that although the rules continue to allow some manoeuvrability, there remains a risk that Revenue Canada will change them in a way that will capture the income you are seeking to protect.

A non-resident company that does not carry on business in Canada will not be liable for Canadian taxes, other than withholding taxes due on certain types of income. FAPI does not attack the offshore corporation, however, but rather seeks to tax the Canadian-resident shareholders of that corporation. FAPI applies to types of foreign-source income that are primarily passive in nature, such as interest, dividends, and capital gains. Only these types of income are subject to the income-inclusion rules given below.

The main purpose of the FAPI rules is to tax the income of certain non-resident corporations even when no income has been distributed to the Canadian-resident shareholders. A Canadian resident (whether a natural person or a corporation) must include in income any share of the earnings from the property of any "controlled foreign affiliate,"[3] whether or not those earnings have been distributed to the shareholder. In other words, if you own a company incorporated in a foreign jurisdiction and that company earns interest, dividends, or capital gains, then you will be required to include your share of that income on your income tax return. The fact that that income may not have been distributed to you does not affect this income-inclusion rule.

Revenue Canada assumes that the income earned by the foreign affiliate will eventually flow to you in the form of dividends. The FAPI rules simply cut short the period between the time the income is earned by the offshore corporation and the time it is paid out to the shareholders (a period during which tax would be deferred). When received, these dividends must be included in your income, but you are entitled to deduct any amounts that were already taxed under the FAPI rules. It is important to note that these income-inclusion rules apply only if the offshore corporation's property income for the year is equal to or greater than $5,000.

The FAPI rules do not apply when the central management and control of a corporation is in Canada, since such a corporation would be considered a resident of Canada and would be taxed on its worldwide income. The typical corporation that triggers the application of the FAPI rules is a foreign investment holding company with the following characteristics:

~ The company has annual passive income equal to or greater than $5,000 per year.
~ The company is incorporated outside Canada.
~ The company's directors are foreigners.
~ The board of directors meets outside Canada.

A corporation satisfying these general guidelines will be subject to the FAPI rules only if its ownership structure meets the following additional criteria:

~ You are a shareholder of a foreign corporation and your equity percentage (see below) of that corporation is equal to or greater than one percent.
~ Your equity percentage of the foreign corporation and the percentage of persons related to you (i.e., spouse, children, siblings, parents) are equal to or greater than 10 percent.
~ The foreign company is controlled directly or indirectly by one of the following:
   i) you;
   ii) a person or persons, whether resident or not, with whom you do not deal at arm's length (i.e., spouse, children, siblings, parents);
   iii) four persons or fewer who are residents of Canada;
   iv) both (i) and (ii) taken together; or
   v) both (i) and (iii) taken together.

The equity percentage is calculated by adding your direct and indirect interests. For example, if you own 5 percent of the shares of a foreign corporation and you also own 50 percent of a Canadian company that holds 20 percent of the shares of the same foreign corporation, then your equity percentage will be calculated as follows: 5 percent + (50 percent x 20 percent) = 15 percent. If, however, the remaining 85 percent of the shares are held by persons who do not reside in Canada and with whom you deal at arm's length, then the FAPI rules will not apply because the third test (i.e., the control structure) would not be satisfied.

To a significant extent, the FAPI rules limit the use of foreign investment corporations by Canadian residents. A corporate structure that successfully avoids these rules is both qualitatively and financially expensive. (Qualitatively expensive means the company is a riskier venture, because by not becoming a shareholder, you have relinquished control.) Professional advice is always required for FAPI-related matters. You should also be aware of the general anti-avoidance rule.

General Anti-Avoidance Rule

The Income Tax Act contains a general anti-avoidance rule (GAAR), which deals with "abusive" tax-planning strategies that are not otherwise specifically addressed by the Act. The GAAR will deny the tax benefit of any transaction or series of transactions that have no bona fide business, family, or investment purpose other than realizing that benefit. In one instance, the GAAR was used to deny a taxpayer the benefit of a capital gains exemption on the sale of shares in a company with no assets other than cash. The court held that the proper transaction would have been to pay a liquidating but taxable dividend to the shareholder.

The rule is far-reaching and potentially gives Revenue Canada tremendous power to overturn or deny the tax savings of many otherwise legitimate transactions. Fortunately, the breadth and discretionary nature of the power is such that Revenue Canada historically has been reluctant to exercise it.

The GAAR's limitations aside, you must always be aware of the risk of it when planning and executing tax-minimizing strategies, particularly when foreign jurisdictions are involved. Only legitimate ventures should be explored, particularly when you consider that offshore transactions figure prominently among Revenue Canada's concerns.

Finally, please note that although the GAAR was introduced in this chapter, it applies to all financial-planning transactions, not only those involving corporations.

SEVEN

The Taxation
of Trusts

In this chapter, you will learn:
~ *How trusts that are resident in Canada can
be identified*
~ *How trusts and their distributions are taxed
in Canada*
~ *How the FAPI rules operate in relation to trusts*

*I*n an earlier chapter, we introduced the trust as a tool for offshore financial planning. You should be familiar with the material in that chapter before reading about the taxation of trusts in this one.

You will recall that the use of trusts is very common in many offshore-planning schemes. Trusts can be used for a number of purposes, such as holding assets for later distribution to family members or shielding assets from lawsuits that may arise in the future. In many offshore jurisdictions, a very simple declaration can create a trust to hold assets, such as the shares of a corporation, on someone's behalf.

The taxation of trusts in Canada is complex, and this level of complexity is only compounded when offshore jurisdictions are involved in the financial planning. This book is not intended to be an in-depth guide to these issues; instead, this chapter acts as a cursory review of the taxation of trusts resident in Canada. This chapter also explains how to determine the residency status of a trust, how Canada taxes non-resident trusts when some or all of the beneficiaries reside in Canada, and how distributions of a resident trust to non-resident beneficiaries are taxed.

Residency of a Trust

The taxation of a trust depends on the residency of the trust. A trust is either a resident of Canada or a non-resident, and the determination of its residency will have considerable impact on its level of taxation.

The residency of a trust is not necessarily the same as the jurisdiction in which the trust is established. In other words, if you establish a trust in Bermuda, it does not necessarily follow that the trust is a resident of Bermuda and, by corollary, a non-resident of Canada. In fact, your trust may be considered a resident of Canada or even deemed to be a resident of Canada (the distinction here is explained later in this chapter).

In general, a trust resides in the jurisdiction or jurisdictions (it can reside in more than one jurisdiction) where it is managed or where the trust assets are controlled. Since it is the trustee who normally controls the trust, it will usually reside in the same country as the trustee. But this is not a definitive rule: if the trustee does not exercise de facto control over the assets, then his or her place of residence may be irrelevant. For example, if you settle a trust and retain material control over the trust assets (in which case, the trustee is only a nominee trustee), then the trust may be viewed as residing in Canada.

There can be additional complications, particularly if more than one trustee is appointed or if one of the trustees is a corporation that operates in many jurisdictions. In situations where more than one trustee is appointed, Canadian jurisprudence requires that you look to the place where effective control of the trust assets is exercised. In evaluating the residency status of your trust, ask yourself whether the non-resident trustees can control the assets without the consent of any resident trustees. If the unanimous consent of the trustees is required and one of the trustees is a resident of Canada, then the trust may be treated as resident in Canada. If non-resident trustees can make decisions that affect the trust assets over the objections of any resident trustees, then the trust is more likely to be considered a non-resident trust. Protectors, whose role was discussed in chapter 3, may also have an impact on the residency of a trust; the same logic that applies to trustees also applies to them.

Taxation of Trusts Resident in Canada

Under Canadian law, a trust is viewed and taxed as a separate entity, distinct from its settlor and its beneficiaries. The trust is deemed to be an individual; its income and taxes are calculated in a manner similar to that of any other individual.

Trusts are subject to the same tax rates that are applicable to individual taxpayers; however, not all trusts benefit from the progressive tax rates (i.e., the tax rates that rise as a person's income rises). *Inter vivos* trusts (trusts established by a settlor that vest, or become enforceable by the beneficiaries, during the settlor's lifetime) must pay tax at the highest marginal tax rate, whereas testamentary trusts (trusts established by a settlor that vest upon his or her death) are taxed according to the progressive rates. A second distinction is that *inter vivos* trusts pay tax on a calendar basis, whereas testamentary trusts can choose a fiscal year-end. It is also important to note that trusts are not entitled to any personal tax credits.

In computing how much of a trust's income is subject to Canadian taxes, you are entitled to deduct income that was paid or is payable to the beneficiaries. The trust is therefore taxed only on accumulated income. An amount is considered payable to a beneficiary if that beneficiary is absolutely entitled to the share of the income (i.e., the trustee does not have complete discretion over the amount and timing of the distributions) and can enforce the payment of the distribution. The income distributed (whether actually received or not) is taxable in the hands of the beneficiaries, and it retains the same character as income received by the trust. For example, dividends received by a trust will, if distributed, flow to its beneficiaries as dividends and will be taxed as dividends in the beneficiaries' hands. The same rule applies to capital gains, interest, non-taxable dividends, and other sources of income.

The rules governing the attribution of income for transfers of property also apply to transfers involving trusts. If you transfer property to a trust of which your spouse is a beneficiary, then any income (or loss) from property and any taxable capital gains (or allowable capital losses) that relate to your spouse's beneficial interest are attributed back to you and included in your income. If the beneficiary is a minor and is related to you (this has been expanded to include nephews and nieces), then any income (or loss) from property, with the exception of a capital gain or a capital loss, will be attributed back to you.

Taxation of Non-Resident Trusts

Generally speaking, trusts are subject to taxation in the country in which they reside. Since some jurisdictions do not tax trusts, many Canadians have sought to avoid tax on income-producing property by transferring such property to a trust in one of these jurisdictions. Accordingly, Revenue Canada has developed very sophisticated rules to tax the income of non-resident trusts.

Your trust may be deemed to be resident in Canada if a Canadian resident has a beneficial interest in it. For your trust to be deemed a resident in Canada, the Income Tax Act requires that the following three conditions be present:

a) the trust is not otherwise a resident of Canada;
b) a person resident in Canada has a direct or indirect beneficial interest in your trust; and
c) the person in (b) directly or indirectly transferred property to your trust.

In other words, a trust will be deemed a resident of Canada and taxed as such only if the settlor (i.e., the person transferring assets to the trust) retains a beneficial interest in it. If the trust is deemed to be resident in Canada, it will be subject to Canadian taxes in the same manner as resident trusts, with two important exceptions.

First, if your trust is a non-discretionary trust (in other words, if the trustee must allocate income based on a distribution formula established by the trust) and a Canadian resident has a beneficial interest of 10 percent or more, then it will be considered to be a corporation resident in Canada with respect to such beneficiaries. Those beneficiaries (i.e., those whose beneficial interests are equal to or greater than 10 percent) must apply the foreign accrual property income (FAPI) rules described in the previous chapter and include on their tax return, as appropriate, their share of the trust's income.

Second, if your trust is a discretionary trust (in other words, if the trustee decides the allocation schedule and the distribution formula, and/or if the trust deed does not name any beneficiaries), it will be subject to tax on income from various sources, including

~ real property situated in Canada;
~ business carried on in Canada;
~ taxable capital gains from the disposition of taxable Canadian property; and
~ FAPI for itself and for any of its controlled foreign affiliates (see the previous chapter for more detail on FAPI).

These provisions of the Income Tax Act are designed to capture income that could otherwise go untaxed in Canada because of the use of residency as the basis of taxation. If you are interested in creating an offshore trust, you should be aware that avoiding these tax rules will necessarily require that you relinquish complete control and legal ownership of the trust assets, and that the trustee be given carte blanche with respect to distributions or beneficiaries. Many common-law jurisdictions do not allow trust deeds that fail to specify the beneficiaries of the trust.

The same income-attribution rules that apply to resident trusts (described earlier) also apply to non-resident trusts. That is, if you are the settlor of a trust and your spouse is a beneficiary, then all income that would otherwise be included on your spouse's tax return must be included on your own. The same basic rule applies if a child to whom you are related is a beneficiary of the trust; all income must then be included on your tax return, with the exception of capital gains, which are taxed in the hands of the minor.

Distributions to Non-Residents by a Trust Resident in Canada

A trust resident in Canada is entitled to deduct from its income any amounts paid or payable to the beneficiaries. It does not matter if those beneficiaries are residents or non-residents of Canada. If the beneficiaries are non-residents, withholding taxes will apply to any amounts accruing to them, whether they are paid or only credited. The trustee must then remit only the net amount (the gross amount less withholding taxes) to the non-resident beneficiaries.

Beginning in 1998, Canadian-resident *inter vivos* trusts that have one or more non-resident beneficiaries became subject to a special tax on income from business carried on in Canada and on capital gains arising from the disposition of taxable Canadian property. This new tax seeks to close a loophole that allowed such income to be taxed through the withholding-tax regime instead of the normal taxation system, which carries higher tax rates. As will be discussed in a later chapter, certain income is subject to normal taxes (not withholding taxes) even when earned by non-residents.

EIGHT

Becoming a Non-Resident

In this chapter, you will learn:
~ *How Revenue Canada evaluates residency*
~ *What tax effects are associated with becoming a non-resident*

*I*n this chapter, we deal with what happens when you, as an individual, become a non-resident. Becoming a non-resident of Canada can provide you with certain tax advantages because residents are taxed on their worldwide income while non-residents are taxed only on certain types on Canadian-source income. But the decision to leave Canada is a difficult one, and one that will significantly alter your lifestyle, sometimes for the worse. Ultimately, the financial advantage is only one of many factors you should consider. Personal and practical factors such as the change to your standard of living, the level of crime, societal values, the quality of health care, and the distance to close family and friends must also be evaluated. It is only when all of these factors have been considered that the right decision can be made.

Criteria for Becoming a Non-Resident

To become a non-resident, you must change your relationship with the place where you reside. The criteria Revenue Canada uses to evaluate whether you have severed your residential ties with Canada are essentially the same as those used to determine whether, for taxation purposes, you are a resident of Canada. Generally, the greater the ties you maintain with Canada, the greater the likelihood that you have failed to sever your residency.

According to common law, you must reside in at least one country, but you can reside in more than one country. The fact that common law recognizes dual-residency status presents a real risk of double taxation for those who do not properly plan and execute their departure from Canada. If you are contemplating a move to a jurisdiction that does not have a tax treaty with Canada, you should be particularly careful because there will be no relief from double taxation. For these reasons, professional advice should always be sought when planning a departure from Canada.

Save for the specific provisions dealing with deemed residency, the rules for determining your residency status are established by the common law. As a result, there are no absolute or strict rules by which to gauge your particular set of circumstances. Over the years, however, a number of key indicators have been developed and used by Revenue Canada to maintain a level of consistency in its treatment of taxpayers. These indicators include the following (listed in order of importance):

Have you established residence in another country?
   ~ Revenue Canada will not consider you to have severed
      your residential ties with Canada until you have established
      residence in another country.

Do you maintain a dwelling in Canada?
   ~ A dwelling in this context is a house, an apartment, or
      another form of lodging that can be occupied year-round
      and is available for use without delay.
   ~ The safest strategy is to sell your Canadian dwelling (or not

to renew a lease, in the case of a rented dwelling), which would effectively sever any residential tie.

~ A riskier strategy, if you own your dwelling, is to lease the property to a tenant. Ideally, the tenant should be an unrelated person. If a family member becomes the tenant, then the lease agreement must not give you the right to terminate the lease within three months. Short-term leases (three- or six-month leases, for example) are likely to be more closely scrutinized by Revenue Canada than leases of longer duration. Please also note that the gross rental payments will be subject to withholding taxes.

~ Another risky strategy is to vacate the dwelling and render it unsuitable for immediate use. All furniture and personal effects should be removed. Serious consideration should be given to stopping all utility services.

Does your immediate family (spouse and dependants) continue to reside in Canada?

~ In general, you cannot become a non-resident if your immediate family remains in Canada. Even couples who have separated should enter into a formal (written) separation agreement to avoid any future problems.

~ This indicator also has an impact on a taxpayer's date of departure, which is discussed later in this chapter.

Do you maintain personal property in Canada?

~ Personal property includes furniture, motor vehicles, bank accounts, clothing, credit cards, and similar items.

Do you maintain social or professional ties with Canadian organizations?

~ Maintaining club and professional memberships may indicate an intention to return to Canada. Memberships should be terminated or your membership status changed to that of a non-resident.

Do you maintain a seasonal residence in Canada?
> ~ Maintaining a seasonal residence such as a cottage should
> not have a great effect on the determination of residency.
> This factor increases in significance only when considered
> in conjunction with all the others.

*Do you continue to benefit from services not otherwise
available to non-residents?*
> ~ Revenue Canada looks unfavourably on taxpayers who seek
> to sever residential ties while retaining provincial health-care
> coverage or receiving family-allowance payments.

These factors — and any others that may link you to a life in
Canada — must always be considered in the aggregate when you
are evaluating whether you have truly severed your residential ties.
In every case, additional factors may be introduced depending on
your particular circumstances.

The Period Abroad

The preceding factors can all be dwarfed by your intention to return
to Canada. That is, a definite intention to return to Canada could
jeopardize your objective of becoming a non-resident. Because it is
difficult for Revenue Canada to establish your subjective intent,
the agency has adopted an administrative rule: if you remain
absent from Canada for two years or more, you will be considered
to have become a non-resident. Of course, this two-year rule must
be examined in the context of the residency indicators: if you sever
no residential ties (i.e., maintain a dwelling, personal property,
memberships, etc.) but leave Canada for two years, you may still be
treated as a resident for tax purposes.

A foreseeable return to Canada in less than two years would also
affect your residency status. For example, if you were awarded a
contract of employment that was set to begin upon your return to
Canada or at some fixed time in the future (within two years), then
Revenue Canada could treat your return as a foreseeable event, thus
negating your attempt to become a non-resident.

On the other hand, an unforeseen return to Canada within two years may not jeopardize your attempt to sever residential ties. A return to Canada owing to loss of employment abroad, for example, may qualify as an unforeseen return. Other unexpected events, such as family emergencies, could also qualify.

Visits to Canada

Non-residents can make occasional visits to Canada for personal or business purposes without affecting their status. The visits must not be regular and must be of limited duration. Extended stays in Canada can change your tax status to that of resident or deemed resident, in which case you would be taxed on your worldwide income.

Date of Departure

The date of departure is the date on which you cease to be a Canadian resident and cease to be subject to certain forms of taxation. The date of departure is the latest of three dates:

   a) the date you leave Canada;
   b) the date your spouse and/or dependants leave Canada; or
   c) the date you establish residency in the country of immigration.

According to these rules, you cannot sever your Canadian residency until your spouse and/or dependants have also left Canada. There is one exception to this rule: if you are returning to a country where you previously resided and your spouse is remaining in Canada only temporarily, then the date of departure will be the later of (a) or (c) above; (b) will not apply.

Advanced Rulings

Revenue Canada's International Taxation Office is responsible for evaluating the residency status of persons leaving Canada. You can request an advanced ruling by filing form NR73. Since no two sets of circumstances are identical, it is highly recommended that you obtain an advanced ruling if you are seriously considering becoming a non-resident. It is also recommended that professional advice be sought, since legislation, jurisprudence, and Revenue Canada pronouncements can all affect the requirements for establishing non-resident status. It is important to note that Revenue Canada's assessment is not binding on Revenue Quebec but is binding on all other provinces.

Tax Effects of Becoming a Non-Resident

By becoming a non-resident, you will no longer be subject to the traditional taxes that apply to Canadian factual residents, but you will become subject to special taxes applicable to non-residents. The taxation of non-residents is discussed in the next chapter. The four sections that now follow deal with the tax effects of becoming a non-resident.

Deemed Disposition

When you cease to be a resident of Canada, you are deemed to have disposed of all of your property, *except actual and deemed taxable Canadian property*. The proceeds of disposition, which are used to compute your capital gain, are deemed to be the fair market value of the property immediately before you became a non-resident. This deemed disposition rule will trigger capital gains and capital losses that must be reported on your tax return for the year of departure. Since the deemed disposition occurs while you are still a resident of Canada, you are entitled to offset capital gains by any unused capital gains exemption (now generally restricted to qualifying shares of a small business or a farming business). Please note that there are special exceptions to the deemed disposition rules if you resided in Canada for less than sixty months in the ten years prior to departing the country.

By including in income for a single year all previously unrealized capital gains, you are more likely to be taxed at the highest marginal tax rates. In contrast, if you disposed of the property over a number of years, the same capital gains could be taxed at lower marginal tax rates. Therefore, you should consider disposing of your property in the years prior to your intended departure. If, however, your current income level already places you in the highest marginal tax bracket, then gradual dispositions generally will not provide you with a significant tax saving.

Important tax savings can also be realized by choosing a departure date wisely. December 31 is the worst possible departure date, since your income will then include all salaries and wages you earned during that year, as well as all accrued capital gains triggered by the deemed disposition rules. You will probably find that your optimal departure date will be in early January; by that time, you will have earned little or no employment income, and only the capital gains caused by the deemed disposition rules will be taxed. As we discussed in an earlier chapter, part-year residents (this category includes individuals who severed Canadian residency during the year) are entitled only to reduced personal tax credits and deductions. It may be prudent to obtain professional advice in determining your optimal departure date.

Please also note that an election can be made to defer the actual payment of tax resulting from the deemed disposition rules (form T2074), but Revenue Canada requires acceptable security and charges interest on the unpaid balance.

Taxable Canadian Property

Taxable Canadian property is a special class of capital property identified by the Income Tax Act. Actual or deemed taxable Canadian property is excluded from the deemed disposition rules described above. In the following chapter, you will discover that non-residents are taxed in the same manner as residents when they dispose of taxable Canadian property. As a result, Revenue Canada is taxing on departure only those assets that will not be subject to tax in the future.

You can elect to treat other types of property as taxable Canadian property. The effect of this would be to defer the inclusion in income of any accrued capital gains and losses until the property is actually disposed. Upon actual disposition of the property, the capital gain, including any increase in the property's value since you severed your residency, will be taxed in Canada. For example, if you become a non-resident and choose to treat your coin collection, which has a fair market value of $100,000 and a cost of $25,000, as taxable Canadian property, then no capital gain will be triggered by your departure from Canada. If you subsequently sell the collection for $150,000, you will have to pay tax on the $125,000 capital gain. This example raises the issue of selectivity. If you had not made the election, you would have triggered a capital gain of only $75,000 (i.e., $100,000 less $25,000). If the collection was then subsequently sold for $150,000, no further capital gain would have been taxable in Canada. The lesson here is to avoid the election on property that will appreciate in the future.

You can also elect to trigger capital gains on property that qualifies as taxable Canadian property. If, prior to departing Canada, you owned shares of a private company with a fair market value of $50,000 and a cost of $10,000, for example, then you could elect to trigger a $40,000 capital gain. Under the election, you are deemed to dispose of the property at fair market value in the same manner as all other property. The election does not, however, change the tax status of the property. The property remains taxable Canadian property and is subject to tax upon actual disposition, even though you are no longer a resident of Canada. However, given that you have already triggered — and paid tax on — the capital gain, only any further increase in the value of the property will be taxed. If the individual shareholder in our example above later sells his or her shares for $75,000, then $25,000 (i.e., $75,000 less $50,000) will be treated as a capital gain. This is a good way to exploit any unused capital gains exemption, since the exemption will not be available to you once you are a non-resident.

The list of property that qualifies as taxable Canadian property is lengthy. The following are included:

~ real property that is located in Canada, but not a mortgage interest in real property;

~ capital property (other than real property) that is used by a non-resident in carrying on business in Canada;

~ shares in a private corporation (other than a mutual-fund corporation) that is resident in Canada;

~ shares of certain Canadian mutual-fund corporations and certain non-resident corporations;

~ partnerships that derive at least 50 percent of their value from real property that is situated in Canada;

~ beneficial interests in trusts resident in Canada (though

note that the interest must be a capital interest, not just an income interest); and

~ property deemed to be taxable Canadian property (by election, as discussed above).

Pension Assets

The deemed disposition rules do not apply to most interests in pension assets, including registered pension plans (RPPs), deferred profit-sharing plans (DPSPs), registered retirement savings plans (RRSPs), and registered retirement income funds (RRIFs). Payments from these plans to a non-resident are normally subject to withholding taxes, but this may be modified by a tax treaty between Canada and the country in which you intend to reside.

Please note that certain penalties apply to funds that are withdrawn from an RRSP under the Home Buyers' Plan, but that are still unpaid at the time you cease Canadian residency.

Proposed Changes

Many important additional rules that were introduced in the federal budget on October 2, 1996, have yet to emerge in final legislative form. One of the proposed changes would require all individuals with total assets greater than $25,000 to file a list of their assets when emigrating from Canada. Property worth less than $10,000 would be exempted from the reporting requirement. Revenue Canada has issued a draft form T1161 for this purpose.

For departures from Canada after October 1, 1996, you will no longer be able to defer the application of the deemed disposition rules for taxable Canadian property. That is, you will be required to include all capital gains and/or losses in your tax return for the year of departure, thus eliminating any possible tax deferment on the accrued gains. In the years following your departure, you will still have to pay Canadian tax on any capital gains resulting from the disposition of taxable Canadian property, but again the tax will be payable only on the increase in value since your departure, as in the earlier example with the shares of the private company. This change has yet to be applied in practice, and it requires substantial clarification before it can be implemented.

NINE

The Taxation of Non-Residents

In this chapter, you will learn:
~ *How non-residents are taxed on certain Canadian-source income*
~ *How to identify income that is subject to Canadian withholding taxes*
~ *Which non-residents must file a Canadian tax return*

*I*n the previous chapter, we discussed how you could become a non-resident of Canada, as well as which criteria Revenue Canada will emphasize in its evaluation of your status. In this chapter, we will discuss in greater depth how non-residents are actually taxed.

It would be a gross oversimplification to state that non-residents are not subject to Canadian taxes. In fact, non-residents must pay Canadian income taxes on certain types of income. In general, income earned by non-residents can be divided into five categories:

  a) income earned from business or employment outside Canada;
  b) capital gains or losses from dispositions of property, other than taxable Canadian property;

    c) income earned from business or employment in Canada;

    d) capital gains or losses resulting from the disposition of taxable Canadian property; and

    e) income from other Canadian sources.

As a non-resident, you are not subject to Canadian taxes on income that falls under category (a) or (b). For income that falls under category (c), (d), or (e), however, you would often be subject to some form of Canadian tax.

Business or Employment Income Earned in Canada and Dispositions of Taxable Canadian Property

(Note: For the balance of this chapter, we are assuming that you are in fact a non-resident.)

If you carry on a business in Canada, earn employment income in Canada, or dispose of taxable Canadian property — that is, if you have income from category (c) or (d) above — *you must file a Canadian tax return and pay Canadian taxes*. Unlike factual residents, who must pay taxes on their worldwide income, you are taxed only on your Canadian-source income. You are also entitled to many deductions and to certain tax credits.

Disposition of Property by a Non-Resident

Any capital gain resulting from the disposition of taxable Canadian property[4] is subject to a special withholding tax. But if you dispose of taxable Canadian property (including property that former Canadian residents elected to treat as taxable Canadian property, as discussed in the previous chapter), you must file a Canadian tax return for the year of disposition. The taxes withheld by the buyer will be credited towards your final tax bill.

A person, either resident or non-resident, who purchases taxable Canadian property, real property situated in Canada, or an interest in such property from a non-resident is required to withhold 33 1/3 percent of the purchase price and remit that amount to Revenue Canada. Since the vendor in these circumstances is a non-resident, Revenue Canada cannot easily force that individual to file a Canadian tax return and to pay the applicable taxes. The withholding-tax process helps ensure that enough money is collected at the time of the sale. Alternatively, the non-resident vendor (you) may prefer not to be subject to withholding taxes; this can be accomplished by filing form T2062 with Revenue Canada and by prepaying the tax liability or providing Revenue Canada with adequate security. If you file form T2062 and it is accepted by Revenue Canada, then the purchaser is not required to withhold and remit any amounts to the agency so long as the final purchase price does not exceed the amount you reported on form T2062. It is highly recommended that you file form T2062, since it will avoid any delay in obtaining a refund of the excess taxes that would otherwise have been withheld.

Similar reporting and withholding procedures apply when you dispose of resource property, depreciable taxable Canadian property, and life-insurance policies. The withholding rate for such dispositions is 50 percent, instead of 33 1/3 percent.

Quebec has similar reporting and withholding requirements for dispositions of real estate, business property, and resource property within that province. The Quebec withholding rate is 18 percent, and double prepayment (Quebec and federal) may be required.

Please also note that dispositions of certain types of property (including Canadian resource property, timber resource property, and income interests in trusts resident in Canada) qualify as ordinary income or loss (fully taxable), instead of capital gains or losses (taxable at 75 percent). If you dispose of such property, you will be required to file a tax return in the year of disposition.

The table below may help explain the rules regarding dispositions of property by non-residents. If you dispose of property located outside Canada, the resulting gain (or loss) is not subject to Canadian taxes. If the property is located in Canada but was not taxable Canadian property, the resulting gain (or loss) also goes untaxed. But if the property is taxable Canadian property or if you elected to treat the property as taxable Canadian property when you became a non-resident (see the previous chapter), the gain (or loss) resulting from the disposition is subject to Canadian tax.

Where is the the property located?	Is the property taxable Canadian property?	Did you elect to treat the property as taxable Canadian property?	Is the resulting capital gain taxable in Canada?	Are you required to file a tax return?
Outside Canada	Not applicable	No	No	No
In Canada	No	No	No	No
In Canada	No	Yes	Yes	Yes
In Canada	Yes	Not applicable	Yes	Yes

Foreign Tax Credits

You are entitled to a foreign tax credit if the disposition of property previously elected to be taxable Canadian property results in double taxation on your departure (i.e., you are required to pay taxes in your country of residence as well as in Canada). A full credit will not be available, however, if you earned other taxable income in Canada during the same year.

Deductions Allowed in Calculating Taxable Income

If you earn income on Canadian-source business or employment and/or capital gains from the disposition of taxable Canadian property, you are entitled to the same deductions that are available to normal residents. However, certain rules may prevent you from using these deductions.

In broad terms, the deductions you claim must relate to the income declared on your tax return. For example, if you sold shares of a private company at a profit, you would be permitted to deduct the interest on the money borrowed to acquire those shares. Some special restrictions apply to the deductions for moving expenses, childcare expenses, and foreign exploration and development expenses. You are entitled to most other deductions only when the income you earn is subject to tax under the general rules (rather than under the withholding-tax rules).

If you are required to file a Canadian tax return, you are subject to tax under the general rules and are *always* entitled to claim the following deductions in calculating your taxable income:

~ qualifying employee stock-option benefits;

~ repayments of Employment Insurance benefits;

~ prospector's exemptions;

~ available loss carryovers;

~ amounts exempt from tax owing to tax treaties; and

~ Canadian workers' compensation or social assistance.

Also, you may claim all of the deductions available to a Canadian resident (i.e., not only those listed above) if all or substantially all (90 percent or more) of your income for the year is Canadian-source employment or business income. If you are a former Canadian resident, you may also satisfy the 90 percent rule by including in your income any scholarships, bursaries, or research grants received during the year.

Deductible Losses and Loss Carryovers

The types of deductible losses are explained below. For now, you need note only two important points. First, losses from business and employment, net capital losses, and allowable business investment losses normally give rise to deductions from income for Canadian residents. Second, if a resident taxpayer has insufficient income to make use of the loss in the year in which it was incurred — that is, if her income from other sources is in aggregate less than her total losses for the year — then she is entitled to carry the loss back to offset income reported in prior years or to carry it forward to offset income in future years. For example, if you were a Canadian resident who incurred a business loss of $15,000 and earned employment income of $10,000, you would have a non-capital loss carryforward of $5,000. The loss would be non-capital in nature because it did not arise from the disposition of capital property. Traditionally, non-residents could not benefit from these carryover rules. However, recent changes have reversed Revenue Canada's policy in this regard. The new administrative rule is as follows: if a loss would have been taxable in Canada had the activity produced income, then the loss may be used to reduce your income.

Losses from Business (Including Farming Losses)

A loss from business arises when the deductible expenses of a business exceed its revenues. You may deduct from income any losses from business activities carried on in Canada. Your deduction is limited to whatever income is subject to Canadian taxes, and may be used to offset your income for the three years prior to and the seven years following the year of the loss. You may not deduct losses from business activities carried on outside Canada. Losses from business activities carried on in Canada when you were a resident may be applied to offset income in years of non-residence and vice versa. For example, if you suffered a business loss of $35,000 in 1998 and had earned employment income of $10,000 in both 1996 and 1998, you would be able to apply the loss to reduce your taxable income to nil for both 1998 and 1996. In addition, you would still be entitled to reduce your taxable income by $15,000 in the future (until 2005).

Losses from Employment

Losses from employment are very rare but are usually incurred by salespeople who pay their own travel expenses. These losses may give rise to a deduction if they are incurred as a result of duties or employment performed in Canada. They could then be applied to reduce income from any Canadian source. Losses from employment may be used to offset income for the three years prior to and the seven years following the year of the loss. Note, however, that losses from employment activities outside Canada will never give rise to a deduction from Canadian income. Unlike losses from business, losses from employment that were incurred during a year of residence cannot be carried to a year of non-residence. The reverse, however, is not true: losses that are incurred in a year of non-residence can be carried to a year of residence. The inconsistency is difficult to explain, particularly when you consider that both losses arose from activities that are subject to Canadian tax.

It would be rare for you to find yourself working in Canada, incurring a loss, and remaining a non-resident all at the same time. If you do find yourself in such a situation, you should evaluate whether your level of worldwide income is such that sojourning in Canada for 183 days or more per year, and thus being taxed on your worldwide income, would be more advantageous. This strategy would allow you to deduct the loss against any other income that would not otherwise have been subject to Canadian tax. Needless to say, professional advice would be required if such a change in residency status was contemplated.

Net Capital Losses

You incur a capital loss when you dispose of capital property (often interpreted as any property except inventory) for an amount that is less than what you originally paid for that property. (Note that there are exceptions to this for property received by way of a gift or a bequest.) An *allowable* capital loss, simply put, is 75 percent of the capital loss described above. In computing your taxable income for the year, you may deduct only allowable capital losses arising from the disposition of any taxable Canadian property (excluding certain types of personal property). Your deduction is limited to the amount of taxable capital gains arising from the disposition of the same type of property and included in your income for the year. Losses from the disposition of any other type of property during the period you are a non-resident will not be deductible. Let's say that in 1999, you sell a cottage in Ontario for $120,000. You had acquired the cottage for $80,000 a few years earlier. Also in 1999, you sell shares of a private Canadian corporation for a capital loss of $100,000. On your 1999 tax return, you will be required to declare a *taxable* capital gain of $30,000 (i.e., 75 percent of the $40,000 capital gain from the sale of the cottage). You will also be permitted to deduct some of the *allowable* capital loss of $75,000 (i.e., 75 percent of the $100,000 capital loss from the sale of the shares), but only to the extent that you had taxable capital gains from the disposition of the same type of property (i.e., taxable Canadian property). Your deduction for 1999 will therefore be limited to $30,000, and the remaining $45,000 will be deductible against capital gains arising from dispositions on taxable Canadian property for three years prior to and for an indefinite number of years following 1999. If you were once a Canadian resident or will be a resident of Canada in the future, losses from the disposition of taxable Canadian property can be carried back or carried forward to years of residence. The reverse is also true: losses arising in years of residence may be used to offset gains realized in years of non-residence.

Allowable Business Investment Losses

Allowable business investment losses (ABILs) are capital losses incurred on the disposition of shares and debts of a small business corporation (SBC). To use the loss to reduce your Canadian-source income, the shares and/or debts of the SBC must qualify as taxable Canadian property. Unlike allowable capital losses, which can be deducted only against taxable capital gains, ABILs can be used to offset income from any source. To be an SBC, the business must be a Canadian-controlled private corporation (as a non-resident, you cannot control the corporation) with active business income that represents all or substantially all (90 percent) of its income. If the corporation for which the shares or debt are sold is not an SBC, then 75 percent of any loss that arises from such disposition will be treated as an allowable capital loss and not an ABIL. If, in our previous example, the company whose shares you sold was controlled by Canadian residents and 90 percent of its income was considered active business income (thus qualifying the company as a small business corporation), then the $100,000 capital loss would give rise to a $75,000 ABIL. If you had also earned Canadian business income of $50,000 during the year, then the entire ABIL would have been deductible, since your total income would have amounted to $80,000 (i.e., $50,000 in business income and $30,000 in a taxable capital gain from the sale of the cottage). The carryover rules for ABILs are essentially the same as those for allowable capital losses (i.e., they may be carried back three years and carried forward an indefinite number of years), with one important exception. If an ABIL is not used within seven years, then it reverts to an allowable capital loss, is added to the pool of net capital losses, and, for non-residents, may be deducted only against taxable capital gains on dispositions of taxable Canadian property.

Personal Tax Credits

You are *always* entitled to personal tax credits for the following items:
- ~ charitable donations;
- ~ gifts to the Crown and gifts of cultural property;
- ~ disability (not a transferred amount);
- ~ qualifying tuition fees (not a transferred amount);
- ~ contributions to the Canada Pension Plan or the Quebec Pension Plan; and
- ~ contributions to Employment Insurance.

The personal tax credits for other items, such as medical expenses, are available to you if 90 percent or more of your income for the year is employment and/or business income from Canadian sources. However, the following special rules apply:
- ~ To transfer your spouse's unused personal amounts, only you need satisfy the 90 percent test.
- ~ The pension income credit is not available, except for those non-residents who choose to file a Canadian tax return under a section 217 election. This topic is discussed later in this chapter.
- ~ Donations to foreign charities do not give rise to a tax credit.
- ~ Medical expenses used in calculating the related tax credit may be incurred in or outside Canada.
- ~ A dependant cannot transfer the disability credit to you unless he or she was a resident of Canada during some part of the year.

Federal Surtax

Any income that cannot be attributed to a particular province is subject to a federal surtax of 52 percent of your basic taxes payable (i.e., the taxes computed using the regular Canadian tax rates). In view of the recent reductions in some provincial tax rates, this federal surtax may well exceed the taxes that would otherwise be owed to a province.

Withholding Taxes

Many payments from Canadian sources to non-residents are subject to withholding taxes. The general withholding-tax rate is 25 percent, but a tax treaty between Canada and your country of residence may reduce this rate. Few of the low- or no-tax jurisdictions studied in this book benefit from a tax treaty with Canada.

Sizeable tax savings may still be realized after you become a non-resident, notwithstanding this 25 percent withholding tax. For example, if you contributed $10,000 to your registered retirement savings plan (RRSP) when you were a resident of Canada and were taxed at a marginal rate of 45 percent, then you would have saved $4,500 in the year of the contribution. If you withdrew the $10,000 after you became a non-resident, then the transferor would be required to withhold $2,500 (25 percent) in withholding taxes. This means, of course, that you would have effectively saved $2,000 in taxes.

There are two distinct tax systems that deal with non-residents. The first system deals with non-residents who carry on business in Canada, are employed in Canada, or dispose of taxable Canadian property during the year. If you have undertaken any of these three activities, you must file a Canadian tax return and pay Canadian taxes according to the normal progressive rates.

The second system is based on withholding taxes, and requires a Canadian taxpayer to hold back a fixed percentage of tax from your income and remit that amount to Revenue Canada. As a non-resident, you are to receive only the net amount. The tax must also be withheld even if the amount is only credited to your account and no actual payment is made. You are not required to file a Canadian tax return under this system, and your tax liability is limited to the amount of tax withheld at the source. For example, let's say you hold $100,000 in Bell Canada bonds that pay an annual interest rate of 10 percent, or $10,000 per year. Every year, Bell Canada will be required to withhold $2,500 (i.e., 25 percent of $10,000) in taxes, remit that amount to Revenue Canada, and send you a cheque for the $7,500 difference. You are not required to file a Canadian tax return, and your tax bill will never exceed the $2,500.

The following Canadian sources of income are subject to withholding taxes:

~ interest (including standby charges and commitment fees);[5]

~ dividends (including stock dividends and dividends paid out of the "capital dividend account" but excluding those paid out of the "pre-1972 capital surplus on hand account");[6]

~ superannuation benefits;

~ pension benefits;[7]

~ deferred profit-sharing plan (DPSP) payments;

~ registered retirement savings plan (RRSP) benefits;

~ registered retirement income fund (RRIF) benefits;

~ retiring allowances (with some exceptions);

~ death benefits;

~ Employment Insurance benefits (rare for non-residents);

~ annuity payments;[8]

~ payments from a registered education savings plan (RESP);[9]

~ rents and royalties for Canadian property;[10]

~ alimony payments made prior to May 1997; and

~ estate or trust income.[11]

Non-Arm's-Length Transfers

The same income-attribution rules that apply to transfers to spouses or children can also apply to transfers involving non-residents. If, as a resident of Canada, you transfer income-generating property to your resident spouse or child, then any income from that property is attributed back to you (except capital gains on transfers to a related child). If you and the person to whom you are transferring the property (i.e., your spouse or your child) are non-residents, then the attribution rules are of little concern because any income generated by the property will be subject to the same rate of withholding tax. However, if you are a resident of Canada but your spouse or child is a non-resident, then any income will be included on your tax return and taxed at the full Canadian rates. Any payments to the non-resident transferee (i.e., your spouse or your child) will be free of withholding taxes.

Old Age Security Benefits

Your old age security (OAS) benefits are subject to withholding taxes if you are a non-resident. An exception exists for U.S. residents: OAS benefits are not taxable in Canada but are taxed by the U.S. in the same manner as U.S. social security (i.e., a minimum of 85 percent of the benefits are taxable). In other words, as a U.S. resident, you must file a U.S. tax return and include in income up to 85 percent of your OAS benefits. The benefits will be remitted to you by the Canadian government, free of any withholding taxes. The new OAS clawback can reduce your OAS benefits to nil if your income for the year exceeds $84,000 or if you failed to file a tax return for the previous year. If you are not required to file a return or if you elect not to under sections 216 or 217 of the Income Tax Act (discussed below), you can report your income for the purposes of the OAS clawback rule on form T1136. Please note that if you reside in a country with which Canada has negotiated a tax treaty, then that treaty may impose limits on Canada's right to withhold taxes and would effectively override the OAS clawback rule. It is this override effect that explains why the OAS payments to U.S. residents are not subject to withholding taxes.

Section 216 Election

Section 216 of the Income Tax Act allows you to file a special Canadian tax return. You may use this section 216 election only if you receive rent from real property situated in Canada, royalties from a timber resource property, and/or a share of partnership income derived from such properties.

Section 216 is only an election: this means that you have the option of filing a tax return using form T1159 or allowing your income to be taxed under the withholding-tax system. You are not required to report your worldwide income or all of your Canadian-source income on form T1159; only the rent, royalties, and share of partnership income mentioned above need be reported. Section 216 allows you to deduct all expenses incurred to earn the income, including capital cost allowance (i.e., depreciation for tax purposes). You cannot use loss carryovers to reduce the amount of income subject to Canadian tax, and you cannot claim any personal tax credits. Your tax burden is computed using the same progressive tax rates that are applicable to Canadian residents. The election does not change the requirement that tax be withheld from payments to non-residents — the taxes withheld are simply credited as taxes paid on form T1159.

The only reason for filing form T1159 is to recover all or some of the withholding taxes. The election should be filed only if it results in a refund of taxes. This is achieved by your deducting expenses that would go unused under the withholding-tax system (because it is the gross amount, not the net amount, that is subject to the withholding taxes). Form T1159 must be filed within two years of the year of receipt of the income.

Section 217 Election

(Section 217 of the Income Tax Act has twice been amended since 1993. The rules discussed here are applicable for calendar years after 1996. The section is very complex, and at the present time any elections under section 217 should be reviewed or prepared by a tax specialist or financial planner.)

Sections 217 and 216 have some important similarities: both apply to non-resident taxpayers (including part-year residents) and both allow the taxpayer to choose whether to file a tax return. The difference between the two elections lies in the fact that section 217 applies to individuals who receive pension income, superannuation benefits, and other similar payments.

Another difference is that if you elect to file a tax return under section 217, you must also include in that return any income from carrying on a business in Canada, any income from employment in Canada, and any taxable capital gains from the disposition of taxable Canadian property. In normal circumstances, you would have to file a separate tax return for these three sources of income using the T1 General Return for Non-Residents and Deemed Residents of Canada. But a new form is likely to be created by Revenue Canada to deal with the complexities surrounding this election. The tax return must be filed by June 30 of the year following the year the income was subject to withholding tax.

With the exception of loss carryovers, normal deductions are permitted so long as they relate directly to the income reported. The calculation of allowable personal tax credits is extremely complex and is discussed here only by way of interest. If your Canadian *taxable* income represents less than 50 percent of your worldwide income, you are entitled to only a few tax credits. More tax credits are permitted if your Canadian *taxable* income represents 50 percent or more of your total worldwide income. Full tax credits are available if your Canadian *net* income represents 90 percent or more of your total worldwide income. Finally, taxes are calculated using the average marginal rates that would have resulted had your total (i.e., 100 percent) worldwide income been subject to Canadian taxes. If the effective tax rate on the return, after applying the appropriate deductions and credits, is less than the withholding rate, then it is in your interest to file a tax return under section 217. Any tax withheld from Canadian-source income may be claimed as a tax payment.

Conclusion

These last few chapters on taxation demonstrate that there are many complex tax issues affecting offshore planning. This fact, however, should not deter you from exploring the possible advantages of using offshore tools in your financial planning.

In most cases, you will find that consulting a reliable and trustworthy tax professional or financial planner will prove extremely worthwhile. The information that has been conveyed to you in these chapters will help you understand the options that a professional adviser will recommend. Ultimately, we hope that you will be in a position to make a more informed decision, based on a more intimate understanding of your personal and financial goals.

Tax Tables

Table 1: Revenue Canada Forms and Publications

Revenue Canada publishes a number of forms, guides, information circulars (ICs), and interpretation bulletins (ITs). Forms give taxpayers a means of providing Revenue Canada with certain information, guides explain how to use the forms, information circulars outline the status of the tax law, and interpretation bulletins clarify Revenue Canada's interpretation of the law. Most forms and publications are available free of charge at Revenue Canada's Web site (www.rc.gc.ca/).

As will be seen in the long list that follows, Revenue Canada has made a concerted effort to publish its pronouncements in many areas affecting non-residents and non-resident transactions. These documents are often short and easy to understand; they are an excellent source of information for anyone devising an offshore (or onshore) tax-planning strategy. The documents listed below deal only with matters that affect non-residents or non-resident transactions; consequently, this list is only a sample of the documents available from Revenue Canada.

Information Circulars

~ IC72-17R4: Procedures Concerning the Disposition of Taxable Canadian Property by Non-Residents of Canada — Section 116

~ IC75-6R: Required Withholding from Amounts Paid to Non-Resident Persons Performing Services in Canada

~ IC76-12R4: Applicable Rate of Part XIII Tax on Amounts Paid or Credited to Persons in Treaty Countries

~ IC76-12R4SR: Special Release

~ IC77-16R4: Non-Resident Income Tax

~ IC77-9R: Books, Records and Other Requirements for Taxpayers Having Foreign Affiliates

~ IC87-2: International Transfer Pricing/Other International Transactions

~ IC94-4: International Transfer Pricing: Advance Pricing Agreements (APA)

Interpretation Bulletins

~ IT59R3: Interest on Debts Owing to Specified Non-Residents (Thin Capitalization)

~ IT68R2: Exemption from Income Tax in Canada — Professors and Teachers from Other Countries

~ IT76R2: Exempt Portion of Pension When Employee Has Been a Non-Resident

~ IT81R: Partnerships — Income of Non-Resident Partners

~ IT106R2: Crown Corporation Employees Abroad

~ IT122R2: United States Social Security Taxes and Benefits

~ IT137R3: Additional Tax on Certain Corporations Carrying On Business in Canada

~ IT137R3SR: Additional Tax on Certain Corporations Carrying On Business in Canada (Supplemental)

~ IT150R2: Acquisition from a Non-Resident of Certain Property on Death or Mortgage Foreclosure or by Virtue of a Deemed Disposition

~ IT155R3: Exemption from Non-Resident Tax on Interest Payable on Certain Bonds, Debentures, Notes, Hypothecs or Similar Obligations

~ IT155R3SR: Exemption from Non-Resident Tax on Interest Payable on Certain Bonds, Debentures, Notes, Hypothecs or Similar Obligations (Supplemental)

~ IT161R3: Non-Residents — Exemption from Tax Deductions at Source on Employment Income

~ IT161R3SR: S.R. — Non-Resident Exemption

~ IT163R2: Election by Non-Resident Individuals on Certain Canadian Source Income

~ IT171R2: Non-Resident Individuals — Computation of Taxable Income Earned in Canada and Non-Refundable Tax Credits [1988 and Subsequent Taxation Years]

~ IT173R2: Capital Gains Derived in Canada by Residents of the United States

~ IT173R2SR: Capital Gains Derived in Canada by Residents of the United States (Supplemental)

~ IT177R2: Permanent Establishment of a Corporation in a Province and of a Foreign Enterprise in Canada

~ IT177R2SR: Permanent Establishment of a Corporation in a Province and of a Foreign Enterprise in Canada (Supplemental)

~ IT183: Foreign Tax Credit — Member of a Partnership

~ IT193SR: Taxable Income of Individuals Resident in Canada during Part of a Year

~ IT194: Foreign Tax Credit — Part-Time Residents

~ IT201R: Foreign Tax Credit — Trusts and Beneficiaries

~ IT201R2: Foreign Tax Credit — Trusts and Beneficiaries

~ IT-221R2: Determination of an Individual's Residence Status

~ IT221R2SR: Determination of an Individual's Residence Status (Supplemental)

~ IT262R2: Losses of Non-Residents and Part-Year Residents

~ IT-270R2: Foreign Tax Credit

~ IT290: Non-Resident-Owned Investment Corporation — Meaning of Principal Business

~ IT298: Canada-U.S. Tax Convention — Number of Days Present in Canada

~ IT303: Know-How and Similar Payments to Non-Residents

~ IT303SR: Know-How and Similar Payments to Non-Residents (Supplemental)

~ IT-351: Income from a Foreign Source — Blocked Currency

~ IT361R3: Exemption from Part XIII Tax on Interest Payments to Non-Residents

~ IT388: Income Bonds Issued by Foreign Corporations

~ IT393R2: Election Re: Tax on Rents and Timber Royalties to Non-Residents

~ IT395R: Foreign Tax Credit — Foreign-Source Capital Gains and Losses

~ IT412R2: Foreign Property of Registered Plans

~ IT420R3SR: Non-Residents — Income Earned in Canada

~ IT447: Residence of a Trust or Estate

~ IT451R: Deemed Disposition and Acquisition on Ceasing to Be or Becoming Resident in Canada

~ IT465R: Non-Resident Beneficiaries of Trusts

~ IT468R: Management or Administration Fees Paid to Non-Residents

~ IT494: Hire of Ships and Aircraft from Non-Residents

~ IT497R: Overseas Employment Tax Credit [1984 to 1987 Taxation Years]

~ IT497R3: Overseas Employment Tax Credit

~ IT-506: Foreign Income Taxes as a Deduction from Income

~ IT520: Unused Foreign Tax Credits — Carryforward and Carryback

Forms and Guides

~ T1: General for Non-Residents and Deemed Residents of Canada

~ T1134-A: Information Return Relating to Foreign Affiliates That Are Not Controlled Foreign Affiliates

~ T1134-B: Information Return Relating to Controlled Foreign Affiliates

~ T1161: List of Properties by an Emigrant of Canada

~ T2061: Election by an Emigrant to Defer Deemed Disposition of Property and Capital Gains Thereon

~ T2061A: Election by an Emigrant to Report Deemed Dispositions of Taxable Canadian Property and Capital Gains and/or Losses Thereon

~ T4055: Newcomers to Canada

~ T4056: Emigrants and Income Tax

~ T4057: Tax Guide for International Students and Teachers in Canada

~ T4058: Non-Residents and Temporary Residents of Canada

~ T4061: Non-Resident Withholding Tax Guide 1997

~ T4131: Canadian Residents Abroad — 1997

~ T4133: Are You a Newcomer to Canada?

~ T4144: Income Tax Guide for Non-Residents Electing Under Section 216 — 1997

~ T4145: Electing under Section 217 of the Income Tax Act — 1997

~ T4155: Old Age Security Return of Income Guide for Non-Residents 1997

~ T5013-R: T1 General Return — Outside Canada 1997

~ T5113-G: General Income Tax Guide for Non-Residents and Deemed Residents of Canada — 1997

~ NR73: Determination of Residency Status (Leaving Canada)

~ NR74: Determination of Residency Status (Entering Canada)

~ NR980804: U.S. Tax Refunds Issued for Canadian Seniors

~ FS1295: Information for Canadians Going to the United States for Extended Periods

~ P151: Canadian Residents Going Down South

These lists are ever-changing. For the latest list of pronouncements, you should check directly with Revenue Canada.

Table 2: Withholding Tax Rates

The table that follows provides a good overview of withholding tax rates applicable to countries with which Canada has a tax treaty. These rates were drawn from two Revenue Canada information circulars — namely, IC76-12R4 and IC76-12R4SR. The statutory tax rate for withholdings is 25 percent, and residents of other non-treaty countries will be subject to that rate of tax.

Management fees paid or credited to residents of treaty countries are normally exempt from withholding tax if they are reasonable in relation to the services performed by the non-resident. If the payment is exempt from withholding taxes, the remitter must still retain 15 percent of the gross amount as a pre-payment on any potential Part I tax. The issue is more complex than it appears, but needless to say some treaty countries are excluded from this rule. Here are some examples:

~ Barbados: 15 percent withholding rate if the management fee is taxable in Barbados, 25 percent otherwise;
~ Guyana: 10 percent withholding rate;
~ India: 25 percent withholding rate;
~ Jamaica: 12.5 percent withholding rate if the management fee is taxable in Jamaica, 25 percent otherwise;
~ Kenya: 15 percent withholding rate.

Country of Residence	Interest	Dividends	Periodic Pension Benefits or Annuity Payments	Lump-Sum Pension Benefits or Annuity Payments	Estate or Trust Income	Alimony	Rents, Royalties, etc. Movable & Intangible Property	Rents, Royalties, etc. Immovable Property
Australia	15%	15%	25% for income-averaging annuities; 15% otherwise	15% for pension benefits; 25% for annuities	15% if taxable in country of residence; 25% otherwise	25%	10%	25%
Austria	15% if taxable in country of residence; 25% otherwise	15%	25%	25%	15%	0%	10% if taxable in country of residence; 25% otherwise	25%
Bangladesh	15%	15%	25% for income-averaging annuities; 15% otherwise	25%	25%	0% if taxable in country of residence; 25% otherwise		25%
Barbados	15% if taxable in country of residence; 25% otherwise	15%	25% for income-averaging annuities; 15% otherwise	25%	15% if taxable in country of residence; 25% otherwise	0% if taxable in country of residence; 25% otherwise	10% if taxable in country of residence; 25% otherwise	25%
Belgium	15%	15%	25%	25%	15%	0% if taxable in country of residence; 25% otherwise	10%	25%
Brazil	15% for companies; 25% for individuals	15% for companies holding at least a 10% equity percentage; 25% otherwise	0% on first $4,000 in the year; 25% on the excess (0% for OAS)	25% for annuities; 0% on first $4,000 in pension benefits in the year; 25% on the excess	25%	0% on first $4,000 per year; 25% on the excess	25% for individuals; 25% for companies re: trademarks; 15% otherwise	25%
Cameroon	15%	15%	25%	25%	25%	25%	15%	25%

Country of Residence	Interest	Dividends	Periodic Pension Benefits or Annuity Payments	Lump-Sum Pension Benefits or Annuity Payments	Estate or Trust Income	Alimony	Rents, Royalties, etc. Movable & Intangible Property	Rents, Royalties, etc. Immovable Property
China (People's Republic of)	10%	10% for companies holding at least 10% of voting stock; 15% otherwise	25%	25%	25%	25%	10%	25%
Cyprus	15%	15%	25% for income-averaging annuities; 15% for other annuities; 0% on first $10,000 of pension benefits in the year; 15% on the excess	25% for annuities; 25% for pension benefits in excess of $10,000	15% if taxable in country of residence; 25% otherwise	0% if taxable in country of residence; 25% otherwise	10%	25%
Denmark	15%	15%	0%	0% for pension benefits; 25% for annuities	25%	25%	15%	15%
Dominican Republic	18% if taxable in country of residence; 25% otherwise	18%	18%	25%	18% if taxable in country of residence; 25% otherwise	0% if taxable in country of residence; 25% otherwise	18% if taxable in country of residence; 25% otherwise	25%
Egypt	15%	15%	25%	25%	15% if taxable in country of residence; 25% otherwise	25%	15%	25%
Finland	15%	15%	0%	25%	25%	25%	15%	15%

Country of Residence	Interest	Dividends	Periodic Pension Benefits or Annuity Payments	Lump-Sum Pension Benefits or Annuity Payments	Estate or Trust Income	Alimony	Rents, Royalties, etc. Movable & Intangible Property	Rents, Royalties, etc. Immovable Property
France	10%	10% for companies holding at least 10% of voting stock; 15% otherwise	25%	25%	15% if taxable in country of residence; 25% otherwise	0% if taxable in country of residence; 25% otherwise	10% if taxable in country of residence; 25% otherwise	25%
Germany	15%	15%	25% for income-averaging annuities; 15% otherwise	25%	25%	0%	10%	25%
Guyana	15%	15%	25%	25%	25%	0% if taxable in country of residence; 25% otherwise	10%	25%
India	15%	15% for companies holding at least 10% of the shares; 25% otherwise	25%	25%	25%	25%	25%	25%
Indonesia	15% if taxable in country of residence; 25% otherwise	15%	25% for income-averaging annuities; 15% otherwise	25%	25%	0%	15% if taxable in country of residence; 25% otherwise	25%
Ireland	15%	15%	0%	15%	15%	15%	15%	15%
Israel	15% if taxable in country of residence; 25% otherwise	15%	25% for income-averaging annuities; 15% otherwise	25%	15% if taxable in country of residence; 25% otherwise	0% if taxable in country of residence; 25% otherwise	15% if taxable in country of residence; 25% otherwise	25%

Country of Residence	Interest	Dividends	Periodic Pension Benefits or Annuity Payments	Lump-Sum Pension Benefits or Annuity Payments	Estate or Trust Income	Alimony	Rents, Royalties, etc. Movable & Intangible Property	Rents, Royalties, etc. Immovable Property
Italy	15%	15%	25% for annuities; 0% on first $10,000 or 12M lira (whichever is greater) of pension benefits in the year; 25% on the excess (maximum average of 15% for pensions)	25% for annuities; 0% on first $10,000 or 12M lira (whichever is greater) of pension benefits in the year; 25% on the excess	25%	25%	10%	25%
Ivory Coast	15%	15%	15%	25%	25%	25%	10%	25%
Jamaica	15% if taxable in country of residence; 25% otherwise	15%	25% for income-averaging annuities; 15% otherwise	25%	15% if taxable in country of residence; 25% otherwise	0% if taxable in country of residence; 25% otherwise	12.5% for equipment rental if taxable in country of residence; 10% for other payments if taxable in country of residence; 25% otherwise	25%
Japan	10%	10% for companies holding at least 25% of voting stock; 15% otherwise	25%	25%	25%	25%	10%	25%

Country of Residence	Interest	Dividends	Periodic Pension Benefits or Annuity Payments	Lump-Sum Pension Benefits or Annuity Payments	Estate or Trust Income	Alimony	Rents, Royalties, etc. Movable & Intangible Property	Rents, Royalties, etc. Immovable Property
Kenya	15% if taxable in country of residence; 25% otherwise	15% for companies holding at least 10% of voting stock; 25% otherwise	25% for income-averaging annuities; 15% otherwise	25%	25%	25%	15% if taxable in country of residence; 25% otherwise	25%
Korea	15%	15%	25%	25%	25%	25%	15%	25%
Malaysia	15%	15% if taxable in country of residence; 25% otherwise	25% for income-averaging annuities; 15% otherwise	25%	15%	25%	15%	25%
Malta	15%	15%	25% for income-averaging annuities; 15% otherwise	25%	15% if taxable in country of residence; 25% otherwise	0% if taxable in country of residence; 25% otherwise	10%	25%
Morocco	15% if taxable in country of residence; 25% otherwise	15%	25%	25%	25%	25%	10% if taxable in country of residence; 25% otherwise	25%
Netherlands	15%	10% for companies holding at least 25% of voting stock; 15% otherwise	25% for income-averaging annuities; 15% otherwise	25%	0% if income is from foreign sources; 25% otherwise	0%	10%	25%

Country of Residence	Interest	Dividends	Periodic Pension Benefits or Annuity Payments	Lump-Sum Pension Benefits or Annuity Payments	Estate or Trust Income	Alimony	Rents, Royalties, etc. Movable & Intangible Property	Rents, Royalties, etc. Immovable Property
New Zealand	15%	15%	0% for first $10,000 of total payments; 25% on the excess for income-averaging annuities; 15% on the excess otherwise	25% for annuities; 15% for pension benefits if total payments exceed $10,000; 0% otherwise	15% if taxable in country of residence; 25% otherwise	25%	15%	25%
Norway	15%	15%	0%	25%	15%	0%	0% for rental of movable property; 15% otherwise	25%
Pakistan	15% if taxable in country of residence; 25% otherwise	15%	25%	25%	15% if taxable in country of residence; 25% otherwise	15% if taxable in country of residence; 25% otherwise	15% if taxable in country of residence; 25% otherwise	25%
Papua New Guinea (Not yet ratified)	10%	15%	25% for income-averaging annuities; 15% otherwise	25%	25%	25%	10%	25%
Philippines	15% if taxable in country of residence; 25% otherwise	15%	25% for annuities; 0% on first $5,000 of pension benefits in the year; variable rate (up to 25%) on the excess	25%	25%	25%	10% if taxable in country of residence; 25% otherwise	25%

Country of Residence	Interest	Dividends	Periodic Pension Benefits or Annuity Payments	Lump-Sum Pension Benefits or Annuity Payments	Estate or Trust Income	Alimony	Rents, Royalties, etc. Movable & Intangible Property	Rents, Royalties, etc. Immovable Property
Poland (Not yet ratified)	15%	15%	25% for income-averaging annuities; 15% otherwise	25%	15% if taxable in country of residence; 25% otherwise	0%	10%	25%
Romania	15% if taxable in country of residence; 25% otherwise	15%	15% for pension benefits if taxable in country of residence; 25% otherwise	25%	15% if taxable in country of residence; 25% otherwise	25%	15% if taxable in country of residence; 25% otherwise	25%
Singapore	15% if taxable in country of residence; 25% otherwise	15%	25%	25%	15% if taxable in country of residence; 25% otherwise	15% if taxable in country of residence; 25% otherwise	15% if taxable in country of residence; 25% otherwise	25%
Spain	15% if taxable in country of residence; 25% otherwise	15%	25% for income-averaging annuities; 15% otherwise	25%	15% if taxable in country of residence; 25% otherwise	0%	10% if taxable in country of residence; 25% otherwise	25%
Sri Lanka	15% if taxable in country of residence; 25% otherwise	15%	25% for income-averaging annuities; 15% otherwise	25%	15% if taxable in country of residence; 25% otherwise	0% if taxable in country of residence; 25% otherwise	15% if taxable in country of residence; 25% otherwise	25%
Sweden	15%	15%	25%	25%	15% if taxable in country of residence; 25% otherwise	0%	10%	25%

Country of Residence	Interest	Dividends	Periodic Pension Benefits or Annuity Payments	Lump-Sum Pension Benefits or Annuity Payments	Estate or Trust Income	Alimony	Rents, Royalties, etc. Movable & Intangible Property	Rents, Royalties, etc. Immovable Property
Switzerland	15%	15%	25% for income-averaging annuities; 15% otherwise	25%	25%	0% if taxable in country of residence; 25% otherwise	10%	25%
Thailand	15%	15%	25%	25%	15%	25%	15%	25%
Trinidad and Tobago	15%	15%	0%	0% for pension benefits; 25% for annuities	25%	25%	15%	25%
Tunisia	15% if taxable in country of residence; 25% otherwise	15%	25%	25%	15% if taxable in country of residence; 25% otherwise	25%	20% for trademarks, films, and equipment if taxable in country of residence; 15% for other payments if taxable in country of residence; 25% otherwise	25%
United Kingdom (Britain and Northern Ireland)	10%	10% for companies controlling at least 10% of the voting shares; 15% otherwise	25% for income-averaging annuities; 10% for other annuities; 0% for pension benefits	25%	15%	0%	10%	25%
Russian Federation	15%	15%	25%	25%	25%	25%	10%	25%

Country of Residence	Interest	Dividends	Periodic Pension Benefits or Annuity Payments	Lump-Sum Pension Benefits or Annuity Payments	Estate or Trust Income	Alimony	Rents, Royalties, etc. Movable & Intangible Property	Rents, Royalties, etc. Immovable Property
United States	15%	10% for companies holding at least 10% of voting stock; 15% otherwise	25% for income-averaging annuities; 15% otherwise	25%	0% if income is from foreign sources; 15% otherwise	0%	10%	25%
Other non-treaty countries	25%	25%	25%	25%	25%	25%	25%	25%

Getting
Out There

TEN

Profiles

In this chapter, you will learn:
~ *About the different types of individuals who may benefit from offshore planning*
~ *About your offshore-planning needs and desires by taking our self-test*

To give you some idea of the breadth of circumstances that have led people to consider offshore investing, we have included a variety of scenarios in this chapter. As you will notice when reading through these, offshore investing is not for everyone and, whatever your circumstances, must be considered with great care.

Scenarios

Inheritance
Joe Smith earns significant annual investment income as a result of money he inherited from his father's estate. He wants to pay as little tax as possible and is interested in diversifying his portfolio

by placing money in some offshore instruments. He resides in British Columbia but owns a winter home in Bermuda, also left to him by his deceased father. Joe wonders how best to structure his financial affairs.

Although Canada (unlike the United States) does not impose restrictions on investment offshore, Joe's wish to diversify his portfolio is not necessarily sufficient reason to create a complex offshore-planning scheme. If Joe continues to reside in Canada, he will be taxed on his worldwide income regardless of whether he holds property elsewhere. His Canadian tax burden will be sizeable, particularly if the investment income comes from interest. He therefore has three options to minimize or defer taxes:

1. Joe can become a non-resident (i.e., move his family and belongings away from Canada) and create an offshore corporation to hold his assets — preferably in a jurisdiction other than Bermuda.

2. Joe can become a shareholder of an international business corporation (IBC) established in a foreign jurisdiction. To avoid triggering the foreign accrual property income (FAPI) rules, Joe must do one of the following:
   ~ limit his shareholding and that of persons with whom he does not deal at arm's length to 10 percent or less; or
   ~ ensure that the IBC is not controlled by himself and four other Canadian residents, or by persons to whom he is related.

   Of course, any income that Joe repatriates to Canada will be taxed in his hands. Therefore, if he depends on the investment income for his living expenses, an IBC structure will provide no tax advantages.

3. Joe can create an offshore discretionary trust by leaving the management and distribution of his money to a trustee. In this case, Joe has no control over the distribution of his assets and cannot name himself or others (i.e., relatives, friends, charities, etc.) as potential beneficiaries. This option may prove unsuitable for investors who rely on the income from their investments. What is more, there is always the

risk of being hit by the FAPI rules if Revenue Canada can prove that you have a beneficial interest in the trust.

Small- to Medium-Size Business Owner

Janet is a consultant to major auto manufacturers and her clients are based mostly in Canada. Janet wants to reduce her taxes and expand her business so she can attract more international clients.

If Janet incorporates offshore, she should not automatically assume that the consultant fees she receives offshore will be free of tax. In fact, if she continues to manage her business from her Canadian base, her company will be considered a resident of Canada for tax purposes and will be taxed on its worldwide income. Furthermore, payments for services are subject to a 25 percent withholding tax. Any attempts by Janet to keep her operations secret, as well as any failure to disclose her income to the revenue authorities, is tax evasion (a crime).

If, on the other hand, the volume of Janet's international business increases to the point where she spends most of her time abroad and manages her operation from there, the company may not qualify as a Canadian resident. Should Janet choose to remain a Canadian resident, she could still create an offshore corporation and become its main shareholder. Consulting fees, minus the withholding tax, would be paid to that business; since consulting fees are not considered passive income, the operation would not be subject to FAPI rules.

Import/Export Business

Doris owns and operates a company that imports fruit juices from South Africa and exports bottled water to Brazil. While on vacation in Portugal, Doris discovered that Madeira has a tax regime that is beneficial to the import and export of goods. Doris would like to profit from this favourable tax structure.

Using Madeira — or many other favourable locations, for that matter — to establish a trading company is not as easy as it first seems. To begin with, if Doris incorporates her business in Madeira, she must either move there or delegate central management and control to someone on the island to avoid having her company considered a Canadian resident. She also must develop a pricing scheme that enables some of the profit to remain in the Madeiran corporation, because her company has to be more than a front for an import/export scheme operated from elsewhere. The company must, in some way, add value to the goods. For example, the Madeiran employees could take orders, organize shipping, and pay invoices — some sort of work beyond simply re-invoicing. Doris's corporation would not be subject to FAPI rules because its income is not passive in nature.

Professional

Dr. Walters is a gynecologist-obstetrician with a practice based in Calgary, Alberta. Recently, a colleague was successfully sued for causing an injury to one of the children he delivered. The court held that the risk of injury could have been reduced through proper prenatal monitoring and care. Since his medical malpractice insurance is capped at $1 million, Dr. Walters is worried that a similar lawsuit directed at him (whether genuine or frivolous) could cost him his life savings.

Dr. Walters would be well advised to set up an asset-protection trust. This set-up is not always foolproof, however. Dr. Walters should be aware that, depending on the jurisdiction, the transfer of assets from settlor to trust can be reversed under certain circumstances (most jurisdictions have fraudulent-disposition acts). For example, under Bermuda law, if a creditor believes that he or she has been prejudiced because a settlor has transferred his or her money or assets to a trust at a significant undervalue, the creditor can apply to a court to have the transfer reversed. The reversal will be granted if the obligation arose either before or within two years of the transfer of assets to the trust.

Let us assume that Dr. Walters, unaware of any pending civil action or claim against him but wishing to protect his assets from future lawsuits, transfers a large portion of his life savings to an asset-protection trust in Bermuda on October 1, 1996. He receives no consideration in return. On October 15, 1997, a malpractice claim similar to the one involving his colleague is launched against him. In March 1998, the court sides with the plaintiff and all appeals are rejected. The damages total $3 million, $1 million of which is covered by Dr. Walters's medical insurance. This leaves $2 million for the doctor to pay personally. In March 1999, the plaintiff's lawyers, unable to get the damages from Dr. Walters, discover the existence of the offshore trust. Since the doctor's obligation to pay the plaintiff arose within two years of the transfer of the assets to the trust — even though he had no knowledge of the lawsuit when he made the transfer — the plaintiff can bring a motion before a Bermuda court to void the transfer. In Bermuda, a claimant has six years from the date when the obligation arose or the date when the transfer was made (whichever is later) to launch a claim. Therefore, the plaintiff is acting within the limitation period. The claimant, however, must prove that the defendant could reasonably have foreseen that the creditor would be prejudiced by the transfer. This was the case with Dr. Walters, as he transferred his assets specifically to protect them from lawsuits. However, the court, if it grants the motion, will void the transfer only for the amount claimed ($2 million in this case).

To avoid such an unfortunate situation, Dr. Walters may wish to establish his trust in a country like Belize, where a court cannot set aside or vary a resident trust. To date, no trust in that country has ever been compromised in this manner, and Belize does not have fraudulent conveyances legislation. However, the country's political and economic instability may make it a somewhat risky venture.

Contract Work Abroad

John is an engineer who has been lured to the United Arab Emirates (U.A.E.) to work on a three-year desalination project. He is married and plans to move his family with him. Although John is slated to begin work in January, his wife and children, in an effort to minimize disruption, plan to leave Canada only after the school year is finished, sometime in June. John and his wife own their matrimonial home, a joint bank account, two cars, and a summer cottage in Quebec. John also owns some shares of a publicly traded corporation. The shares cost him $20,000 but now are valued at $120,000.

John's present situation is complex as far as taxes are concerned because although he may wish to become a non-resident to take advantage of the U.A.E. tax structure, he will not immediately be considered a non-resident upon his departure from Canada. In fact, Revenue Canada will continue to view John as a Canadian resident until he either becomes a resident of the U.A.E. or his wife and children leave Canada (whichever is later). Furthermore, to become a non-resident, John and his wife will have to dispose of their assets (i.e., sell their home; dispose of things like the car and the bank account — the cottage is not critical; and stop or change the residency status of any memberships in associations such as engineering societies or golf clubs). They would also be well advised to forego provincial health coverage and family-allowance payments. Alternatively, they could rent out the family home to a third party (not a relative) for an extended-period lease that cannot be terminated within ninety days.

Until John severs his Canadian residency, he will be taxed on his worldwide income. He will also be deemed to have disposed of his shares at their fair market value on the date he became a non-resident. His capital gains on the $120,000 will be taxed, and 75 percent of that must be included in his taxable income for the year. Alternatively, he may elect to treat the shares as taxable Canadian property and defer the capital gain until he actively disposes of the shares. While this option would avoid the deemed disposition rules temporarily, it would mean that when he eventually sells the shares, he will have to pay taxes in Canada on the capital gain. This capital gain will be calculated using the shares' fair market value at the time of their disposal — an amount that includes any gains that accrued from the time he became a non-resident.

Armed Forces

Major Snow is a high-ranking member of the Canadian armed forces who has been assigned to a peacekeeping mission in Cyprus. He is a widower with a child who is nineteen and has recently been admitted to Princeton University without a scholarship. He would like to help his child with tuition and remains uncertain about the tax implications of his upcoming move. Major Snow expects to receive a moving allowance, as well as a living allowance while abroad. He plans to rent his home in Canada to his twin brother, who has promised to care for his car and furniture.

Since Major Snow is a member of the military, the Income Tax Act deems him to be a Canadian resident and he will be taxed on his worldwide income. It is futile for him to dispose of his personal property and to sever his residential ties. His moving and living allowances may not be taxed if they are reasonable. If his child has little income, Major Snow may be entitled to tax credits for some of his child's tuition.

Extended Visit to Canada

Hans Bayer is a renowned German anthropologist whose scholarship is recognized throughout the world and whose books earn him considerable royalty income. Throughout his illustrious career, Dr. Bayer dreamed of exploring the Canadian Arctic, and now he has made plans to spend nine full months living with the polar bears, arctic seals, and wolves in an isolated region north of Whitehorse. Before leaving, Dr. Bayer wants to know what taxes he will have to pay.

Because Dr. Bayer will be spending nine months in Canada, his stay will exceed the 183-day limit and he will be deemed to have been a resident of Canada for the entire year. This means that he will be taxed on his worldwide income for the entire fiscal year, not just for the period he spends in Canada. He will, however, be entitled to the housing-benefit deduction for northern residents.

Under the Canada-Germany tax treaty, the German government should credit Dr. Bayer for the tax he paid to Canada. Nevertheless, although he is obliged to file a tax return in Canada, this does not absolve him of any obligations he may have towards the German tax authorities, whom he would be well advised to consult before leaving.

Snowbirds

Jack and Ida have retired from successful teaching careers. They currently spend the entire winter months (from October to March) in Florida. Their summer months are spent at their cottage in the Muskoka region, north of Toronto. They realize that U.S. tax rates are lower than Canadian ones, and wonder if it would be possible to change their current tax status without affecting their lifestyle.

Although renouncing Canadian residency to benefit from American tax rates may seem an appealing idea at first, it requires careful scrutiny, especially by those who are not young and whose health may not be perfect. In Jack and Ida's case, they cannot become U.S. citizens without severely compromising their lifestyle. To begin with, they should think twice, given their age, before abandoning Canadian health-care privileges. (They have paid into the system all their lives. Why should they forego it when they might need it the most?) Also, Jack and Ida cannot become non-residents without giving up their bank accounts, golf memberships, and other assets in Canada. Assuming that the couple returns to Canada on April 1 and leaves October 1, they will be deemed Canadian residents because they have sojourned in Canada for 184 days. They can't just decide to stay in the United States an extra week, because the regularity and length of their visits to Canada can also help establish the residential ties necessary to be considered factual residents. What is more, Jack and Ida may have to file tax returns in the United States as well.

The snowbird option is not as easy as it first seems and requires much planning to be successful.

Retirement in the Caribbean

Harriet and Gordon are public servants who have accepted early retirement packages from their respective employers. Their only child, Michael, is married and lives in France. Harriet and Gordon have long enjoyed Caribbean cruises and have always dreamed of living on one of the islands they visited. While surfing the Internet, Gordon found a property for sale in Nevis; it was listed at approximately the same price as the value of their current home. Harriet and Gordon are contemplating becoming non-residents upon retirement, but they worry that they will be unable to continue receiving their pension income if they move to Nevis. Also, they wonder how they will be able to benefit from the sizeable savings in their registered retirement savings plans (RRSPs).

The disposal of their home and assets, as well as their move to another country, is likely sufficient to establish Harriet and Gordon as non-residents. Nevis levies no tax. Their rights to their pension payments are normally unaffected by a change in residency status. Both Harriet and Gordon, therefore, should receive their pensions, subject to a 25 percent withholding tax. The same withholding tax applies to withdrawals from their RRSPs. Like Jack and Ida, however, Harriet and Gordon should consider strongly what they are giving up in terms of health-care benefits, friends, and community before making the final decision. Many couples leave for warmer climates only to discover that they are homesick and want to return. This revelation is often expensive and sometimes comes too late. An alternative would be to rent a home in the area for a while before making a final commitment to buy.

Successions

A medical scare suffered by Mrs. Morgan has her thinking about her legacy. She owns a sizeable estate and is afraid that Canada will follow the lead of other countries by introducing burdensome probate fees. She wants to know how to structure her assets to avoid any potential reduction in her children's inheritance.

Mrs. Morgan would be well advised to establish a trust with her children as beneficiaries. This trust should be set up in a jurisdiction that does not impose inheritance tax (of which there are many). Mrs. Morgan should pay special attention to selecting trustees. They should be people in whom she has full confidence and who will abide by her instructions. To further ensure that her wishes are respected, she should establish a non-discretionary trust with a deed providing for the distribution of assets upon her death.

Despite what some financial planners may assert, Mrs. Morgan should still draft a will and not rely solely on the trust deed to distribute her assets. Canadian courts look unfavourably upon people who do not leave wills, particularly where the deceased has transferred assets to a trust.

The Offshore Entrepreneur

Mr. Diamond has been looking for a business to get into. He does not have a lot of capital available but has a strong spirit and a good knowledge of the latest developments in technology. He is a firm believer in the Internet and its potential as an economic tool. Recently, Mr. Diamond and his friend Mr. Wiley got together and decided that they wanted to develop an e-commerce business. Because both Mr. Diamond and Mr. Wiley have limited money available, they were considering developing an informational product that would not require much in the way of upfront investment and storage space. They thought about developing software but realized quickly that neither of them possessed the necessary skills and that hiring programmers would be a very expensive endeavour. Furthermore, they could not agree on what a good software product might be. After two days spent contemplating the problem, they came up with the idea of an on-line casino. But after contacting their lawyer, they learned that running such a business in Canada would violate the Canadian Criminal Code.

Fortunately, their lawyer knew of a client with a similar set-up in an offshore jurisdiction, and he advised the would-be partners to do the same. By setting up their server and operation in an offshore jurisdiction, Mr. Diamond and Mr. Wiley will have access to a global market. Furthermore, many offshore jurisdictions would be willing to grant the pair a licence to set up such a gambling operation.

Setting up on-line businesses in an offshore jurisdiction makes good sense. In some cases, you will set these up in order to limit the taxes payable. In other situations, such as the one described above, using an offshore jurisdiction may allow you to avoid certain regulations in your home country. For Mr. Diamond and Mr. Wiley, owning a corporation that runs a gambling operation in an offshore jurisdiction should not cause them problems under Canadian law so long as the corporation does not promote its services or allow Canadians to gamble. Similar rules may limit the pair's activities in other countries. However, some countries will not have sophisticated gambling laws, and there such an operation may not be considered illegal. As long as the pair is willing to implement technology that blocks users from the restricted countries from accessing their on-line services, there should be no problem.

The use of gambling as an example is extreme. Gambling generally has a strong stigma associated with it. It is therefore strictly regulated in many countries. In other cases, however, regulations concerning products and services will be approached in the same universal way. In other words, moving operations offshore is a good way to attract international customers, and to sell goods or services that you would not be able to sell domestically because of some form of regulation. Of course, in all cases involving such matters, it is absolutely essential to consult lawyers in both the onshore and the offshore jurisdictions.

Although the scenarios outlined above cover a range of situations, they are only some of the events that may lead a person to consider offshore investing. Needs vary from person to person, and it is wise to consult the relevant professional advisers and establish a plan tailored exactly to your particular needs.

Self-Test: Is Going Offshore for You?

Here we present a self-test that may help you decide whether you should — and are prepared to — consider offshore investing. The test is divided into two sub-tests: a straightforward quantitative test and a more reflective qualitative one.

Quantitative Test

1. Estimate the income you earn from interest, dividends, and capital gains.
2. Deduct losses or expenses relating to that income.
3. Estimate the amount of taxes you pay on this income annually.
4. Compare the annual tax with the cost of setting up various structures offshore (see the country profiles for an idea of the prices).
5. To amortize the unusually high first-year costs that are a result of start-up fees, compare taxes with offshore costs over a five-year period.

Take Samantha Jones as an example. Samantha lives in Toronto and earns $75,000 in employment income per year. She owns

$200,000 in government bonds, which pay her 6.5 percent ($13,000) per year. She estimates her incremental tax rate as 53 percent, and she incurs no additional costs with this investment. Samantha has an unrelated friend who resides in England and has a similar portfolio. Samantha and her friend are considering establishing an IBC in the Bahamas to hold their investments. We can assume that Samantha and her friend will each own 50 percent of the shares of the IBC (note that this avoids FAPI rules, because de facto control is not in Canada), and that the set-up and annual fees for the IBC are $4,173 (U.S. $2,782) and $3,675 (U.S. $2,450), respectively. Samantha's circumstances could be analyzed as follows:

Annual Income from Investments	$13000
Less: Associated Costs	Nil
Incremental Effect on Taxable Income	$13000
Taxes on Incremental Income (53 percent)	$6890
Less: IBC Set-up Costs ($4173 x 20 percent x 50 percent)	($417)
Less: IBC Annual Costs ($3675 x 50 percent)	($1838)
Less: Canadian Withholding Taxes ($6890 x 25 percent)	($1723)
Potential Annual Tax Savings	**$2912**

Note, however, that as wealth accumulates in the IBC, Samantha will be subject to taxes on capital gains when she ultimately disposes of her shares. But the IBC allows her to defer $2,912 in taxes per year. She could organize the disposition of the shares so that it coincides with a year in which she has less income, thus creating a smaller tax burden. And again, only 75 percent of the capital gain would be taxable in Canada. Samantha should also be aware, however, that this tactic could trigger the Income Tax Act's general anti-avoidance rule (GAAR), because her main goal may be to obtain a tax benefit.

Qualitative Test

This test may not be as easy, because it asks potential investors to be honest with themselves. It might be a good idea to conscript the help of a close friend or spouse (someone who really knows you) to double-check the answers.

1. Are you prepared to abandon full control of your assets, so that you are neither a director nor a shareholder in your company? Are you prepared to give a trustee full discretion over your assets? (Inevitably, the answer to these questions will depend on who you are entrusting the assets to.) Would you be comfortable entrusting them to your best friend? Would you be comfortable entrusting them to a well-qualified professional?

2. Have you extra time to research and learn about offshore planning? You shouldn't trust your money to professionals without understanding what they are doing. The more you can help them by telling them what you want, the more lucrative an offshore venture will prove to be.

3. Are you sufficiently interested in world affairs to read international newspapers or surf the Internet to keep up to date on legislative changes that may occur in the various countries where your money is placed? (This is not necessary, but it helps.)

4. Are you able to move without missing your friends, family, and community? While this may seem a trivial question, it is extremely important that you assess what you have in Canada and what you may take for granted (such as reliable health care, honest government officials, access to cultural institutions, etc.).

5. Can you deal with the stigma often associated with going offshore? While your financial affairs are your business, you have to be comfortable with your decision. In fact, it is probably a better idea not to share your financial dealings with others.

ELEVEN

Investors Beware:
The Scam Alert Chapter

In this chapter, you will learn:
~ *About some of the more popular scams in the offshore world*
~ *How to avoid being taken in*

Before investing offshore, you should realize that there are many con artists who are waiting to part you from your money. You should also be wary of the not-so-legitimate uses of otherwise perfectly respectable offshore instruments such as trusts, bank accounts, and credit cards. Knowing about these things will save you time, money, and anguish. Although it's not exhaustive — the nature and number of scams change daily — this chapter describes some of the best-known scams, as well as some shady uses of legitimate investment tools. It also provides several tips to help potential investors spot and avoid scams.

Bad Attitudes

Many intelligent and vigilant people fall victim to scams and shady dealings because they approach offshore investing with two self-destructive attitudes: greed and a blind fear or resentment of government.

In the world of offshore investing, greed is without a doubt a deadly sin, and con artists play on this with promises of extraordinary returns on investment. Knowledge and persistent work, however, are far more likely to bring rewarding results than get-rich-quick schemes. Investors should not count on hitting the jackpot in one easy shot, but rather should concentrate on saving and earning money in bits and pieces, here and there. The amounts quickly add up. Remember that two important rules of thumb, although cliché, apply to offshore investing: (1) There is no free lunch; and (2) If something seems too good to be true, it probably is!

A second attitude that is guaranteed to get investors into trouble is the one promoted by the yahoos of offshore investment: government is inherently evil and is out to take every hard-earned penny you ever made. This is ludicrous. In Canada, in matters of taxation, the government and the taxpayer are both forced to play by the same rules — the Income Tax Act — and neither party can go to any lengths to get around them. (As an aside, we might point out that it is hard to conceive of a government that returns the money taxpayers have overpaid as duplicitous and penny-pinching!) This book does not advocate duping the government but rather endorses playing by the rules and maximizing your *legal* financial opportunities.

A belief that government is out to get them, however, leaves many investors vulnerable to scams that involve contracts with disclaimers preventing the investor from seeking advice. These investors, needlessly afraid of government bodies that exist to protect citizens (one of the reasons we pay such high taxes is to maintain these bodies), sign agreements without receiving proper information. A quick call to a lawyer or a financial planner, or even a visit to Revenue Canada, the provincial securities commission, or RCMP Web sites, could prevent the loss of many life savings.

Any investor who is serious about venturing offshore should learn to master these fears, or at least refrain from acting on greed and mistrust of government.

Scams

Although new scams emerge every day, a general knowledge of how scams work and a familiarity with the most popular ones will go a long way to protecting you as an investor.

Our research has found that most offshore-investment scams fall into three categories: (1) the advanced-fee scam; (2) the pyramid or ponzie scam; and (3) the telemarketing scam. In this chapter, we will describe these three types of scams, and we will list some actual scams that have been thwarted in the past.

Advanced-Fee Scam
This type of scam asks the investor to pay an advanced fee to participate in a project that promises huge returns. Before any profits materialize, the scam organizers disappear with the money that has been advanced to them. Many of the scams described below fall into this category.

Pyramid or Ponzie Scam
This scam requires that the individual invest a certain sum of money to earn interest. The interest, however, is contingent on the investor recruiting new members, because it is the money from the new recruits that goes to pay the original investor's interest. Eventually, the pool of new recruits dries up; only those at the absolute top of the pyramid ever receive any money. Although this sounds straightforward enough, there are often complicated variations of the pyramid that dupe even the most cautious investors. The pyramid scheme is sometimes incorporated into another type of scam.

Telemarketing Scam
Believe it or not, Canadians excel at perpetrating these scams. In fact, telemarketing fraud has become so widespread that some

American television stations run advertisements telling people what to do if they receive a call offering them "an investment opportunity of a lifetime." The chief characteristics of a telemarketing scam are that through some form of deceit, people are led to part with their money and to place their property at risk. The relationship between the victim and the con artist is initiated and maintained through telephone calls. These scams can be aimed at the wealthy, in the form of investment opportunities in precious metals and gemstones; at the poor, in the form of advanced-loan scams (a person is guaranteed a $2,000 loan if they send $500, then neither the loan nor the advance is ever seen again); or at the average person, in the form of "truck loading" or straight fraud (the victim receives a phone call saying that he has won a prize, but then is told that he must send money to claim it; again, neither the money nor the prize is ever seen again).

While advanced-fee, pyramid, and telemarketing scams are some of the most common, there are others. As you will see below, some scams don't even come packaged in elaborate structures — they merely involve selling overpriced books or attending conferences describing ludicrous get-rich-quick schemes.

Prime Bank Instrument Scam

Estimated to make $10 million a day in North America, this scam involves a con artist passing off impressive-looking documents with a purported value of $100 million or more. The investor is told that these are notes issued by the big banks when they lend each other money; that they are limited in number; that they can be obtained at a discount rate; and that they can be resold quickly for a huge profit. They are, allegedly, a risk-free investment. Brokers get involved because small investors have to pool their money to build up a minimum of $10 million to $100 million. Investors are required to sign a non-disclosure statement, which prevents them from talking to lawyers or financial advisers upon risk of forfeiture of their investment.

The reality of this scam is that while names of banks such as Chase Manhattan, Barclays, and Lloyd's are bandied about, these notes are not backed by any financial institution and are worthless.

While foreign banks use bank guarantees, these are never traded or sold on any kind of market. Meanwhile, the unsuspecting investor has deposited money in a foreign account to purchase these notes. This money is then transferred to the con artist's offshore account and laundered. The investor never sees it again.

Some warning signs that point to this fraud or variations on it are, as follows:

1. The investor is approached as an investor, not as a principal, which means that he receives no personal security. The investor is told not to worry, because his money is secured by a letter of credit or other guaranteed bank certificate, both of which are actually worthless.
2. The investor is told not to contact the bank involved because it cannot acknowledge the scheme unless the investor is a principal.
3. A high degree of trust is required from the investor.
4. The investor is discouraged from seeking professional advice.
5. The scheme is wrapped in complicated terms and name-dropping. Investors are duped because they are afraid to ask questions, either for fear of appearing stupid or because they are impressed with the big names.

Nigeria Scam

This scam, purported to be the third-largest industry in Nigeria, perpetually changes in order to attract new people. The basic structure, however, remains the same. Victims receive an unsolicited fax or a letter from Nigeria describing a project — usually, but not always, illegal — with which the correspondent wants help. Here are some of the most common requests:

~ A person's parent has died, leaving him millions of dollars that he wants to take out of the country. Before he does so, he needs an investment of capital with which to bribe officials.
~ A company has sold crude oil in Nigeria and wishes to get the money out of the country. Again, it requires an investment of capital to bribe officials.
~ The Nigerian government has overpaid a contractor, and he wants to get the extra money out of the country before the

government realizes its error. To do this, the contractor
needs a bank-account number and an authorizing signature.
~ The national petroleum company has discovered oil, and its
administrators, as insiders, want to acquire more land. They
need a foreign front man to purchase it for them.

In return for the investor's help, the con artist promises a high
commission fee, usually in the millions of dollars. The investor is
asked to provide an advanced fee of some sort (alternately called an
advanced fee, a transfer tax, or a performance bond) to extend credit
or to grant C.O.D. privileges. If the investor pays the fee, a series of
complications follows, requiring the payment of additional fees.
The requests for money stop only when the investor's funds have
run out.

Some warning signs that point to this fraud or variations on it
are, as follows:

1. There is sense of urgency in the initial unsolicited document.
2. A request to travel to the country is made (this is to be
   avoided like the plague).
3. Many foreign-looking documents, which may actually
   come from Nigerian officials who are involved in the scam,
   are used.
4. The investor is asked to provide blank letterhead and his
   bank-account numbers.
5. Many bribes and processing fees are required.
6. The investor must keep the transaction confidential.
7. Nigerians in the United States, Canada, or Britain act as
   intermediaries or clearing-houses to close the transactions.

The most frightening thing about the Nigerian scam is that it
can be physically dangerous for the investor. If an investor loses
money on this scam, he should simply accept the loss and chalk it
up to experience. By no means should he go to Nigeria to attempt
to recover it. Once in the country, he risks being blackmailed,
robbed, or thrown in a Nigerian jail at best, or at worst, killed.

A new twist on this scam is Nigerians posing as law-enforcement officials who claim that for a small fee, they will try to

retrieve the money the investor has lost. They too are con artists and should not be entrusted with your money.

Bankroll or Bank-Debenture Schemes

This scam is a prime example of the destructive effects of greed. By promising an extraordinarily high return on investment, it plays upon people's belief that they can get rich quick. The investor is told that there is a banking and trading system, closed to the general public, that produces exorbitant returns on investment (at least 50 percent). Since the secret system is open only to people with $1 million or more, investors are encouraged to pool their money to receive a 50 percent return in the short term. Although a trading system that is not generally open to the public does exist (INSTINET), institutional trading does not produce astronomical rates of return (usually just one percent or 2 percent).

In some cases, the sceptical investor may choose to invest only $1,000, for which she will receive $1,500 in return. Encouraged by this result, she places $10,000 and may receive $15,000. It is only when she is fully convinced of this scheme's ability to deliver high returns, and places her life savings, that she is told this trade didn't work. The con artists disappear with the money, leaving the investor unwilling to report the scam because she signed a confidentiality agreement and is afraid of being sued or charged for having done something illegal. The confidentiality agreement is not valid, however, because the scam underlying it was against the law; the investor is not likely to be prosecuted, because she has done nothing wrong.

Like a pyramid scheme, the bank-debenture scam may also lure the defrauded investor into more illegal activity. Once the investor has discovered that her money will not be returned, she is used by the con artists, who tell her that if she attracts others to the scheme, she will receive a cut of the money. If the investor is foolish enough to do this, she may be guilty of fraud, securities fraud, embezzlement, or aiding and abetting fraud, securities fraud, or embezzlement.

Tapes, Books, and Seminars

The con artists in these scams either sell books and tapes for hundreds of dollars or give seminars with a registration fee of thousands of dollars that claim to reveal the "secrets" of offshore investing.

For example, one $99 book describes tools such as the self-liquidating, or arbitrage, loan. The investor is advised to borrow $100 million to $500 million in long-term loans, and he is then instructed to dispose of this money in the following ways: (1) by buying collateral, which he then pledges against the money he borrows; (2) by investing it and using income to pay off the loan; (3) by paying his stockbroker; and (4) by keeping what is left over, because even 10 percent of the loan is still a substantial amount of money. The main problem with this scheme (other than the fact that the figures don't add up) is that no bank will lend the average person anywhere near that kind of money. The scam is that the investor bought the book for the high price and is out $99. There is also a book for $149 describing how to make the bank-debenture scam work!

Upgrade Scam

This scam is perpetrated by some investment companies. They offer to give their clients B-class shares for free that they will upgrade to A-class shares for a small sum (several dollars per share). They then claim the shares will go to market at double the price of the upgrade, which they never do.

Passport and Titles Scam

Some foreign companies provide people with citizenships and diplomatic titles to countries that don't exist. These foreign ties, the victim is told, mean that the Canadian citizen is no longer a resident of Canada for tax purposes. This claim is false.

Encumbering Your Property So As to Avoid Equity

In this scam, the con artist suggests to the investor that he allow his property to be encumbered with phony loans. The payments are tax-deductible, but in the end the investor has received no loan money and has given away (pledged) his assets.

Misuse of Valid Offshore Instruments

In addition to outright offshore-investment scams, there are illegitimate uses of valid investment instruments to which victims may fall prey. These are sometimes difficult to avoid because they are often promoted by respectable-looking investment operations. Some offshore havens such as the Bahamas have, in an attempt to keep their reputations as legitimate investment areas, set up Web sites warning people of these tricks and of the companies that run them.

The following are some examples of the misuse of otherwise valid offshore structures and techniques.

The $200 Credit Card

Some offshore-investment companies have been offering a credit card for $200 that allegedly will enable the user to obtain $5,000 worth of credit. Avoid these. What seems to happen is that the potential cardholder pays her $200 and never sees the card.

Any investor interested in obtaining an offshore credit card can do so by visiting or contacting a reputable offshore bank; it will issue a secured credit or debit card at a small cost.

The Offshore Private Bank

This is a perfect example of something that seems — and is — too good to be true. Some companies purport to sell private banks for $5,000. The incentive is that once the bank is set up, the investor will make millions from other wealthy investors who want to place their money there. In reality, such a venture will cost the investor tens of thousands in consulting fees alone for advisers to review the situation. This does not include licensing, incorporation, and all the other fees involved in such a huge operation.

If, however, an investor has $10 million in disposable income, setting up a private bank may be a good idea. It is certainly to be avoided by the average investor.

Various Trusts

Because trusts come in so many different forms, they are one of the preferred tools of con artists seeking to part people from their money.

Living Trust

Although a living trust is a perfectly legitimate estate-planning tool, it is not a cure for all fiscal ailments. Claims that it will reduce income tax, reduce estate tax, be cheaper than a will, and act in place of a will are misleading, if not utterly false.

To begin with, a living trust is simply a trust that is revocable — that is to say, the settlor entrusts his or her property to a trustee for the settlor's benefit during his or her lifetime. The settlor retains the ability to cancel the trust at any time, and the beneficiaries at death are the settlor's heirs. No probate proceedings are required for the property to pass to the heirs.

The living trust cannot meet the above claims due to the following:

1. The government, knowing that the trust is for the settlor's benefit, taxes the settlor as if the trust didn't exist. It is useless to get a separate tax identification number for this trust because the settlor and the trust will have to pay taxes on the same property.
2. The trust property is deemed part of the settlor's estate at the time of death — unlike the property in an irrevocable trust — and therefore is subject to estate taxes.
3. It is not cheaper than and cannot replace a will. The settlor has to pay to convey assets into a trust, whereas with a will, a testator simply has to state to whom the assets will go. Filing the necessary trust tax returns will take as much effort as creating a will. Since the trust covers only the property that is in trust, a will is required for the settlor's other assets anyway.

Pure Trust

Also referred to as a constitutional, patriotic, or freedom trust, these American trusts are completely fraudulent and are not recognized by any state. Although they have been around for more than five years, these trusts have never protected money from anyone, be it creditors, ex-spouses, or the Internal Revenue Service (IRS), and have not saved any income, estate, probate, property, or other taxes. People promoting these trusts will make two arguments. First, they will claim that the trusts find their origin in the American constitution, which ensures that no state will impair the obligation of contract. The con artist will interpret this to mean that the constitution allows people to set up any structure they want. The con artist will support his or her argument by citing court cases in which constitutional trusts have not had to pay taxes. What the con artist fails to tell the victim is that the trusts themselves don't pay taxes because they are not recognized as legitimate instruments. In fact, the court considers that the money has never left the settlor.

Second, the con artist may argue that these trusts are used by very wealthy families, like the Rockefellers and the Astors, as well as by corporations such as Texaco. Potential victims may have lists of authorities and court cases cited to them to further convince them. These claims are fraudulent and taken out of context.

Hiding Money in a Foreign Trust

Many far-too-trusting individuals fall prey to this scheme. Investors are told that they should place their money in a trust in a foreign country. By claiming that this money is not theirs, investors protect it from creditors, as well as from Revenue Canada. The money is then free to grow tax-free. Two problems emerge with this scheme:

1. The person or company entrusted with the money keeps it, leaving the investor without recourse, because any attempt to report the theft will result in the investor being charged with tax evasion.
2. The person or company entrusted with the money, aware of the investor's fear of reporting the theft, blackmails him or her for more money in return for keeping quiet.

The above list represents only a fraction of the scams in existence. There are many others that involve inappropriate uses of insurance or telephone (not telemarketing) fraud. A familiarity with these major scams, however, will help to protect you from becoming a victim.

Tips to Help You Avoid Becoming a Victim

While you may not be able to avoid all the scams, the following rules of thumb may help to protect your money from con artists.

1. The most important rule, and the one that is most difficult to follow, is to use common sense and to have faith in your own judgement. If something seems too good to be true, it is. If something appears twisted and unclear, ask for further explanations. A legitimate company will be more than happy to inform its clients about its products; a scammer will not. Self-confidence is also essential in offshore investing. Many people are fooled by big words and fail to ask questions for fear of seeming ignorant. This is a mistake. If you don't understand something, you are not at fault — the people you're dealing with must be able to express themselves clearly. Remember: there is not a concept in the world that cannot be explained in plain English. If a company's employees prove incapable of expressing an idea simply, and insist on throwing big words around, run while you still have your money. Legitimate companies don't behave in that manner.

2. If someone asks you not to speak to a consultant, a financial adviser, or a lawyer, these are the first people you should consult. Confidentiality clauses are frequently used to prevent investors from consulting experts who will tell them they are dealing with a scam. Even if something seems straightforward and clear, the law is tricky and the project may have hidden hitches that an expert in the field can spot. Successful business people generally surround themselves with a team of lawyers and accountants for good reason.

3. Don't view government as the enemy. One of the many

reasons Canadians pay high taxes is to maintain services and agencies that protect investors against bad deals. Indeed, some of the best anti-scam Web sites are funded by the government. Government institutions are there to help you, not harm you; it is better to pay consultants and forego unrealistic profits than to lose your money altogether.

4. Check the Internet for advice on scams. A search using the terms "offshore" and "scam" will yield several sites with invaluable information, including links to other sites of interest. Frequently, these sites have e-mail addresses of people you can contact to help investigate schemes. Always check a number of sites to confirm your findings.

5. Do your own due diligence. Offshore investment advisers and managers should have substantial tax and international-law training. These are not things a manager can teach herself, no matter how clever she may be. Avoid fee-based planners who also charge sales commissions. Also, check the dates of incorporation of various companies. A company boasting a great track record is obviously suspect if it has been incorporated for only a week.

6. If you decide to set up a trust, seek the services of a well-established international firm. Local management firms can be unreliable. They can make off with your money, leaving you with little or no recourse. A large firm will offer greater accountability. Again, large firms may be more expensive, but in the long run they provide worthwhile protection and peace of mind.

TWELVE

Pulling It All Together

In this chapter, you will learn:
~ *What to look for in an offshore jurisdiction*
~ *Which jurisdictions provide strong support for various offshore instruments*

Now that we have described various offshore instruments, explained the Canadian Income Tax Act, warned you of some scams, and sketched a portrait of the type of people who might consider offshore planning, you should be ready to integrate all this information and make it more personally relevant. But be forewarned, this chapter will not tell you where to set up or what structures to use. Those are personal choices that you must make with the help of a professional financial planner.

Where you decide to go depends on what you hope to accomplish. Each jurisdiction has its advantages and disadvantages. For example, you may find yourself sacrificing asset security for the opportunity to realize greater gains; alternatively, you may want to play it safe and take a smaller return on your investment. Also, you will find that some areas are great for banking but less attractive for companies because of their high corporate tax rates. You should also bear in mind that mutual funds and development bonds can be a reasonable option for those who do not have a lot of disposable income but would still like to explore the possibilities of offshore planning. If these investments work out, then you could move to a more complex structure. There is no shame in starting small. In fact, you would be wise to gradually acquire a feel for offshore investing rather than throwing a lot of money at a venture with which you are not entirely comfortable.

This chapter provides an overview of the most popular regions for offshore planning and suggests what to consider in deciding where to invest and where to establish a bank account, an international business corporation, and a trust. To supplement this chapter, we have included, in the Country Profiles section, extensive details on thirty specific countries.

General Information

Ten Things to Look for When Choosing an Offshore Centre

The following ten characteristics of an ideal tax haven were listed in a United Nations' preliminary report entitled *Financial Havens, Banking Secrecy and Money Laundering*. With the exception of item 6, this list is equally useful for selecting an offshore jurisdiction in which to focus your financial planning.

1. The jurisdiction has no agreements with other countries for sharing tax information.
2. Shelf companies are available.
3. The jurisdiction has strong corporate-secrecy laws.
4. The jurisdiction has excellent communications facilities.
5. The jurisdiction has strict bank-secrecy laws.
6. A thriving tourist trade exists in the area and will help mask large cash influxes.
7. A major world currency is used in the country as local money.
8. The local government is not likely to be influenced by outside pressures.

9. The jurisdiction depends heavily on its financial-services sector.
10. The country's geography makes it accessible to its neighbours.

There are three other important but non-essential characteristics:
1. The jurisdiction is in a favourable time zone (for telecommunications access).
2. There exists a free-trade zone in the country.
3. A shipping registry is available.

Since finding a single jurisdiction with all these characteristics is difficult, we suggest you break the search down by instrument and region. That is to say, you may choose one country for a bank account, one for a trust, one for mutual funds, and another for an international business corporation. To make this task a little easier, we have provided an overview of the various regions, as well as advice on the things to look for when selecting a jurisdiction for each of the offshore instruments.

Regional Rundowns

In general, there are six types of offshore centres:
1. countries that levy no income taxes on their residents (e.g., Andorra, the Cayman Islands, the Bahamas);
2. countries that tax domestic income but exempt foreign earnings (e.g., most Latin American countries, Cape Verde);
3. countries that tax foreign profits but not local income (e.g., Monaco);
4. countries that tax their residents' worldwide income only moderately (e.g., the Channel Islands, some cantons in Switzerland);
5. countries that tax visible wealth by levying some accumulated assets yearly;
6. countries without strict laws, or at least with laws that they barely enforce, against their citizens' activities abroad (e.g., Italy, Portugal, Spain).

Although there has been an emergence of favourable tax laws in countries such as Labuan, the Seychelles, Hong Kong, Israel, and others, traditionally tax havens have been located in three areas:

1. Europe, including several Mediterranean countries and the British Isles;
2. the Caribbean and Bermuda; and
3. the South Pacific.

Each of these three areas has its distinct problems and advantages.

The Caribbean

While this region is the preferred location for offshore investment for Canadians and Americans (mostly for geographical reasons), caution is strongly recommended when investing there. The islands differ widely. While the Cayman Islands and Bermuda are reputable and stable, places like Anguilla, Panama, and Montserrat are, at the moment, best avoided by the honest investor. The major problem facing the Caribbean islands is the ever-increasing American pressure to weaken their secrecy laws. In fact, the United States has, in the past, threatened to withhold foreign aid to islands that wouldn't co-operate with its law-enforcement objectives. Some islands have proved more immune to these threats than others. The Cayman Islands, for example, has used its status as a British protectorate to shield itself against American pressures. But even this tactic is not foolproof, as evidenced by recent changes to Cayman secrecy regulations.

A second problem with the Caribbean is that while a particular country may have strong secrecy provisions, nothing prevents its financial-services professionals (for example, bank clerks) from divulging information in return for a bribe. So although the region has a tradition of offshore planning, you must be careful of the particular jurisdiction you choose. We recommend the Caribbean for mutual funds, international business corporations, and trusts but not necessarily for bank accounts. If you do choose this region for a bank account, choose a country with a well-established reputation, such as the Cayman Islands or the Bahamas.

Europe

When it comes to offshore planning, Europe can be subdivided into three areas: the Channel Islands (Guernsey, Jersey, Sark) and the Isle of Man, which offer good services at a reasonable price and a favourable fiscal environment for companies, but whose secrecy provisions have been weakened; the Mediterranean countries (Gibraltar, Malta, Cyprus, Madeira) and Ireland, which provide an excellent corporate environment with little or no tax on certain enterprises; and the continental European countries (Switzerland, Luxembourg, Liechtenstein, and Austria), which are best known for their excellent secrecy provisions.

We recommend the banks in these last four countries for your offshore account despite the inconvenience of cost, geography, and time zone. Not only have these four countries designed bank accounts to be as confidential as possible, they actually make the disclosure of information a criminal offence. That said, however, you should be aware that in the same way as the United States poses a threat to the Caribbean, the European Union may pose a threat to certain practices in the various European nations. Pressure from France has prevented both Monaco and Andorra from becoming pure tax havens, for example, while Luxembourg has been under (but so far withstood) tremendous pressure from Belgium and Germany concerning its secrecy regulations.

The stiffer regulations under which European financial-service providers operate may at first seem disadvantageous, but they serve to protect the average investor — which may not be a bad thing if you are just starting out. All in all, Europe is still an excellent place to engage in offshore planning. This is particularly true if you are willing to set up your various structures in the country best suited for each (for example, a trading company in Madeira, a bank account in Luxembourg, a trust in Gibraltar).

South Pacific

The South Pacific jurisdictions are relatively young offshore centres that, with the exception of Hong Kong, were created to compensate for the lack of agricultural and industrial capacity in the region. Generally, the level of offshore services offered in these areas ranges from adequate to very good and usually will not cost investors a fortune in fees. The weakness of this region is the time zone, which renders same-day transactions nearly impossible unless you live on the west coast of Canada or the United States.

On the other hand, the distance of the South Pacific countries from Europe and the United States protects them from the type of pressure that European and Caribbean countries have been subjected to from the bigger powers. South Pacific centres, however, have not been completely free from scrutiny. Countries such as Vanuatu, for example, are under pressure from international law-enforcement authorities for their money-laundering activities.

It is interesting to note that the offshore centres in the South Pacific are, for the most part, former colonies of New Zealand; Australia prevented its colonies from becoming tax havens. It is not unreasonable to assume, therefore, that in the future, if these islands start to attract excessive capital from Australia, they may too find themselves under pressure for increased disclosure. Thus far, Australia has been content to deal with this issue through internal regulations.

Although the favourable tax rates and secrecy regulations provide an excellent environment for international business corporations and trusts, we suggest you avoid this region for banking. The Cook Islands and Nauru (a country we have not described in the country profiles) are the most highly recommended islands, while Western Samoa, Niue, and Vanuatu are also worth keeping an eye on.

Offshore Instruments

Development Bonds

Although we are not detailing the wide range of offshore instruments that exist, it is important to give mention to two of the more popular ones available to middle-income investors: mutual funds and development bonds. We will deal first with development bonds.

Development bonds are simply bonds issued by developing countries for large infrastructure projects. Repayment of these bonds is typically guaranteed by the host country, which makes for a rather secure investment in many cases. Contrary to popular belief, it is rare for a country that encounters economic difficulties to default on the repayment of its debts. There are many organizations, including the International Monetary Fund and the World Bank, that have been put in place by the international community to prevent the economic failure of countries. Country-backed bonds are generally more secure than their corporate equivalents.

To attract foreign investment, developing-country bonds typically pay high rates of return. These countries know that they face scepticism in the investment community. Because of this perception of heightened risk, they must provide increased returns on investment. When purchasing such bonds, be sure to determine the currency of the investment. While these bonds are available in the currency of the country issuing them, this usually increases an investor's risk because currency fluctuations for developing countries are not uncommon. However, these countries often offer their bonds in more stable Western currencies as well. It is not uncommon to find bonds issued in either U.S. dollars or pounds sterling.

Purchasing developing-country bonds is not a complicated task. Often, state-owned banks will offer such bonds. These banks also often have branches in big international centres, so gathering information on the investments that are available is as simple as visiting one of these branches or writing a letter to them. In some cases, there will be restrictions on who may purchase these bonds. It is not uncommon, for example, for a state bank to limit the purchase of the bonds to expatriates or to children born in the issuing country. A good example is the State Bank of India, which often makes available development bonds in either Indian rupees or pounds sterling. These bonds provide a high rate of return, but they are available to only Indian citizens, those born in India, or those whose parents were born in India.

If you or your parents are of non-Canadian origin, check with financial institutions in your country of ancestry to determine whether you can benefit from investment opportunities that are designed to build links with expatriates and their children. These opportunities are almost always underwritten by the government, or are the result of some government policy or legislation. As they restrict the type of investor, they are typically not underwritten solely by private-sector actors such as banks, which are interested in attracting the widest possible audience. Because these opportunities are a result of a government policy — meaning profit is not necessarily the only motivating factor — they often provide sound economic advantages to those individuals who invest in them.

Once you have found the investment that suits you, purchasing the bond is as simple as writing a cheque to the bank. They will then send you a bond certificate and will communicate with you as the bond's expiry date nears. Cashing out is as simple as completing a form provided to you by the bond issuer. On the bond's expiry, you may typically roll over the money into another bond or demand a bank draft in the amount of the bond with interest.

Investment Funds

We turn now to offshore investment funds. A fundamental principle in investing internationally is to view the world as a global marketplace. You must abandon ideas of equity markets as being only nationally based.

With the dramatic increase in the popularity of mutual funds (also known as investment funds) over the past two decades, it is not surprising that a host of offshore funds have begun to emerge. These funds are registered in a foreign jurisdiction, but may not, in fact, be administered from that jurisdiction. In other words, you may get not only the quality of fund-management experience available in financial centres such as New York or London, but also the advantages of having a fund located in an offshore jurisdiction. As with onshore mutual funds, offshore funds may invest in securities of all sorts. A fund located in an offshore jurisdiction such as the Bahamas may invest its assets in securities in Southeast Asia, Europe, South America, or any other jurisdiction.

There are two advantages to investing in offshore funds. First, many offshore jurisdictions have few restrictions on which instruments or vehicles a fund may invest in. Also, there are often lower administrative and regulatory burdens. The second chief advantage is that offshore jurisdictions do not tax funds in the same way as countries such as Canada and the United States do. As a result, these funds earn greater profits, after paying taxes, than equivalent funds located onshore. In other words, they will have more money to invest, and thus so will you. We will now discuss each of these advantages in turn.

First, let us examine the regulatory differences between onshore and offshore funds. Offshore funds offer the typical array of mutual-fund products, including money-market funds, equity funds, income funds, and balanced funds. There are also, however, many products that are not typically seen in onshore jurisdictions. These include derivative funds, which invest in derivative products such as futures and options. The regulatory vacuum that exists in offshore jurisdictions allows fund companies to develop these products much more quickly than their onshore cousins can. As a result, investors can have access to the latest instruments, which would have to go through a complex and lengthy regulatory approval process in an onshore jurisdiction such as Canada. These offshore funds also do not have the same reporting requirements or administrative regulatory burden as their onshore cousins do.

Of course, as with many good things, this regulatory vacuum has its downside. Securities legislation and regulation was originally set up as a form of consumer protection. It was to protect investors from unscrupulous brokers and other unethical vendors of financial instruments. It was also to provide a system of disclosure, whereby companies raising capital would be forced to disclose, in detail, aspects of their operation considered relevant to an investor's ability to make a sound and reasonable investment decision. Nevertheless, investors should be aware that they may not be afforded the same regulatory protections in offshore jurisdictions as they will in more sophisticated onshore jurisdictions.

In terms of companies offering services, Canadian investors may be surprised to learn that some of Canada's biggest chartered banks own investment houses in these offshore jurisdictions. The Royal Bank and Scotia Bank, to name two, have a particularly strong presence. Once again, however, investors should be aware that these offshore Canadian-owned banks are regulated only as much as the jurisdictions within which they operate. Dealing with a Canadian-owned bank or financial-services group in a foreign jurisdiction is not the same as dealing with its parent in Canada. Remember, the banks are interested in one thing only: profit.

Before moving on to our discussion of the impact of low- or no-tax jurisdictions on foreign investment funds and their earnings, it is important to mention that for nationals of some countries, there may be limits on investing in offshore funds. Although these limits do not apply to Canadians, they do affect our American neighbours. American citizens are, under U.S. law, prohibited from owning certain types of foreign instruments (e.g., bearer bonds or bonds issued by countries such as Cuba). If an American wishes to bypass these regulations, he or she should speak to an investment planner.

We now turn to a discussion of tax savings. As mentioned, one of the chief advantages of investing in an offshore fund is that it is not subject to Canadian tax laws. In other words, undistributed income held by such funds is subject to the tax laws of the offshore jurisdiction, which may require the payment of little or no tax. Income earned by these funds is also not subject to Canadian taxation rules. Once the income is distributed to a Canadian resident or to a controlled foreign affiliate of a Canadian resident (this is a term used in the Income Tax Act in dealing with the FAPI rules), however, the income becomes taxable in the hands of the Canadian as part of his or her worldwide income. But until the income has been distributed, it may continue to grow at a rate that is higher than if the fund was paying tax on such income (after all, the more money you have, the more money you earn).

By investing in offshore funds, Canadians have the ability to effectively defer tax on income and realize capital gains retained by the funds. Because the income retained by the fund drives up the fund's unit share price, the fundholder, when he sells his units, will be incurring a capital gain that is taxable at a lower rate than if it was merely distributed as income (Canadians are taxed on only 75 percent of their capital gains). In other words, this presents an opportunity to further reduce your taxes payable. Although existing anti-avoidance rules permit Revenue Canada to tax residents on their holdings in these funds where the primary motivation was to avoid taxes (for example, by deeming a dividend issue), this is difficult to prove and has rarely been used by the agency. Furthermore, it has been extremely difficult for Revenue Canada to gather information regarding Canadian taxpayers' holdings in these foreign funds.

For these reasons, investing in an offshore fund currently presents an excellent opportunity for Canadians. However, as with all things in the offshore game, the government is in the process of closing the loopholes.

The 1999 Budget

Finance Minister Paul Martin's 1999 budget will likely be remembered as the budget that put money back into the social system. But the budget also contained many important fiscal changes designed to eliminate tax advantages derived from structures such as foreign-based investment funds and non-resident trusts. In fact, the budget's Annex 7, in which these changes appear, represents the last steps in a scheme developed over the past few years to render traditional offshore tax-reduction strategies unattractive to most Canadians.

To begin with, the budget's proposed offshore rules take the concept of voluntary disclosure to new heights. The budget tries to remedy the fact that some Canadians, by investing in foreign-based funds, defer taxes on both income and realized capital gains, as well as convert income to capital gains (which are taxed at a lower rate). The budget recommends that Revenue Canada begin taxing such investors on their pro rata share of a fund's undistributed income on an annual basis. As with the rules concerning non-resident trusts (which follow), the budget proposes a host of exceptions, including limiting the assessment of taxable income in such funds to cases where no tax has been levied by any other jurisdiction. This will require that the federal government obtain information on the offshore investment that remains consistent with the new foreign investment reporting requirements, which came into force on April 1, 1999. On a brighter note, while the new rules limit the tax-reduction aspects of foreign investment funds, they do not affect their strong investment potential. Given the continued under-performance of many Canadian funds, it is a sound investment strategy to keep your portfolio partially invested in foreign-based funds. (Remember, though, that your RRSP invest-ments are limited in their allowable percentage of foreign content.)

Bank Accounts

Selecting a jurisdiction for your offshore bank account is a task that must be taken seriously. After all, this is where your money is going to be kept. Political and economic stability are absolutely essential. Once these factors have been addressed, there are other character-istics to look for.

What to Look For

When you're selecting a jurisdiction for a bank account, three ele-ments are key:

1. secrecy laws;
2. stability and reputation of the bank; and
3. access (both financial and physical).

Good bank-secrecy laws — like those of Switzerland and Luxembourg — make it a crime to disclose information about accounts and account holders. These laws can be bypassed only when criminal activity is suspected, but even then the activity has to be considered a crime in that particular country before a court will order information to be disclosed. In Switzerland, for example, tax evasion is not a crime, so a court will not order a bank to pro-vide information to foreign tax authorities. Money laundering, however, is a crime, and a court may very well collaborate with foreign officials if it suspects such activity.

Bank secrecy comes in many forms. Some of the most common types of secret accounts are, as follows:

~ Totally anonymous accounts (such as exist in Austria) where no one knows the owner. These may be becoming extinct.
~ Accounts opened by a lawyer for a client to protect his or her identity. As with the totally anonymous accounts, these accounts have been abolished in Switzerland and are under threat of being abolished in other jurisdictions.
~ Accounts protected by bank-secrecy legislation and by a nominee owner, who is bound to the beneficial owner by a civil contract or simple bond of trust.

~ Coded accounts. Only the top managers in a bank know the owners of these accounts, and confidentiality is protected through strict bank-secrecy laws.

~ Coded accounts whose owners can ask that secrecy be lifted (should the owner be pressured by foreign officials, for example).

~ Non-coded accounts that are protected by bank-secrecy laws and whose owners are known only by the bank managers.

In judging the effectiveness of bank-secrecy laws, you must closely examine the pressure that may be placed on a country by outside jurisdictions — in the case of the Caribbean by the United States, and in the case of European banks by the European Union. Have the banks been able to withstand these pressures? Have there been instances in which secrecy was lifted? If so, do these circumstances resemble your situation?

Stability and reputation are also key features to consider in selecting a bank. There is no point placing your money offshore if you are going to lose it when the bank goes under. Check banking agency reports to find out which institutions are the most stable. Deposit insurance, though not likely available, is also worth looking into.

Although maintaining access to your bank and your money is essential, bear in mind that the most reputable institutions will not let you walk in with a bag of money and establish an account. Most insist on appointments and recommendations from lawyers or financial advisers. This may be tiresome, but it is worth taking the time to do properly. You should also avoid, if possible, taking the easy route by using banks with branches in your own country, especially if you are an American citizen. There have been incidents in the past where branches in the United States were harassed into divulging information about clients' accounts abroad.

If you need easy access to your money, consider getting an offshore debit card or credit card, but remember that your secrecy will be diminished with the creation of a credit trail.

Where to Go

To meet the above criteria, we feel that the best places to keep your accounts are still the traditional European banking capitals of Switzerland, Austria, Liechtenstein, and Luxembourg. These countries are economically and politically stable, and have a record of enforcing their strict bank-secrecy regulations. Furthermore, they have a comparatively long tradition of banking and rely heavily on their strong financial infrastructure. Although there has been much recent discussion about the falling secrecy standards in Switzerland, the country still has a long way to go before the honest investor need worry. Also, despite this concern, many accounts have been moved to Switzerland from the big Caribbean banking centres such as the Cayman Islands because of American pressure on the islands. Owing to its totally anonymous accounts, Austria is probably the best country for general bank secrecy, followed by Luxembourg and Liechtenstein. In general, however, you can't go wrong in any of the four continental European centres.

International Business Corporations

International business corporations (IBCs) can be used for a variety of purposes, including as holding companies and trading companies. However, an IBC's activities often cannot include owning real estate in its home jurisdiction, or undertaking insurance, re-insurance, asset management, banking, or other activities in that country. For greater secrecy, some IBCs can issue bearer shares, whereby the holder of the shares is recognized as the rightful owner of the company. A bank or trust company in the offshore jurisdiction can hold the bearer shares through a simple declaration of trust. You should also note that some countries use exempt companies instead of IBCs, although both often share many of the same features.

What to Look For

When establishing an IBC, the features you should look for — in addition to political and economic stability — are these:

~ bearer shares;
~ limited fees;
~ limited reporting requirements;

~ secrecy;

~ no residency rules for shareholders or directors;

~ no registration of office in the jurisdiction;

~ no tax on income or capital;

~ availability of shelf companies; and

~ availability of corporate management services.

Where to Go

Very few jurisdictions offer all of the features described above. In the Caribbean, the Cayman Islands and Bermuda offer the greatest level of service, while Belize and Nevis provide the highest level of secrecy. Since low fees and a stable political environment are two of the most important features, the Cayman Islands and the Bahamas are probably the most desirable jurisdictions for IBCs in the Caribbean. In the South Pacific, only Hong Kong and the Cook Islands offer the degree of service and accessibility required for an IBC. In Europe, top marks must be awarded to the British Isles (Jersey, Guernsey, and the Isle of Man) for their long tradition of high-quality service and their easy trade access to the European Union.

Trusts

There are many reasons to consider making a trust part of your off-shore structure, including estate planning, asset protection, and general secrecy. While passive income accrued in a trust is subject to FAPI rules, this structure offers a different kind of protection for your money by sheltering it, to a certain extent, from your creditors. Be forewarned, however, that common-law courts may allow creditors to have access to trusts if they can prove that the instrument was formed specifically to defraud them of what was rightfully theirs. To protect trusts against this eventuality, international trust jurisdictions have adopted one of three approaches:

1. They require the creditor to prove fraudulent intent.
2. They require the settlor to prove that he or she was able to meet all of his or her obligations at the time of formation.
3. They limit the recourse available to the creditor.

Trusts cost around $15,000 (U.S.) to establish and require several thousand dollars annually in trustee fees. Canadian law will not recognize the transfer of immovable property into an offshore trust. There are also certain features you may wish to consider in drafting your deed, such as a "flee clause" that compels the trustee to shift the trust if it is threatened by things such as political instability or probing authorities. Also, some jurisdictions, such as Niue, allow the settlor to be the beneficiary of the trust. If common-law trusts don't quite offer what you are looking for, you might consider the Liechtenstein *Anstalt*, which combines features of a trust and a corporation. You should note, however, that these have been red-flagged by law-enforcement authorities for their money-laundering activities.

What to Look For

In addition to political and economic stability, a reputable juridical system, and a reliable communications system, you should look for three things when establishing a trust:

1. Strong financial privacy laws.
2. A trustee you can depend on. With foreign asset protection, this is essential, because your money is offshore and not as easily accessible.
3. A jurisdiction that allows a protector and letters of wishes. These are essential if you wish to retain some control over the instrument.

Where to Go

Some countries provide a more hospitable environment than others for asset protection. Because trusts are mostly a common-law creation, it is advisable to establish them in countries that adhere to this particular legal system. Among the Caribbean countries, the Cayman Islands, the Bahamas, Nevis, the Turks and Caicos Islands, and Belize are probably best for trusts. These jurisdictions have strong secrecy laws and have made it difficult for creditors to attack a trust (in Belize, for example, it is almost impossible for creditors to gain access to trust assets). In Europe, Gibraltar, the Isle of Man, and Jersey are reliable areas for trusts. In the South Pacific, the

Cook Islands offer excellent asset protection. Although Vanuatu and Niue also provide these services and boast strict secrecy laws, it is too soon to tell whether they will be able to maintain them. Vanuatu has been red-flagged by money-laundering officials — a situation that may eventually lead to a deterioration of its secrecy laws.

THIRTEEN

Using the Internet

In this chapter, you will learn:
- ~ *How to trust Internet communications*
- ~ *Why you should avoid using cyber-jurisdictions as a substitute for offshore centres*
- ~ *How Internet-based businesses can use offshore planning to their benefit*

*N*o book that discusses communicating globally would be complete without some mention of the Internet. For offshore investing, good communication is critical. The Internet is the network of networks that allows for instantaneous digital communications all over the globe. For the offshore investor, the Internet has allowed us to bend time and space. Offshore accounts and other instruments can be manipulated instantaneously from computer networks halfway around the world. The offshore-investment industry has embraced this popular technology not just for its communications potential but as a driver of change in terms of how the offshore-planning business works. For example, it is now possible to incorporate offshore companies and to conduct other traditionally complex and high-level transactions on-line with a click of a mouse. This short chapter addresses this revolutionary new technology in the context of offshore planning. It begins with a discussion of the history of the Internet, examines security measures in conducting Internet transactions, moves to an analysis of virtual cyber-jurisdictions (islands in cyberspace that are purporting to offer investors offshore products) and concludes with a discussion of electronic commerce and the opportunities it presents.

Some Internet History

The Internet is not a single network and it is not owned by any one organization, company, or government. Rather, it is a standardized set of protocols that allow digital information to flow on and between networks. It is, in effect, a system of information-sharing that produces a virtual network of networks. In other words, once disparate networks such as the telephone system, the cable system, and computer networks can all interact to transfer data between users. It no longer matters whether you are accessing information via cable television or the telephone. The two work together, and communications can be made between users of each.

Traditionally, the telephone was the only instrument for establishing contact with financial institutions in offshore jurisdictions. The telephone networks were often substandard, and there were no other means of communicating other than by mail. As the financial-services industry grew in these jurisdictions, telephone networks gradually improved, but only at a limited rate; accessing long-distance communications was still an expensive proposition, and communication services could expand only in response to demand.

That all changed with the Internet. One of its great features is that there are no long-distance charges. Users pay to connect to a local Internet service provider (at a cost of roughly ten to twenty dollars per month). There are no other costs for using this service, and the availability, in terms of use, is often unlimited. Consequently, most offshore jurisdictions are in the process of increasing their internal communications infrastructure dramatically to take advantage of the low-cost availability of the Internet. With communications being available for relatively little money, there is a bigger potential client base for these "Internet-ready" jurisdictions.

Trusting Internet Communications

Should you trust a communication on the Internet? One of the key features of the Internet, and the reason for its low user fees, is its design. The Internet routes communications through connected computers that sit between the sender and the recipient. For example, if there are ten computers between points A and B, each of the ten computers will receive and pass on the message on its way to its intended destination. Another important feature of the Internet is its ability to encrypt information. Traditionally, communications have been unencrypted. Encryption is the art of rendering a communication indecipherable by all but authorized parties. Encrypted communications use a key to code information, which is then sent over a network. When the information is received, a key (either the same one or a different one, depending on the technology used) is used to decipher it.

Two of the most common forms of Internet communication, and those most popular in dealing with offshore financial institutions and advisers, are electronic mail (e-mail) and the World Wide Web. Both of these modes of communication operate, by their nature, in unencrypted form. Therefore, it is possible that communications between sender and receiver may be intercepted and read. In terms of offshore planning, this will frustrate the private nature of transactions, which is often one of the primary goals of using an offshore jurisdiction for your investments.

Fortunately, encryption technology has developed for these two modes of communication, but it must be implemented by both sender and receiver for communications to be secure. The security level of these communications can be quite high (to the level where even government authorities cannot decrypt the communications without the requisite key).

If you are considering using the Internet to communicate with your offshore institution, you should ensure that an appropriate level of encryption is used. But you should be aware that even though the communication is encrypted, this does not guarantee that secrecy will be maintained at the other end, a problem that can be resolved only by tough secrecy laws and enforcement in the offshore jurisdiction.

When it comes to insuring secrecy through technological means, today's modern Web browsers provide a high level of encryption. However, this 128-bit key encryption is not yet widely available to users outside of the United States and Canada. This is because the technology used to form this level of encryption falls within the class of technologies protected by U.S. export laws. In other words, in order to supply the software to a country other than the United States or Canada, you would need to apply for an export licence with the U.S. government. These are not readily given.

For those within Canada and the U.S. who are interested in obtaining a copy of the security version of these browsers, you simply need to go to the Netscape (for Netscape Navigator and Communicator) or Microsoft (for Internet Explorer) Web site. You will then be prompted to complete an on-line affidavit (essentially an on-line form). After the completion of this affidavit, you will be allowed to download the browser. Once the browser is connected, you will be able to engage in secure communications with servers that are 128-bit-key-enabled. Offshore banks, brokerage houses, on-line shopping, and other electronic-commerce outfits are generally encryption-enabled in this way (it is easier for these organizations to obtain the export licences for their servers). You may communicate with them secure in the knowledge that the information travelling back and forth will be encrypted using a very high level of technology. Anyone who intercepts the material will not be able to decode it. As a result, you may send your credit card numbers or other private and confidential information over the Internet with relatively little risk of interception.

Virtual Cyber-Jurisdictions: Should You Trust Them?

With the recent growth of the Internet, it is not surprising to see the development of new schemes related to offshore planning springing up in the virtual world. Some of these schemes, such as on-line banking, provide investors with effective tools and valuable offshore opportunities. Other schemes, however, are simply doomed to failure. For example, virtual cyber-jurisdictions, while an interesting theoretical project, cannot presently be made into a workable operation. Virtual cyber-jurisdictions are self-declared nations that exist only in the on-line world (i.e., as a Web site). They often adopt a constitution and a set of laws and try to promote citizenship. These jurisdictions do not have any sovereign recognition, nor do they have any geographical boundaries separate and apart from those of existing states.

We considered including virtual cyber-jurisdictions in the chapter on scams, but it is not always clear to us that the motivation for setting up such structures is fraudulent. It is our feeling that some of these Web sites are set up with the best of intentions and without any fraudulent intent. However, for the serious offshore investor, these cyber-jurisdictions are to be avoided. Their currencies are not recognized; there is little you can do to enforce interest rate payments if their central bank refuses to pay (you would have to bring a lawsuit in an existing jurisdiction); and there is no recognition of their citizenship, sovereignty, or existence by any extant country.

Electronic Commerce: Setting Up an Offshore On-Line Business

The term "electronic commerce," also known as "e-commerce," has come into common parlance over the past two years. It refers to business transactions that occur over some sort of an electronic medium. Broadly speaking, this includes the telephone (i.e., touch-tone banking) as well as the computer. As the Internet grows in popularity and accessibility, e-commerce will increasingly come to mean commercial transactions that are affected using the Internet as the electronic carriageway. For small- and medium-size businesses, which have traditionally operated within local markets, the Internet provides access to global markets. Most discussions of the e-commerce topic, both in the media and in books, focus on this aspect: access by domestic firms to clients located in other countries. Little has been written about the use of offshore planning as a springboard to structuring an e-commerce business. Because the revenues being derived from a globalized e-commerce set-up come from all over the world, it makes good sense to take advantage of offshore-planning techniques to minimize taxes and take advantage of regulatory differences.

In terms of minimizing taxes, a company that is operating in an offshore jurisdiction, deriving its money from other offshore jurisdictions but owned by Canadians, will not necessarily be subject to foreign accrual property income (FAPI) rules. (FAPI is discussed in the chapters dealing with taxation.) If goods are manufactured or processed in an offshore jurisdiction and sold by a company incorporated in that jurisdiction (the business has to be carried on principally in the offshore jurisdiction), the FAPI rules may not apply. Similarly, it is possible to avoid the FAPI rules by structuring offshore joint ventures owned in part by non-Canadians dealing at arm's length with Canadian residents. Setting up operating businesses in an offshore jurisdiction to avoid FAPI rules is clearly easier to do when the offshore company is structured to earn active (i.e., operational) income, as opposed to passive (i.e., investment) income. However, it is still essential to speak to a tax adviser conversant in offshore-planning techniques and Canadian taxation rules before embarking on such a venture. Nevertheless, it is interesting to note that operating an on-line business based in an offshore jurisdiction, while full of fantastic opportunities, has not attained the level of popularity that one would expect.

PART FOUR

Country
Profiles

Introduction

We now turn to the country profiles. In this section, you will learn about the offshore offerings of twenty-nine jurisdictions. The list is by no means exhaustive; there are many other jurisdictions that specialize in offshore financial products, and their omission from this book should not in any way deter you from investigating them further. Our list is purely subjective and reflects what we feel are either traditional offshore centres or up-and-comers. The information presented on each country will vary based on its reliability; the traditional tax havens, for example, have more reliable information in circulation. Furthermore, you will observe that not all countries offer the same services.

We gathered our information from various sources, including atlases, world-fact books, reference books, companies providing financial services in these jurisdictions, government registration authorities, and professionals involved in the offshore-planning field. In many cases, we were provided with conflicting information for everything from fees to the political/economic situation. We have done our best to cross-check the information provided. If we were unable to cross-check sources, we either omitted the information from the discussion or marked it as not available (N/A). Any figures or fees set out in the following profiles are estimates; they are the result of averaging several pieces of information, and are subject to change. These profiles should serve as a guide only; the information provided should not be relied upon for pinpoint accuracy. As we have mentioned throughout the earlier chapters of the book, if you plan on venturing into the offshore world, you must first obtain the advice of a qualified professional.

Explanation of the ★ Rating System

Wherever possible, we evaluated the business infrastructure of each jurisdiction based on six criteria: economic stability, political stability, costs of entry, available services, secrecy, and other. The last category was used to evaluate factors such as the extent to which the local government supports the offshore-services industry, the relative strength of the local legislation in dealing with offshore planners, and any other items considered relevant to the jurisdiction.

Our rating system is based on stars (★), with five stars being the highest possible score for any single category. The higher the score, the more attractive the jurisdiction is to the offshore investor. For example, a five-star score in secrecy means that the jurisdiction in question, in our opinion, will protect your privacy effectively. On the other hand, a five-star rating with respect to costs means that, in our opinion, the costs for financial services and structures in the jurisdiction in question are relatively low. The profiles themselves and the rating of each jurisdiction are generally based on information gathered from several sources. You should be aware that this information is liable to change as the local business infrastructure changes. We have made every effort to reconcile the many conflicts in what we were told, but we cannot assert with absolute certainty that the information contained in these profiles is both accurate and up-to-date.

Geographic location	Andorra is located in the Pyrenees mountains of southwestern Europe, between France and Spain. The country is a triangular shape of 450 square kilometres.
Climate	Temperate
Estimated population	64,000 (70 percent are foreign nationals)
Capital city	Andorra la Vella
Currency	Andorra has no particular currency, but within the country Andorrans use the French franc and the Spanish peseta.
Time zone	GMT plus one hour in winter; GMT plus two hours in summer
Official language	Catalan, but French and Spanish are also spoken
Form of government	The country has been a parliamentary democracy since 1993, with a co-principality consisting of the French president and the Spanish bishop of Seo de Urgel as heads of state.
Legal system	Civil law

Business Infrastructure

Economic stability	★★★★	Secrecy	★★★★
Available services	★★★½	Cost of entry	★★
Political stability	★★★★	Other	★★

Political climate: Although it achieved independence in 1278, Andorra adopted its first written constitution only in March 1993. As a parliamentary democracy, the country is stable politically but is reputed to have problems respecting the rights of foreigners. It is also neutral, leaving its defence to Spain and France.

Economic climate: Andorra has a high GDP. Its main source of income is tourism. It has low agricultural production because there is little arable land, and its manufacturing industry seems confined to things such as furniture and tobacco products. The country's reputation as a tax haven has helped develop its economy substantially.

Andorra has adopted a liberal approach to business, and its trade agreement and customs alliance with the European Union may be attractive to potential investors. The country levies no direct taxes on its residents. Enterprises that create jobs are welcome, but pure trading activities are frowned upon. Since Andorra does not want to become a paper-company haven, it is not the best place to establish an international business company (IBC).

Financial and professional services: Andorra has a well-developed corporate infrastructure.

Communications services: Although Andorra has no airports and no railway, it is accessible by both air and rail via France and Spain. Its telephone, telex, and facsimile systems are connected to international networks. The country has one AM radio station and no television stations.

Secrecy: Specific laws and the penal code protect bank secrecy. Andorra has no tax treaties and will not divulge information about transactions to any foreign fiscal authority.

Exchange controls: Andorra has no exchange controls. Business may be transacted in any internationally quoted currency.

Residency and/or citizenship requirements: The president, general manager, or sole director of a company must be an Andorran citizen. Two-thirds of the company's capital must be owned by Andorrans.

Tax treaties: None

Company Information

Types of companies: Andorra allows three types of companies — the *societat per acciones,* the *societat de responsabilitat limitada,* and the *societat colectiva* — provided that two-thirds of the capital is owned by Andorrans. The country has no laws providing for trusts. Partnerships and sole traders (for citizens and residents of more than ten years' standing) are also permitted. The only type of finance company permitted in Andorra is an insurance company.

Fiscal policy: Andorra levies no direct taxes on citizens, but limited companies and companies limited by shares must pay an annual fixed tax of 110,000 pesetas. They must also pay import duties, an indirect goods tax of 4 to 7 percent, an insubstantial municipal tax, a utilities tax of 10 percent, and an annual registry charge.

Directors and officers: Andorra allows one or more directors, but the functions of president, general manager, and sole director must be carried out by an Andorran citizen.

Shareholdings and types of shares: Andorra allows common or preferred shares but will not permit shares with more than one vote. All shares must be registered. For a *societat per acciones,* the minimum required number of shareholders is three; for a *societat de responsabilitat limitada,* the number is between two and ten.

Capitalization requirements: For a *societat per acciones* and a *societat de responsabilitat limitada,* the minimum required capital is 5 million pesetas or 250,000 French francs; for a *societat colectiva,* no minimum is required.

Meetings and local office: Both are mandatory.

Filing requirements: Companies in Andorra are required to maintain their books and to prepare annual financial statements within five months of the company's year-end. Although these must be submitted to the shareholders for approval, they need not be officially filed unless the enterprise is a bank, a financial company, or an insurance company.

Typical time to incorporate: Thirty days. A company wishing to incorporate in Andorra must first send a draft of its articles of association to the government, which approves the foreign participation. Incorporation then takes place by notarial deed before a public notary. The act of incorporation is recorded in the register of companies in the ministry of commerce. Once a company is registered, it can operate in Andorra or internationally.

Estimated Minimum Corporate Fees

Ongoing Fees	
Annual tax or exemption fees	N/A
Directors' fees	N/A
Office and agency fees	N/A
Audit fees	N/A
Annual return filing fees	N/A
Banking fees	N/A
Total Ongoing Fees	**N/A**

Non-Recurring Fees	
Costs of incorporation (including legal fees)	N/A
Costs of establishing an international bank account	N/A
Provision of corporate VISA card	N/A
Total Non-Recurring Fees	**N/A**

Trust Information

Trusts are not recognized in Andorra.

Geographic location	The Bahamas consists of approximately 700 islands scattered across 250,000 square kilometres of the Atlantic Ocean. One of the largest islands, Grand Bahama Island, lies less than sixty kilometres east of Miami. New Providence is the most populated island in the Bahamas.
Climate	The Bahamas enjoys a tropical climate and warm Gulf Stream waters.
Estimated population	280,000
Capital city	Nassau
Currency	The Bahamian dollar (BAH) is valued at par with the U.S. dollar.
Time zone	GMT minus five hours
Official language	English
Form of government	The Bahamas is governed by a bicameral legislature with a sixteen-member senate. Members of the house of assembly are elected every five years; senators are appointed for a term of five years by the governor general on the advice of the prime minister and the leader of the opposition.
Legal system	Common law, strongly affected by statutory law

Business Infrastructure			
Economic stability	★★★★	Secrecy	★★½
Available services	★★★★½	Cost of entry	★★½
Political stability	★★★★½	Other	★★★½

Political climate: The Bahamas has long benefited from a stable political climate. The country gained its independence from the United Kingdom in 1973, but Queen Elizabeth II remains the head of state and is represented by a governor general, whom she appoints on the advice of the Bahamian prime minister. Two political parties, the Progressive Liberal Party (PLP) and the Free National Movement (FNM), dominate the political arena. The FNM has formed the government since August 1992, and the next elections are scheduled for the year 2002.

Economic climate: The country is heavily dependent on the tourism and offshore-banking industries. Tourism represents 50 to 60 percent of the GDP. The GDP growth rate can fluctuate along with the tourism sector, but government policies such as the Housing Development Program have helped alleviate some of these effects.

Financial and professional services: The Bahamas Investment Authority is part of the Office of the Prime Minister; it seeks to enhance the investment climate of the Bahamas. There are more than 400 financial institutions licensed to provide banking and trust services in the Bahamas. Professional services abound; there is a disproportionate number of accountants, lawyers, insurance companies, and financial-management services in the country.

Communications services: The Bahamas benefits from a highly developed communications infrastructure; telex, fax, and telephone services are readily available. A new satellite and an underground cable connecting the Bahamas to West Palm Beach, Florida, ensure continuous service. Direct dialling is available to the United States, Canada, and most other countries. Relatively good courier and postal services are also available. A number of airlines fly to the Bahamas, and direct flights are available from Toronto, New York, Miami, and London.

Secrecy: The Bahamas claims to possess strict bank-secrecy laws, but recent legislative changes reveal that these laws are not as firm as those of other jurisdictions. In an effort to curb the laundering of money in the country's banks, the Bahamian government passed the Money Laundering (Proceeds of Crime) Act, which imposes positive duties on financial institutions to identify and investigate any suspicious transactions. In addition, there are new reporting requirements for bank deposits in excess of BAH$100,000. Penal sanctions deter unauthorized disclosure of information by banks and management companies, but foreign authorities can apply to the court to obtain information pertinent to a criminal investigation. In one recent case, David Walsh (former president of Bre-X

Minerals Ltd.) was forced to provide a Bahamian court with the details of his personal holdings before that court would direct a local bank to release his funds. The Money Laundering Act was intended to drive away money launderers and improve the international image of the Bahamas, but its ambiguous language can serve many other purposes. Generally, persons not involved in any criminal activity should be unaffected, but the movement to diminish the level of secrecy must be considered.

Exchange controls: There are exchange controls for Bahamian citizens, but most offshore entities can carry out their activities in any currency and are exempt from exchange controls. Foreign-currency bank accounts are readily available.

Residency and/or citizenship requirements: The Bahamian immigration policy is more flexible than that of many other jurisdictions. Work permits are easily obtained for key personnel. Applications for residency may be accelerated for investors or homeowners with a net worth exceeding BAH$250,000. The recently enacted International Persons Landholding Act facilitates the acquisition of real property by individuals seeking residency status.

Company Information

Types of companies: Only international business companies (IBCs) are available to foreign investors. As is the case in most tax havens, an IBC is not authorized to carry on financial-service activities such as insurance, re-insurance, banking, and investment consultation. An IBC cannot offer its shares to the public, nor can it receive deposits.

Fiscal policy: An IBC is subject to an annual licence fee that ranges between US$100 and US$1,000. The licence fee is based on the authorized share capital and is payable on July 31 of each year. No taxes are payable on the company's income or capital gains. In addition, there are no wealth, gift, or inheritance taxes. Income can be earned offshore without fiscal effect, but the country is not a party to any double-taxation agreements. Stamp taxes apply to many transactions, including transfers of foreign currencies from a Bahamian bank, but IBCs (see below) are exempt from such taxes for twenty years.

Directors and officers: The minimum number of directors required is one. Corporate directors are permitted. The directors may be of any nationality and need not be residents of the Bahamas. The directors may register with the proper government authority, but there is no requirement that such registration occur.

Shareholdings and types of shares: The Bahamas allows shareholders considerable flexibility in determining the classes of shares to use. Bearer shares are available and allow complete anonymity. If bearer shares are not used, then the shareholders must be registered with the proper government authority. A minimum of two shareholders is required, but one shareholder may assign his or her shares to the other.

Meetings and local office: Directors must meet at least once a year. Meetings may be held abroad, by telephone, or through other means. An IBC is required to maintain a local registered office at the address of a licensed management company or law firm.

Annual filing requirements: IBCs are required to maintain accounting records that reflect their financial position; however, there is no requirement that they file annual financial returns. There is also no requirement that the records be audited.

Time to incorporate: A total of eight days is required to incorporate and register an IBC. Registration includes the filing of a memorandum of association and the articles of association.

Availability of shelf companies: Shelf companies are available (pre-formed companies).

Estimated Minimum Corporate Fees

International Business Companies (IBCs)

Ongoing Fees	
Annual licence fees	US$100.00
Directors' fees	500.00
Office and agency fees	750.00
Accounting fees	1000.00
Audit fees	Nil
Annual return filing fees	Nil
Banking fees	300.00
Communication costs	132.00
Total Ongoing Fees	**US$2782.00**

Non-Recurring Fees	
Costs of incorporation (including legal fees)	US$850.00
Costs of establishing an international bank account	500.00
Local duty	350.00
Provision of corporate VISA card	750.00
Total Non-Recurring Fees	**US$2450.00**

Trust Information

Types of trusts: A whole gamut of trusts may be created in the Bahamas, including family trusts, marriage-settlement trusts, charitable trusts, financial-planning trusts, and asset-protection trusts.

Effectiveness of the asset-protection trust: Under the Fraudulent Dispositions Act, a creditor can void any disposition of property if he or she has been unduly prejudiced. To set aside a transaction, however, the creditor must demonstrate that the debtor wilfully defrauded him or her by significantly undervaluing the property transferred. In addition, a statute of limitations requires that the creditor bring any court action within two years of the date of the transfer. The act appears to provide asset-protection trusts with an adequate defence against creditor claims.

Disclosure and registration: Discretionary trusts are permitted and trustees are not required to disclose the names of beneficiaries. There is no requirement to register the trust deed with a public body.

Letter of wishes: The Bahamas does not allow the use of a letter of wishes.

Applicable legislation: The Fraudulent Dispositions Act applies to trusts, especially asset-protection trusts.

Protector: A protector may be appointed to oversee and help direct some of the trustee's actions. The protector can act as a counsellor to the trust to ensure congruence between family/business objectives and the actions of the trustee.

Estimated Minimum Trust Fees

Ongoing Fees	
Trustee fees (two)	US$2000.00
Protector fees	500.00
Accounting fees	1000.00
Banking fees	300.00
Communication costs	132.00
Total Ongoing Fees	**US$3932.00**

Non-Recurring Fees	
Costs of settling the trust (including legal fees)	US$1000.00
Costs of establishing an international bank account	500.00
Local (stamp) duty	Nil
Total Non-Recurring Fees	**US$1500.00**

Geographic location	Barbados is an island in the British West Indies, roughly 400 kilometres northeast of Venezuela. The surface area is approximately 430 square kilometres. Barbados is the easternmost island in the Caribbean.
Climate	The country's climate is subtropical. The rainy season spans the months of June and October.
Estimated population	260,000
Capital city	Bridgetown
Currency	The exchange rate for the Barbados dollar is fixed at 2.0113 per U.S. dollar.
Time zone	GMT minus four hours
Official language	English
Form of government	The Barbados government is composed of a twenty-one-member senate (upper house) and a twenty-eight-member house of assembly (lower house). Senators are appointed by a governor general, who represents the head of state, Queen Elizabeth II. Members of the house of assembly are elected by general adult suffrage every five years. The next elections are scheduled for January 2004.
Legal system	Common law

Business Infrastructure			
Economic stability	★★★★	Secrecy	★★½
Available services	★★★★½	Cost of entry	★★★
Political stability	★★★½	Other	★★½

Political climate: Barbados declared its independence from the United Kingdom in 1966, at which time a new constitution was adopted. The country continues to be a member of the Commonwealth. Barbados has historically been stable. Its Parliament is the third oldest in the Commonwealth, after the parliaments of Britain and Bermuda. Barbados has responded to the changing offshore financial-services market by introducing favourable fiscal policies, but the country has not been as aggressive as others in pursuing offshore business. The legislative focus has been on improving the quality of Barbados as a corporate domicile by negotiating new tax treaties with various countries and improving existing ones.

Economic climate: While traditional Caribbean activities such as sugar-cane cultivation once dominated the economic landscape, a more diversified economy that relies on manufacturing, tourism, and financial services has emerged. A marine port and a new tax incentive for manufacturers have played important roles in this transformation. Unemployment in Barbados is high, hitting 22 percent in 1994 before dropping to 16 percent in 1996. Most food must be imported, as agriculture plays only a small role in the economy.

Financial and professional services: The financial- and professional-services sectors are well developed in Barbados. All major accounting firms have offices in Bridgetown, as do some large international banks (including the Royal Bank of Canada). The services of management companies are readily available.

Communications services: Barbados boasts a broad and reliable telecommunications infrastructure, and has a high number of telephones for the Caribbean. Daily direct flights from Toronto and Miami and next-day courier services are available.

Secrecy: The confidentiality of shareholders and trust beneficiaries is protected, although overall secrecy is inferior to that of other countries. Since Barbados is not a pure tax haven (in that corporations and trusts must pay income taxes), secrecy does not apply to investigations by local tax authorities. Also, to maintain its strong international relationships and tax treaties, Barbados must co-operate with foreign tax authorities in their investigations. Revenue Canada, for example, is authorized to conduct audits of Barbadian entities.

Exchange controls: Exchange controls require that corporations, trusts, and individuals demonstrate that they have satisfied all tax liabilities before the central bank will allow the repatriation of funds. Companies geared towards international business are automatically exempt from the exchange controls.

Residency and/or citizenship requirements: Work permits have traditionally been granted to a great number of non-residents, but concerns with high unemployment levels among the local work-force will likely put pressure on the government to restrict the flow. The single greatest advantage of making Barbados a country of residence is that it has negotiated tax treaties with many countries, a fact that has the potential of reducing withholding taxes on foreign-source income.

Company Information

Types of companies: There are many types of business structures used by non-residents in Barbados, including international business corporations (IBCs), foreign sales corporations (FSCs), societies with restricted liability (SRLs), and exempt (captive) insurance companies. On incorporation, an IBC is guaranteed certain benefits and exemptions for a period of fifteen years. An SRL is given the same guarantee, with the period extended to thirty years if the SRL carries on qualifying business activities. The business of captive insurance is very popular in Barbados.

Fiscal policy: As mentioned earlier, Barbados is not a pure tax haven: corporations and trusts are subject to tax. Corporations are taxed if their central management and control is exercised in Barbados (same test of residency as in Canada) or if they are incorporated in Barbados (similar to Canadian deemed residency provisions). IBCs and SRLs are taxed at the rate of 2.5 percent on profits below US$15 million and one percent on the excess. SRLs are generally exempt from tax on passive income such as interest, dividends, and royalties. Capital gains are not taxed, and payments to non-residents are exempt from withholding taxes. Both types of companies can claim credits for foreign taxes paid to a country with which Barbados has negotiated a tax treaty, so long as the effective rate of local tax does not fall below one percent. Barbados has concluded tax treaties with Canada, the United States, the United Kingdom, Switzerland, Sweden, and Finland. The treaties with Canada, Sweden, and the United Kingdom do not apply to IBCs. Interestingly, dividends received from a controlled foreign affiliate resident in Barbados (i.e., with central management and control based in Barbados) that earned active business income may not be subject to tax in Canada.

Directors and officers: IBCs and SRLs must have at least one director.

This director need not be a resident of Barbados. There is no requirement to appoint a corporate secretary.

Shareholdings and types of shares: Barbados, unlike other jurisdictions, does not allow great breadth in the types of shares that a company may issue. It does not appear that bearer shares are permitted. Redeemable shares are allowed, and a company has the power to buy back its shares.

Capitalization requirements: There are no minimum capitalization requirements.

Meetings and local office: A company must have a local office and agent. A number of management companies provide this service in Barbados. Directors can meet in any country, or even by telephone.

Annual filing requirements: IBCs and SRLs are exempt from filing annual financial statements; however, they must calculate their local tax liability, prepare a corporate tax return, and file this return with the local taxing authority. The pre-payment of tax is required in most circumstances. Unpaid balances are assessed penalties and interest.

Typical time to incorporate: The precise time needed to incorporate is unknown, so one should probably expect at least a two-week delay.

Availability of shelf companies: Shelf companies do not appear to be available.

Estimated Minimum Corporate Fees

Ongoing Fees	
Annual licence fees	US$500.00
Directors' fees	500.00
Office and agency fees	2500.00
Accounting fees	1000.00
Audit fees	Nil
Annual return filing fees	Nil
Banking fees	300.00
Communication costs	148.00
Total Ongoing Fees	**US$4948.00**

Non-Recurring Fees	
Costs of incorporation (including legal fees)	US$3000.00
Costs of establishing an international bank account	Nil
Local duty	Nil
Provision of corporate VISA card	750.00
Total Non-Recurring Fees	**US$3750.00**

Trust Information

Types of trusts: Barbados is not a popular jurisdiction for international trusts. An ordinary Barbadian trust is taxable only on the income that has not been distributed during the year. An international Barbadian trust is exempt from tax on income earned from foreign assets and foreign currencies. An international trust must have a Barbadian offshore bank act as trustee.

Effectiveness of the asset-protection trust: No specific legislation reinforces a Barbadian asset-protection trust. To make a successful claim against the settlor, a creditor need only demonstrate that the settlor could have reasonably foreseen that the transfer would prejudice the creditor's claim.

Disclosure and registration: No disclosure is required.

Letter of wishes: A letter of wishes is permitted, but it is not legally enforceable.

Applicable legislation: With the exception of the taxation rules described above, no legislation appears to apply to Barbadian trusts.

Protector: A protector may be appointed to oversee the trustee's activities.

Geographic location	Belize is located in Central America. It shares borders with Mexico to the north, Guatemala to the west and the south, and the Caribbean Sea to the east. Its total surface area is approximately 23,000 square kilometres.
Climate	The climate is subtropical, with both dry and rainy seasons. The average temperature is about 27°C.
Estimated population	200,000
Capital city	Belmopan is the capital city, but the financial and business centre is Belize City.
Currency	Since 1976, the Belize dollar has been tied to the U.S. dollar at the rate of US$1:BZ$2.
Time zone	GMT minus six hours
Official language	English is the official language, but Spanish is widely spoken.
Form of government	Belize has a bicameral legislature, with a twenty-nine-member house of representatives and an eight-member senate. Members of the house of representatives are elected by general adult suffrage for periods not exceeding five years. Senators are appointed for terms of five years. Queen Elizabeth II is the head of state, and she is represented in Belize by a governor general. The governor general, the prime minister, and his or her cabinet constitute the executive branch of government.
Legal system	English common law, supplemented by local legislation

Business Infrastructure

Economic stability	★★★	Secrecy	★★★★★
Available services	★★★	Cost of entry	★★★½
Political stability	★★★½	Other	★★★★

Political climate: Belize, formerly known as British Honduras, became a British crown colony in 1862. The country gained its independence from the United Kingdom in 1981, at which time it adopted its own constitution. Belize remains a member of the British Commonwealth. Two parties — the United Democratic Party and the People's United Party — dominate the political landscape. Both parties are committed to Belize's continued economic development.

Economic climate: The economy of Belize depends heavily on the export of sugar, fruits, and fish products. In fact, exports represent more than 50 percent of the country's GDP. With the election of a government that pledged to diversify Belize's economy, more emphasis has been placed on developing the tourism and offshore financial-services industries. Belize has negotiated preferential market-access arrangements with the United States, Canada, and the European Economic Community (through the United Kingdom). In an effort to encourage foreign investment, the government has even instituted a fifteen-year holiday from import duties on capital equipment and raw materials.

Financial and professional services: Belize is the host to four commercial banks, including Barclays Bank PLC (one of the world's largest) and the Bank of Nova Scotia. Two major accounting firms have offices in Belize, and both provide incorporation and management services. Overall, the financial sector is still in its infancy, but further expansion is expected to attract a greater number of professionals.

Communications services: The fully automated telecommunications system in Belize is above average. Individuals can reach all major countries in the world through direct dialling. Daily flights to Belize City are available from Miami, Houston, Los Angeles, and New Orleans. Overnight courier services are also available.

Secrecy: Belize maintains very strict confidentiality laws. There are no requirements to file the names of directors, officers, or shareholders with any public body. Also, a recent decision by the Belize supreme court suggests that the country will assert its sovereignty even in the face of considerable U.S. pressure. International business companies (IBCs) are not subject to the double-taxation agreements or the exchange-of-information agreements that Belize has negotiated.

Exchange controls: Belize law does impose certain exchange controls; however, IBCs and exempt trusts (discussed below) are excluded. As a result, IBCs and exempt trusts can hold foreign-currency bank accounts and can repatriate funds without limit.

Residency and/or citizenship requirements: No information relating to becoming a resident or citizen of Belize could be found. It is known, however, that most visitors with a valid passport can stay in Belize for up to one month without a visa. Also, the local government is likely to accommodate the needs of the growing offshore financial-services sector by granting a greater number of work permits.

Company Information

Types of companies: The International Business Companies Act of 1990 provides for the incorporation of IBCs with limited liability. With certain exceptions, IBCs can be used for a wide range of purposes, including financial management, investment holdings, ship or property ownership, share ownership of other companies, leasing of assets, holding intellectual property and/or licensing, and general commercial trading. An IBC cannot carry on business with residents in Belize; own real estate in Belize; carry on business as a bank (except as an offshore bank), a trust company, or an insurance company; provide registered office services; or carry on collective investment schemes.

Fiscal policy: An IBC is not subject to taxes in Belize so long as the company does not carry on business with residents of the country. The annual registration (licence) fee for IBCs is only US$100. Unlike most tax havens, Belize has negotiated double-taxation agreements with the United Kingdom, Sweden, Denmark, and the countries of the Caribbean Community (CARICOM). Most Canadian-source income is subject to a 25 percent withholding tax when paid or credited to Belizean IBCs.

Directors and officers: An IBC must have at least one director. Corporate and non-resident directors are permitted, and directors can be of any nationality. In addition, an IBC must appoint a corporate secretary who can also fill the role of director. There is no requirement that the company disclose the names of its directors and officers to the registrar of companies.

Shareholdings and types of shares: An IBC may issue shares in any currency, and it must have at least one shareholder. Bearer shares, registered shares, and shares with or without par value are permitted. IBCs are not required to disclose the names of their shareholders to a public body, even when they issue registered shares. The share register for IBCs may be viewed only by shareholders.

Capitalization requirements: There are no minimum capitalization requirements, but the standard authorized share capital is US$50,000. With authorized share capital of US$50,000, the annual registration (licence) fee is US$100. This fee increases to US$1,000 for IBCs with authorized share capital greater than US$50,000, and to US$350 for IBCs with no par value share capital.

Meetings and local office: An IBC must maintain a registered office in Belize. Meetings may be held anywhere in the world and attended by telephone, facsimile, other electronic means, or proxy.

Annual filing requirements: IBCs are not required to maintain accounting records or to have their financial statements audited. IBCs do not have to file financial information with the registrar of companies.

Typical time to incorporate: Two days are required to incorporate an IBC.

Availability of shelf companies: Shelf companies are available.

Estimated Minimum Corporate Fees

Ongoing Fees	
Annual licence fees	US$100.00
Directors' fees	500.00
Office and agency fees	500.00
Accounting fees	1000.00
Audit fees	Nil
Annual return filing fees	Nil
Banking fees	300.00
Communication costs	206.00
Total Ongoing Fees	**US$2606.00**

Non-Recurring Fees	
Costs of incorporation (including legal fees)	US$750.00
Costs of establishing an international bank account	250.00
Local duty	Nil
Provision of corporate VISA card	250.00
Total Non-Recurring Fees	**US$1250.00**

Trust Information

Types of trusts: Belize permits the creation of all forms of trusts, including variant trusts (which are trusts peculiar to a settlor's law, religion, or nationality). The trust may be an exempt trust if, at the time of settlement of the trust, neither the settlor nor the beneficiaries were residents of Belize and the trust property did not include real property situated in Belize. Exempt trusts are not subject to taxation or to exchange controls.

Effectiveness of the asset-protection trust: A Belize asset-protection trust is extremely secure. No court in the country can set aside or vary one of these trusts. No Belize trust has been compromised since the enactment of the Trusts Act in 1992. There are no laws relating to fraudulent transfers or bankruptcies, and it is not within the authority of a Belize court to enforce the judgements of foreign courts (i.e., there is no reciprocal enforcement). It would appear that Belize asset-protection trusts are impervious to claims by creditors and ex-spouses.

Disclosure and registration: Trusts may be registered with the registrar of trusts for US$100, but it is optional for the settlor to do so.

Letter of wishes: Both settlors and beneficiaries may provide the trustee with a letter of wishes (called a memorandum of wishes in Belize).

Applicable legislation: The Trusts Act of 1992 provides a comprehensive body of law for Belize trusts. The act abolishes the rule against perpetuities and provides for a maximum life of 120 years for trusts (except charitable trusts, which may have an indefinite life). The act also allows settlors to be beneficiaries of a spendthrift trust (i.e., a trust that provides for the beneficiary's personal expenses over the course of his or her life). Trustees are liable for losses or the devaluation of trust assets resulting from a breach of trust duty.

Protector: Belize law allows for the appointment of a protector, who may also be a settlor, a trustee, or a beneficiary. A protector owes a fiduciary duty to the beneficiaries.

Geographic location	Bermuda consists of more than one hundred small islands and is located in the Atlantic Ocean, approximately one thousand kilometres east of North Carolina. The islands cover roughly fifty-three square kilometres.
Climate	Bermuda enjoys a subtropical climate, although it is not part of the Caribbean per se.
Estimated population	62,500
Capital city	Hamilton
Currency	The Bermuda dollar is at par with the U.S. dollar.
Time zone	GMT minus four hours
Official language	English
Form of government	Bermuda is governed by a bicameral Parliament consisting of an eleven-member senate and a forty-member house of representatives. Representatives are elected every five years and senators are appointed by a governor general. The government is formed by the political party or coalition with the greatest number of seats in the house of representatives, and is headed by a prime minister and his or her cabinet.
Legal system	English common law

Business Infrastructure

Economic stability	★★★★	Secrecy	★★½
Available services	★★★★★	Cost of entry	★½
Political stability	★★★★½	Other	★★★

Political climate: Bermuda is a dependent territory of the United Kingdom. Queen Elizabeth II is the head of state, and she is represented by an appointed governor general. Bermuda is self-governing, and historically it has been quite responsive to changing international business climates. A 1995 vote to gain independence from the United Kingdom failed partly because of the growing importance of international business to Bermuda and the fear that independence might discourage such business.

Economic climate: Bermuda boasts one of the highest per capita income rates in the world. A high level of international business drives the Bermudan GDP, and financial services and tourism dominate the economic landscape. Agriculture does not figure prominently in its economy because of the low proportion of arable land. Approximately 80 percent of the food in Bermuda is imported.

Financial and professional services: Bermuda offers first-class financial and professional services. The capital city, Hamilton, hosts three large banks (no foreign banks are permitted in Bermuda) and many accounting, legal, and trustee firms. The financial- and professional-services sector is highly regulated for increased reliability.

Communications services: Bermuda possesses a modern communications infrastructure that is composed of three submarine cables and two satellite earth stations. Direct dialling is available from most countries. Courier services are readily available, and direct flights arrive daily from Toronto, New York, Boston, Philadelphia, Charlotte, Atlanta, and London.

Secrecy: Bermuda does not offer the same level of secrecy as other tax havens. The country also does not permit the issuance of bearer shares, and it requires the registration of the beneficial owners of a trust. Historically, however, Bermudan banks have provided a high level of confidentiality.

Exchange controls: Exempt companies and non-residents are not subject to any exchange controls; they may maintain bank accounts in any currency and repatriate funds without restriction. Trusts can also repatriate funds without restriction; however, they may not hold bank accounts in Bermudan dollars.

Residency and/or citizenship requirements: Bermuda imposes some important limitations on persons going to work there. For example, the employer must demonstrate that he or she has exhausted all efforts to fill the position with a local employee. Only persons with fewer than three children are entitled to work permits. Immigration for persons wishing to take up residence in Bermuda with no intention of seeking employment is less restricted; however, a residence-certificate application must be completed and approved by the government.

Company Information

Types of companies: Limited liability companies (LLCs) are the most common in Bermuda. LLCs may be classified as local companies, exempt companies, or permit companies. Exempt companies are the most appropriate business structure for foreign investment activities. They cannot engage in business activities in Bermuda, and they cannot engage in any banking, insurance, re-insurance, fund management, or other financial-services activities. Also, exempt companies cannot hold domestic real property.

Fiscal policy: Bermuda does not impose any income, withholding, or gift taxes; it is immaterial whether the income is derived from capital gains, dividends, interest, or other sources. The Bermudan government grants exempt companies a certificate of tax exemption, upon application, in accordance with the Exempt Undertakings Tax Protection Act of 1966. If Bermuda was to introduce a taxation scheme, the act specifies that exempt companies would continue to benefit from tax exemption until 2016. Bermuda is not a party to any double-taxation treaties.

Directors and officers: LLCs require at least two resident directors. Non-resident directors are permitted, but a sufficient number of local directors are required to form a quorum. In addition, LLCs must have a corporate secretary, who may or may not be a director. The directors and the corporate secretary must be natural persons.

Shareholdings and types of shares: Shares must be registered; preferred shares are permitted. Shares may or may not carry voting rights. Bearer shares and shares with a par value are not permitted. The minimum number of shareholders is one and the maximum is twenty-five.

Capitalization requirements: The minimum allowable share capital is BMD$12,000.

Meetings and local office: Local meetings are required at least once a year. LLCs must maintain a local office and agent. There are many management companies that offer such services.

Annual filing requirements: There is no requirement to file accounts; however, accounting records must enable the shareholders and the directors to ascertain the financial position of the company. Original accounting records or a copy of those records must be kept at the company's registered office. LLCs must appoint an auditor, but the audit requirement may be waived with the unanimous consent of the shareholders and the directors.

Typical time to incorporate: The incorporation process in Bermuda is very complex and time-consuming. It includes advertising in a local newspaper one's intention to form an exempt company and providing the Bermudan authorities with bank references. Incorporation can take approximately three weeks. Trusts are easier to establish.

Availability of shelf companies: Shelf companies are not available, owing in large part to the complex incorporation procedures.

Estimated Minimum Corporate Fees

Ongoing Fees	
Annual licence fees	US$1680.00
Directors' fees	2000.00
Office and agency fees	1000.00
Accounting fees	500.00
Audit fees	Nil
Annual return filing fees	Nil
Banking fees	300.00
Communication costs	136.00
Total Ongoing Fees	**US$5616.00**

Non-Recurring Fees	
Costs of incorporation (including legal fees)	US$3300.00
Costs of establishing an international bank account	500.00
Local duty	Nil
Provision of corporate VISA card	750.00
Total Non-Recurring Fees	**US$4550.00**

Trust Information

Types of trusts: Bermuda permits varied types of trusts, including purpose trusts and asset-protection trusts. With few exceptions, Bermudan trusts cannot hold local currency, shares of local companies, or real property (or an interest in real property) situated in Bermuda.

Effectiveness of the asset-protection trust: A Bermudan asset-protection trust is less effective than similar trusts established in other jurisdictions. First, a creditor may institute a claim if the obligation arose before or within two years of the date of the transfer of assets into the trust. Second, the statute of limitations bars a claim only if the action is not taken within six years of the later of the date of transfer or the date on which the obligation arose. In other words, a creditor could bring an action to reverse the conveyance to the trust up to eight years after the date of transfer. Finally, creditors must prove their case on a preponderance of evidence, rather than beyond a reasonable doubt, as is the case in most other jurisdictions.

Disclosure and registration: Discretionary trusts are the most popular in Bermuda; they provide trustees with much greater flexibility in determining the timing and extent of any asset distributions. Generally, no bank reference or other personal information is required to establish such a trust. There is also no requirement that the trust document be registered with a public body.

Letter of wishes: Bermudan law permits a settlor to provide his or her trustee with a letter of wishes to help ensure the better administration of the trust assets. The letter may be amended at the discretion of the settlor.

Applicable legislation: There are three principal legislative enactments that govern the law of trusts in Bermuda. The Trusts (Special Provisions) Act of 1989 gives a general structure for trusts in Bermuda and provides rules for resolving legal conflicts. The Perpetuities and Accumulations Act of 1989 amends the common-law rule against perpetuities and restricts the duration of trusts to one hundred years. The Conveyancing Amendment Act of 1994 provides the legal framework for challenging the transfer of assets to an asset-protection trust.

Protector: A settlor can name a protector, whose role is to oversee the administration of the trust assets by the trustee. A protector can ensure that the trust assets are administered in accordance with the settlor's wishes.

Geographic location	The British Virgin Islands (BVI) are located in the eastern Caribbean, approximately one hundred kilometres east of Puerto Rico. The BVI are a group of forty islands, the largest and the most heavily populated of which is the island of Tortola. The total surface area is approximately 150 square kilometres.
Climate	The BVI enjoy a subtropical climate: warm and humid.
Estimated population	17,000
Capital city	Road Town
Currency	The U.S. dollar is the official currency.
Time zone	GMT minus four hours
Official language	English
Form of government	The BVI have a legislative council that is composed of thirteen members who are elected for no more than five-year intervals. Cabinet ministers, including a chief minister, are chosen from among the elected members. These ministers and an attorney-general (ex-officio member of the legislative council) form the executive council, which is overseen by a governor. The British Crown appoints the governor. The next elections are expected before February 2000.
Legal system	Common law

Business Infrastructure

Economic stability	★★★½	Secrecy	★★★½
Available services	★★★★½	Cost of entry	★★★★½
Political stability	★★★★½	Other	★★★★

Political climate: Although the islands are a dependent territory of the United Kingdom, they became self-governing in 1967, when they adopted their own constitution. The country is a recognized member of the Commonwealth, and has enjoyed considerable political stability since 1967. The United Kingdom appoints a governor, but he or she is officially responsible for only the police force, foreign affairs, the public service, and certain legal matters.

Economic climate: The economy relies heavily on two industries: tourism and offshore financial services. There is little industrial production and even less raising of livestock. Nearly all food is imported. Despite this high degree of international reliance, the British Virgin Islands enjoy one of the highest standards of living in the Caribbean. The local government has been responsive to changing economic climates: in 1991, a dramatic decline in tourism was met with a number of successful legislative changes that helped encourage the domestic economy.

Financial and professional services: Professional expertise is readily available on the British Virgin Islands. The islands host two of the largest international banks in the world, Barclays Bank (U.K.) and Chase Manhattan (U.S.). Most of the large accounting firms and major European trust companies also have offices in Road Town.

Communications services: The communications infrastructure is modern and includes phone, telex, and facsimile services. There are daily flights to Puerto Rico and many flights to the continental United States. Overnight courier services are available. Of note is the country's ability to recover quickly from natural disasters: in the case of Hurricane Bertha, electricity was restored to the islands within twenty-four hours.

Secrecy: Legislation provides for the blanket confidentiality of financial matters, though this does not apply to criminal investigations that may or may not be conducted in accordance with a mutual legal-assistance treaty. For corporations, there is no requirement to disclose the names of shareholders or directors. Trust deeds need not be registered.

Exchange controls: There are no exchange controls.

Residency and/or citizenship requirements: We could find no legal information for those wishing to immigrate to the British Virgin Islands; however, it is interesting to note that the population of the islands has more than doubled in the past ten years.

Company Information

Types of companies: The International Business Companies Ordinance of 1984 provides for a versatile business structure: the international business company (IBC). An IBC can engage in any lawful business activity, including holding investments or real property, operating trading companies or mutual funds, and reinforcing an asset-protection trust. A licence is needed to conduct banking, trust, insurance, and other financial-services activities. To create an IBC, you must submit a memorandum and your articles of association to the public registrar of companies, at which time a certificate of incorporation will be issued. In addition to IBCs, the British Virgin Islands also accommodate limited life companies (LLCs) and international limited partnerships (ILPs).

Fiscal policy: An IBC is exempt from all taxes, including income, estate, inheritance, succession, wealth, and gift taxes, and from any stamp duties. To maintain this tax-exempt status, an IBC cannot conduct business with local residents, cannot own real property situated in the British Virgin Islands, and cannot provide the services of a local registered office. IBCs must pay an annual licence fee, which varies based on the capital structure of the company: it is fixed at a minimum of US$300 (for companies with an authorized share capital of less than US$50,001 par value shares) and at a maximum of US$1,000. The country is a party to tax treaties with Japan and Switzerland; however, these treaties are of limited use to tax-exempt IBCs.

Directors and officers: An IBC must have at least one director, and this director can be an individual or a corporation. Directors can be of any nationality and need not reside in the British Virgin Islands. There is no requirement to disclose the names of the directors to the registrar of companies.

Shareholdings and types of shares: An IBC can issue no par or par value shares, bearer or registered shares, preferred shares, non-voting shares, and/or redeemable shares. Shares may be issued in any currency and even in multiple currencies. An IBC need not register the names of its shareholders. Nominee shareholders are permitted.

Capitalization requirements: There are no minimum capitalization requirements for IBCs, but the standard authorized capital is US$50,000. An IBC must have at least one shareholder.

Meetings and local office: An IBC must maintain a registered office and agent in the British Virgin Islands. Meetings of directors can take place in any location or by any means, including by telephone.

Annual filing requirements: IBCs are not required to file an annual information return or to prepare financial statements. There are no audit requirements.

Typical time to incorporate: Two days are required to incorporate a company.

Availability of shelf companies: Shelf companies are available.

Estimated Minimum Corporate Fees

Ongoing Fees	
Annual licence fees	US$300.00
Directors' fees	500.00
Office and agency fees	750.00
Accounting fees	1000.00
Audit fees	Nil
Annual return filing fees	Nil
Banking fees	300.00
Communication costs	146.00
Total Ongoing Fees	**US$2996.00**

Non-Recurring Fees	
Costs of incorporation (including legal fees)	US$850.00
Costs of establishing an international bank account	300.00
Local duty	Nil
Provision of corporate VISA card	750.00
Total Non-Recurring Fees	**US$1900.00**

Trust Information

Types of trusts: Trusts may be used to protect the settlor's assets (i.e., an asset-protection trust), to perform estate planning, or to hold investments. Fixed-term and purpose trusts are also permitted. To allow trusts to evolve along with the needs of the settlor, the British Virgin Islands let existing trusts be rearranged without triggering any local tax or duty.

Effectiveness of the asset-protection trust: There is no specific legislation that reinforces the asset-protection trust. To overturn a transfer of assets by the settlor of the trust, a creditor must demonstrate that he or she was prejudiced by the settlor's action, and that the settlor should reasonably have foreseen that the creditor would be so prejudiced.

Disclosure and registration: No registration of the trust is required and the names of the beneficiaries of the trust need not be disclosed.

Letter of wishes: There is no prohibition against the use of a letter of wishes, but there is also no requirement that the trustee adhere to the instructions in the letter.

Applicable legislation: BVI trusts are governed by the Trustee Ordinance of 1961, the Trustee Amendment Act of 1993, the Banks and Trust Companies Act of 1990, and the common law. Trusts have a maximum life of one hundred years.

Protector: The country permits the appointment of a protector by the settlor. The protector will help ensure that the distribution of assets is performed in accordance with the settlor's wishes.

Geographic location	The Cayman Islands are a group of three islands located in the northwestern region of the Caribbean, near Cuba. Grand Cayman is the main island, and it is located approximately 800 kilometres south of Miami, Florida. The two smaller "sister" islands are Cayman Brac and Little Cayman. The total surface area of the islands is approximately 260 square kilometres.
Climate	The climate is semi-tropical, with a very predictable rainy season.
Estimated population	30,000
Capital city	George Town
Currency	The Cayman Islands' dollar is not tied to any currency, but it is valued at approximately CI$1.00:US$1.20.
Time zone	GMT minus five hours
Official language	English
Form of government	The country is a British crown colony. The head of state, Queen Elizabeth II, is represented by a governor. A local legislative assembly is elected every five years, and the next elections are scheduled for November 2000. The legislative assembly is composed of fifteen members: twelve elected members, a financial secretary, an attorney-general, and an administrative secretary. The governor presides over the executive council, which includes four members of the legislative assembly.
Legal system	English common law is the basis of the legal system; however, Cayman law is greatly affected by locally enacted statutes.

Business Infrastructure

Economic stability	★★★★½	Secrecy	★★★★
Available services	★★★★★	Cost of entry	★★★★½
Political stability	★★★★½	Other	★★★★½

Political climate: The Cayman Islands enjoy an extremely stable political and social climate. The local government has entered into a partnership with the private sector to ensure that the islands are responsive to the changing legislative environment, and that there is a strong and competitive legal framework for business. The government is committed to maintaining a well-organized and stable financial-services sector.

Economic climate: The Cayman economy is dominated by the tourism and financial-services industries. Tourism represents approximately 70 percent of the GDP, with total annual tourist visits in excess of one million persons for 1995 and 1996. Unemployment is approximately 5.5 percent, which is very low for a Caribbean country. The islands boast one of the highest GDPs per capita and one of the highest standards of living in the world. Business is not unduly or overly restricted by local legislation.

Financial and professional services: The Cayman Islands are the fifth-largest financial centre in the world. There are more than 500 banks (including the fifty largest in the world) and approximately one hundred trust companies operating in George Town. All major accounting firms have offices in the Caymans, and a great number of management companies offer a broad spectrum of services. In short, the financial-services infrastructure is extremely well developed.

Communications services: The Cayman Islands boast an advanced telecommunications infrastructure. In fact, one source of information claims that the islands now have the highest per capita number of fax machines and cellular telephones in the world. It is not surprising that one of Canada's major exports to the Cayman Islands is telecommunications equipment. The country may be reached by direct dialling from almost any telephone in the world. There are several daily flights to and from Miami (a little more than a one-hour flight) and many frequent flights from other large Canadian, American, and European cities. Overnight courier and local postal services are readily available.

Secrecy: Strict confidentiality laws protect bona fide business transactions and provide for severe sanctions, including prison sentences and fines, for any breach of the law. In accordance with the U.S.-U.K. Mutual Legal Assistance Treaty, the Cayman Islands have agreed to share information on activities that are criminal in nature, particularly with respect to drug trafficking and money laundering. Exchanges of information with foreign revenue or taxation authorities are excluded from the aforementioned treaty, and are prohibited by the Confidential Relationships (Preservation) Law of 1976. This statute applies to all persons who would have access to financial information, including bankers, lawyers, accountants, and government officials.

Exchange controls: There are no exchange controls in the Cayman Islands, and bank accounts may be kept in any major currency. Funds may be repatriated without restriction.

Residency and/or citizenship requirements: Individuals wishing to immigrate to the Cayman Islands must first obtain permission from the local government. Demand for financial-service professionals is high, and obtaining a work permit is not difficult.

Company Information

Types of companies: An exempt company is the most common form used by offshore investors. An exempt company cannot carry on business within the Cayman Islands, but it can maintain any facilities needed to administer its business, including an office, a bank account, and a brokerage account. Banks, trust companies, and insurance companies require a special licence to operate in the Cayman Islands. An exempt company can have a limited life of up thirty years (this is called a limited duration company). Other company structures available to foreign investors are the ordinary company (resident and non-resident) and the exempted limited partnership; however, these three structures all require more extensive disclosure than the exempt company. A non-resident ordinary company can hold title to a vessel registered in the Cayman Islands, while a resident ordinary company can carry on business and hold real property in the islands.

Fiscal policy: The absence of all forms of taxation makes the Cayman Islands a pure tax haven. There are no taxes on income, profits, or gains, nor are there any inheritance taxes, gift taxes, wealth taxes, or withholding taxes. An exempt company can obtain a tax-exemption certificate that ensures that it will not be subject to tax for a period of twenty years even if the local government introduces such legislation. The certificate is renewable on expiry. Exempted limited partnerships can obtain a similar certificate that covers a period of fifty years. The Cayman Islands are not a party to any bilateral tax treaty.

Directors and officers: An exempt company must have at least one director, who may be of any nationality or residence. A corporate secretary is recommended, and the same person can fill both that role and that of director. Natural persons or bodies corporate can act as directors. The names of a company's directors and officers must be filed with the registrar of companies, but this register is not available for inspection by the public.

Shareholdings and types of shares: A Cayman exempt company that is not a limited duration company (LDC) may issue shares of all forms (including bearer shares) in any currency and even in multiple currencies. The company must have at least one shareholder, and it may be authorized to issue different classes of shares, each carrying different rights. An LDC must have at least two subscribers. There is no requirement to disclose the names of the shareholders to the registrar of companies, but the company's local agent must retain that information.

Capitalization requirements: There are no minimum capitalization requirements; however, most exempt companies are incorporated with an authorized share capital of US$50,000.

Meetings and local office: An exempt company is required to maintain a local registered office and mailing address. Each calendar year, the board of directors must hold at least one meeting in the Cayman Islands. The mandatory meeting can be held by telephone, by videoconference, or by proxy. There is no requirement to have an annual meeting of the shareholders.

Annual filing requirements: Every year, the corporate secretary or a director must file a statement with the registrar of companies declaring that the company's operations were carried out mainly outside the Cayman Islands, and that it complied with certain provisions of the Companies Law. Every company is require to keep proper books, so as to give a true and fair view of its state of affairs and to explain its transactions. There is no statutory requirement that any accounts be audited or filed with the Cayman government (though this is not applicable to banks, trust companies, insurance companies, and management companies). An ordinary company must file an annual return listing its shareholders and their shareholdings.

Typical time to incorporate: A period of three to four days is required to incorporate an exempted company.

Availability of shelf companies: Shelf companies are readily available.

Estimated Minimum Corporate Fees

Ongoing Fees	
Annual licence fees	US$500.00
Directors' fees	850.00
Office and agency fees	900.00
Accounting fees	500.00
Audit fees	Nil
Annual return filing fees	Nil
Banking fees	300.00
Communication costs	145.00
Total Ongoing Fees	**US$3195.00**

Non-Recurring Fees	
Costs of incorporation (including legal fees)	US$1500.00
Costs of establishing an international bank account	Nil
Local duty	Nil
Provision of corporate VISA card	750.00
Total Non-Recurring Fees	**US$2250.00**

Trust Information

Types of trusts: Cayman Islands legislation accommodates virtually all forms of trusts — only trusts whose object is unlawful or contrary to public policy are prohibited. The most common types of trusts are ordinary trusts and exempted trusts; the ordinary trust is much preferred by foreign investors because of the considerably less onerous reporting requirements.

Effectiveness of the asset-protection trust: To defeat a transfer of assets to a trust, a creditor must demonstrate that the settlor intended to defraud the creditor, that the settlor's obligation towards the creditor existed on or prior to the date of the transfer of assets to the trust, that the transfer was effected at an undervalue, and that the creditor was prejudiced by the transfer. According to the Fraudulent Dispositions Law of 1989, the creditor must institute proceedings within six years of the date of the transfer of assets to the trust. Under the Bankruptcy Law (Revised), transfers of assets dating back up to ten years may be declared void if, at the time of the transfer, the settlor was a resident of the Cayman Islands, was present in the Cayman Islands, carried on business in the Cayman Islands, or was a member or partner of a firm that carried on business in the Cayman Islands. It is immaterial whether the transferor was solvent. Nevertheless, a transfer of assets to a Cayman trust will be set aside only to the extent necessary to satisfy the obligation to the creditor.

Disclosure and registration: No registration of the trust deed is required for ordinary trusts. The trust deed of an exempted trust must be registered with and approved by the registrar of trusts. Also, the trustee of an exempted trust may from time to time be required to furnish information about the trust to the registrar. Ordinary trusts are subject to a one-time stamp duty of US$50. Exempted trusts must pay a registration fee of approximately US$480 and an annual fee of approximately US$120.

Letter of wishes: A letter of wishes, more commonly referred to as a memorandum of wishes in the Cayman Islands, is permitted. Since the trustee is given full legal control of the assets, the memorandum is not a legally binding document; however, few responsible trustees would ignore its contents.

Applicable legislation: The law of trusts is heavily regulated in the Cayman Islands. There are many Cayman laws directed at trusts beyond the Fraudulent Dispositions Law and the Bankruptcy Law (Revised), discussed above. The provisions of the Trusts Law (Revised) establish mechanisms for the appointment and discharge of trustees, for the restructuring of trusts, for the protection and indemnity of trustees, and for the vesting of trust assets in trustees. The Perpetuities Law of 1995 provides for a perpetuity period of 150 years for most trusts. Almost any trust with a lawful object can be created under the Special Trusts (Alternative Regime) Law of 1997. The Trusts (Foreign Element) Law of 1987, as amended, offers a choice of governing law provision that permits the continued existence of a Cayman trust even if the laws of the settlor's country of residence forbid trusts or do not recognize the concept of a trust.

Protector: Settlors may assign a protector to review the work of the trustee. The practice is popular in the Cayman Islands.

Geographic location	The country consists of fifteen islands located in the South Pacific, 3,000 kilometres west of Tahiti, 4,000 kilometres south of Hawaii, and 3,200 kilometres northeast of New Zealand.
Climate	Tropical
Estimated population	20,000
Capital city	Avarua, on the island of Rarotonga
Currency	New Zealand dollar and local Cook Islands currency
Time zone	GMT minus ten hours, or daylight savings minus five hours
Official languages	English (trade and commerce) and Maori
Form of government	Parliamentary democracy
Legal system	Common law

Business Infrastructure

Economic stability	★★★	Secrecy	★★★
Available services	★★★	Cost of entry	N/A
Political stability	★★★½	Other	★★★

Political climate: This relatively stable country obtained its independence from New Zealand through a written constitution in 1965. A Westminster-style democracy, the Cook Islands are governed by a prime minister acting on the advice of a cabinet, with the Queen of England as head of state. New Zealand, however, remains responsible for the country's defence.

Economic climate: This is a relatively poor country that has a low GDP and still receives government aid. Its main exports are fresh and canned citrus fruit, clothing, coffee, and fish. In 1996, the country declared bankruptcy and began to cut its public service in half, as well as sell off government assets. Since 1981, government and industry have been working in tandem to create a prime offshore business centre.

Financial and professional services: The country has trustee companies and several banks.

Communications services: The islands have well-developed telephone, telex, and facsimile services that offer direct dialling from many countries and operator-assisted dialling from most others. The country has AM, FM, and short-wave radio stations. Travellers can reach the Cook Islands via one of seven airports (one with a paved runway) or via one of two ports — Avarua or Avatiu.

Secrecy: To protect offshore investors, the islands have strong secrecy provisions that require government officials, trustee companies, and bank employees to maintain confidentiality under the threat of penal sanctions. Legislation such as the Trustee Companies (Due Diligence) Regulations of 1996 and the Offshore Industry (Criminal Provisions) Act of 1995–96 require trustee companies to ensure, before registering a trust, that the money was not derived from illegal activity. A monetary board can apply to the court to have companies de-registered if it suspects criminal activity and trustee companies de-licensed for not reporting suspicious behaviour. The country allows bearer shares, and trusts do not have to be registered.

Exchange controls: None. All major currencies are accepted for bank accounts.

Tax treaties: Although the country maintains that it has no tax treaties, New Zealand's treaties with Canada, the United States, Sweden, and the United Kingdom still include the islands. The islands have no power to revoke the treaties but will not enforce them.

Residency and/or citizenship requirements: Although a director need not be a resident of the Cook Islands, a secretary must be a resident and the registered office is required to be in the islands.

Company Information

Types of companies: The country allows domestic companies, international companies (which are most frequently used in offshore ventures), foreign companies, and registered listed companies. The international companies are regulated by the International Companies Act, which allows organizations to carry on any legal business except banking, insurance, or trustee services (unless licensed to do so by the Cook Islands Monetary Board). The information provided hereafter pertains only to international companies.

Fiscal policy: International companies are exempted from filing tax returns, from paying capital gains or withholding taxes, and from paying taxes on dividends received from international companies. They are also exempt from stamp taxes, import duties, turnover taxes, and licence fees.

Directors and officers: Only one director is required, and that person need not be a resident of the Cook Islands. Corporate directors are permitted. In addition, the company must have a secretary who is a resident of the country and is also either a trustee or an officer of a trustee company. The company is also required to have an office registered with a trustee company in the Cook Islands.

Shareholdings and types of shares: Only one shareholder is required. Registered and bearer shares are permitted, as are shares with or without par value.

Capitalization requirements: There are no minimum capitalization requirements.

Meetings and local office: General annual meetings are not required unless requested by a shareholder. In such a case, a meeting must be held within three months of the shareholder providing notice to the company. a resolution may be passed instead of the meeting If the shareholders agree, a resolution may be passed instead of the meeting, which need not be held in the Cook Islands.

Annual filing requirements: An annual return is required within twenty-eight days of the anniversary of incorporation. The accounts do not have to be lodged with the registrar.

Typical time to incorporate: At least one day. To incorporate a company, an officer must file an original and unsigned true copy of the memorandum and articles of association with the registrar of international and foreign companies. The registrar then issues a certificate of incorporation for a twelve-month period; this certificate is renewable upon payment of the prescribed fees.

Availability of shelf companies: Shelf companies are available.

Estimated Minimum Corporate Fees

Ongoing Fees	
Annual tax or exemption fees	N/A
Directors' fees	N/A
Office and agency fees	N/A
Audit fees	N/A
Annual return filing fees	N/A
Banking fees	N/A
Total Ongoing Fees	**N/A**

Non-Recurring Fees	
Costs of incorporation (including legal fees)	N/A
Costs of establishing an international bank account	N/A
Provision of corporate VISA card	N/A
Total Non-Recurring Fees	**N/A**

Trust Information

Types of trusts: Non-resident offshore trusts are available for estate planning, asset protection, and family businesses. Minimum fees start at US$2,000 to establish a trust and US$5,000 in annual trustee fees.

Effectiveness of the asset-protection trust: Unless fraud is suspected, it is extremely difficult for creditors to break a trust in the Cook Islands. Disinherited heirs cannot challenge a trust because it interferes with their right to inherit, and foreign judgements are not enforceable.

Disclosure and registration: Although you are not required to register a trust, it is a good idea to do so, because international trusts are not liable for taxes.

Applicable legislation: The International Trusts Act of 1984 and the Trustee Companies Act of 1981–82 apply.

Protector: A protector may be appointed.

Cyprus

Geographic location	Cyprus is an island in the Mediterranean Sea, south of Turkey.
Climate	Mediterranean temperate
Estimated population	More than 7 million
Capital city	Nicosia
Currency	Cyprus pound (considered one of the most stable currencies in the world)
Time zone	GMT plus two hours, or daylight savings plus seven hours
Official languages	The official languages are Greek and Turkish, but English is used in most financial and legal documents.
Form of government	Republic
Legal system	Common law

Business Infrastructure			
Economic stability	★★★★	Secrecy	★★★½
Available services	★★★★½	Cost of entry	★★★★
Political stability	★★★½	Other	★★★★

Political climate: Cyprus gained independence from Britain in 1960, becoming a republic with a president as head of state. Turkey invaded the island in 1974 and now controls 40 percent of it (in the north). Although the Greek government is the only one officially recognized, Cyprus remains politically unstable and the United Nations has established a buffer zone occupying 4 percent of the island.

Economic climate: The Turkish part of Cyprus is economically weak and attracts little investment. In contrast, the Greek part prospers thanks to a low inflation rate and to developed service, finance, tourism, and agricultural sectors. In 1996, the island satisfied the Maastricht convergence criteria, but it is still prone to economic fluctuation caused by external factors.

Financial and professional services: To take advantage of its growing popularity with offshore investors, Cyprus has developed a strong financial infrastructure.

Communications services: Cyprus offers direct dialling to one hundred countries, as well as good postal and courier services. The island has fourteen airports, four heliports, and five seaports. It also has radio and television stations.

Secrecy: No bearer shares are permitted and all banks must submit accounts for annual inspection. These accounts are confidential and not for general viewing. Trusts need not be registered, but beneficiaries and interests must be identified in the trust deed.

Exchange controls: Exchange controls exists in Cyprus but not for offshore companies. Non-residents may hold foreign-currency accounts.

Residency and/or citizenship requirements: Offshore companies must belong to non-resident owners and derive their income from an outside source. For offshore trusts, the trustees, the beneficiaries, and the settlor cannot be residents.

Tax treaties: Cyprus has tax treaties with Canada, the United Kingdom, and the United States.

Company Information

Types of companies: Cyprus recognizes two types of companies: those limited by shares and those limited by guarantee. Companies are governed by the Companies Law of 1951. Offshore companies cannot trade with residents, individuals, or other companies, and they cannot engage in banking, insurance, assurance, re-insurance, building-society, or trust-management activities without a specific licence. Offshore companies may own property in Cyprus.

Fiscal policy: Offshore companies are taxed at 4.5 percent, payable August 1. They are exempt from capital gains taxes, except for those payable on property owned in Cyprus.

Directors and officers: Offshore companies require at least one director; this director need not be a resident and can be a corporate entity. No secretary is required, but a registered office in Cyprus is. General meetings do not have to be held in Cyprus.

Shareholdings and types of shares: Shares must be registered and can be par value shares, preferred shares, redeemable shares, or shares with no voting rights. The minimum number of shareholders is two and the maximum is fifty.

Capitalization requirements: No minimum share capital is required.

Meetings and local office: An annual meeting is required, but it need not take place in Cyprus. A company must have a local registered office.

Annual filing requirements: Companies are required to prepare accounts, maintain proper books, have independent auditors examine accounts, and prepare financial statements that are to be presented at annual meetings.

Typical time to incorporate: One week. To incorporate, a company must submit a memorandum and its articles of association to the registrar of companies with a declaration of compliance and a registration fee.

Availability of shelf companies: Shelf companies are available.

Estimated Minimum Corporate Fees

Ongoing Fees	
Annual fees (management fees, fee for submission of annual returns to the registrar of companies, and cost of registered office)	US$560.00
Directors' fees	200.00
Nominee shareholders' fees	200.00
Total Ongoing Fees	**US$960.00**

Non-Recurring Fees	
Costs of incorporation	US$1450.00
Costs of establishing an international bank account	300.00
Provision of corporate VISA card	N/A
Total Non-Recurring Fees	**US$1750.00**

Trust Information

Types of trusts: Cyprus offers discretionary, fixed, trading, and purpose trusts. Although the settlor and the beneficiary cannot be residents, at least one trustee must be. A trust cannot hold immovable property and cannot last longer than one hundred years.

Effectiveness of the asset-protection trust: Normally an international trust is irrevocable unless creditors can prove that it was formed for the purpose of defrauding them.

Disclosure and registration: Trusts need not be registered, but bank accounts have to be disclosed to the Central Bank of Cyprus. The names of the trustees need not be mentioned.

Applicable legislation: Trustee law is based on the English Trustee Act of 1925 and the International Trusts Law.

Geographic location	Gibraltar is a six-square-kilometre stretch of land located at the southernmost tip of the Iberian peninsula.
Climate	Mediterranean
Estimated population	30,000
Capital city	Gibraltar
Currency	Gibraltar pound, which is at par with the British pound
Time zone	GMT plus one hour, or daylight savings plus six hours
Official language	English
Form of government	British dependent territory and crown colony of the United Kingdom
Legal system	Common law

Business Infrastructure			
Economic stability	★★★★	Secrecy	★★★½
Available services	★★★★½	Cost of entry	★★★
Political stability	★★★★½	Other	★★★★

Political climate: Although Gibraltar is a colony of Britain, which is responsible for its defence, foreign affairs, and financial stability, it is otherwise self-governing. An elected house of assembly legislates on domestic matters. The country is a member of the European Union but is exempted from the union's agricultural policy, the common customs tariff, and value-added taxation.

Economic climate: Gibraltar has primarily a service economy consisting of tourism and finance (banking and shipping). It produces tobacco, beer, and canned fish but is a recipient of foreign aid. The country's economy is stable, with a low deficit. The termination, in 1985, of Spain's economic blockade, and the closing of the frontier between Gibraltar and Spain in 1969, has improved their relations and traffic dramatically.

Financial and professional services: Gibraltar has an excellent infrastructure consisting of major accounting firms, banks, and trust companies. Financial services in Gibraltar are regulated by the Financial Services Ordinance of 1989, which is based on the U.K. Financial Services Act of 1986 (an act enforcing European Community financial directives) and the Financial Services Commission Ordinance of 1989 (an act that established a financial-services commission and enforces the provisions of the FSO).

Communications services: Gibraltar has completely rebuilt its telecommunications system (telephone, telex, facsimile), and it is now excellent. The country has two radio stations (AM and FM) and four television stations. Several flights to London leave the country's airport each day, and there are plans to have daily flights to Frankfurt and Zurich. Gibraltar has good port facilities.

Secrecy: The Banking Ordinance insures banking secrecy and confidentiality. The Drug Trafficking Ordinance of 1989 and the Gibraltar Criminal Justice Ordinance of 1995 together enable authorities to take the necessary measures to prevent money laundering and other criminal offences. Gibraltar allows bearer shares, but not for exempt companies. Only charitable trusts must be registered with the government; the register is maintained by the Financial Services Commission. The recording of any transfer of assets to asset-protection trusts is closed and its contents privileged.

Exchange controls: None

Residency and/or citizenship requirements: Either the company director or its secretary must be a resident, and the company's office must be registered in Gibraltar. Although trustees need not be residents, it is strongly recommended that at least one of them is.

Tax treaties: None

Company Information

Types of companies: There are four types of companies permitted in Gibraltar: companies limited by shares; share-capital companies limited by guarantee; companies without share capital limited by guarantee; unlimited companies with or without share capital. Only companies with share capital qualify for exempt status for international trade and investment. Hereinafter all information pertains to these exempt companies. The Companies Ordinance, which is based on the English Companies Act of 1929, regulates the formation of companies. Exempt companies can't be owned beneficially by residents of Gibraltar, but residents can hold shares as nominee or acting directors. Exempt companies cannot trade within Gibraltar or take deposits, insure, assure, re-insure, manage funds or assets, or engage in any other financial activity.

Fiscal policy: Exempt companies are excused from local taxation and duties (including estate duties) on their shares and from all withholding taxes. As non-residents, shareholders are exempt by definition from tax on dividends, interest, royalties, and distributions on a liquidation; withholding taxes; estate taxes; transfer taxes; gift taxes; and any other form of taxation in Gibraltar.

Directors and officers: Gibraltar requires only one director. Either the director or the secretary must be a resident of the country. Corporate directors are permitted; for private companies, directors don't have to be shareholders.

Shareholdings and types of shares: Only one shareholder is required. For exempt companies, registered shares are required. These may be in the form of preferred or redeemable shares, with limited or no voting rights. Par value shares are not permitted.

Capitalization requirements: Exempt companies must have a minimum authorized and issued capital of 100 GIP. There is a 0.05 percent duty on authorized share capital, with a minimum fee of 10 Gibraltar pounds.

Meetings and local office: A local annual meeting is required, as is a local registered office.

Annual filing requirements: There is no requirement to file financial statements for public companies, but a company must prepare audited financial statements each year and present these to the shareholders for approval at a general meeting. The statement must be filed with the registrar of companies and the accounts must be kept in Gibraltar.

Typical time to incorporate: Three days to three weeks. To incorporate, a company must file its articles of association, a Statement of the Situation of Registered Office, a statement declaring the authorized share capital, and a declaration of compliance. To obtain exempt status, a company must apply to the financial and development secretary and send a letter of reference from a banker, a lawyer, or an accountant concerning future activities. A certificate of exemption lasts twenty-five years.

Availability of shelf companies: Shelf companies are available.

Estimated Minimum Corporate Fees

Ongoing Fees	
Annual tax for exemption status	US$375.05
Provision of two directors	N/A
Provision of two shareholders	500.00
Office and agency fees	417.00
Fee for maintaining registered office, secretaries, and company records, and for filing statutory returns	417.00
Auditing fees	584.00
Audit compliance certificate	42.00
Annual return filing fees	59.00
Banking fees	N/A
Total Ongoing Fees	**US$2392.05**

Non-Recurring Fees	
Application for exempt status	US$167.00
Costs of incorporation (including legal fees)	N/A
Costs of establishing an international bank account	2000.00
Provision of corporate VISA card	167.00
Total Non-Recurring Fees	**US$2334.00**

Trust Information

Types of trusts: Gibraltar permits charity, fixed, or discretionary trusts. Trusts can be used for estate planning, asset protection, accumulation of assets, and as unit trusts. Their maximum duration is one hundred years, except for charitable trusts, which are unlimited. For a trust or a beneficiary to be exempt from taxation, the trust must be created on behalf of a non-resident and have its income derived from outside Gibraltar.

Effectiveness of the asset-protection trust: The Trusts Ordinance of 1990 ensures that forced heirship and other civil-law concepts that threaten trusts are not enforceable in Gibraltar. Under the Fraudulent Conveyances Act of 1571, a creditor may invade a trust if transfers into it lacked legal propriety.

Disclosure and registration: Only charitable trusts need to be registered. In a discretionary trust, the beneficiaries need not be named as long as they are included in a nominated class of beneficiaries. Beneficiaries must be non-residents to gain exemption from taxation.

Letter of wishes: N/A

Applicable legislation: Trustee Ordinance, based on England's Trustee Act of 1893; Variations of Trusts Act of 1958; Trustee Investments Ordinance; Perpetuities and Accumulations Ordinance of 1986; Trusts Ordinance of 1990

Protector: A protector may be appointed.

Geographic location	The bailiwick of Guernsey consists of a group of islands. The largest, with a total surface area of sixty-three square kilometres, is the island of Guernsey. The islands are located in the English Channel, approximately fifty kilometres northwest of France and 130 kilometres south of England.
Climate	Guernsey is mild and often overcast. The average temperature varies between 6°C in the winter and 17°C in the summer.
Estimated population	63,000
Capital city	St. Peter Port
Currency	The Guernsey pound is set at par with the British pound sterling. The exchange rate with the U.S. dollar is approximately US$1.00:£0.60.
Time zone	GMT, with daylight savings between March and October
Official language	English
Form of government	The Assembly of States (Guernsey's legislative assembly) is composed of sixty elected members. Among these members, there are thirty-three conseillers (who are elected every six years) and twenty-seven deputies (who are elected for three-year terms). There are no political parties in Guernsey: all members of the Assembly of States are independents. To be properly enacted, local laws must be approved by the lieutenant-governor, who represents Queen Elizabeth II, the chief of state.
Legal system	Guernsey law is rooted in Norman (French) customary law, though local statutes have introduced many common-law concepts to the island. English common law is used where custom is non-existent or irrelevant.

Business Infrastructure

Economic stability	★★★★	Secrecy	★★
Available services	★★★★½	Cost of entry	★★★★½
Political stability	★★★★½	Other	★★

Political climate: Guernsey has had a long and peaceful history since Henry III formally annexed it to the Crown of England in 1254. Guernsey is a British Crown dependency, but laws of the United Kingdom do not apply to the island. Guernsey also maintains a separate judicial system, with final appeals going to the privy council. Guernsey is not a member of the European Union (EU), but it enjoys all the trade benefits of member countries. Under Protocol 3 of the Treaty of Accession of the United Kingdom, industrial and agricultural goods manufactured or cultivated in Guernsey may be shipped to EU countries free of any customs duties. If the goods originate outside Guernsey, then normal U.K. customs levies apply. In general, Guernsey is not subject to EU laws or policies.

Economic climate: Favourable tax policies and flexible business structures have transformed Guernsey into a leading offshore financial centre. The financial-services sector now accounts for 55 percent of the bailiwick's total income; tourism, manufacturing, and horticulture are in decline. The local government remains committed to further developing the financial-services sector, and the Guernsey Financial Services Commission was created to ensure the development and effective control of the industry.

Financial and professional services: Guernsey is host to more than seventy banking institutions, and to numerous law firms, trust and insurance companies, and accounting firms. In fact, only banks that are among the 500 largest in the world may carry on business in Guernsey.

Communications services: The Guernsey telecommunications infrastructure and postal services are modern and efficient. Direct flights are available from the United Kingdom, France, Holland, Switzerland, and Germany; flight times range between one and two hours. Public telegrams, international and local telex, and facsimile and courier services are also available.

Secrecy: While confidentiality is important in Guernsey, the local government is more concerned with ensuring that the islands remain a leading offshore financial centre. As a result, great efforts have been undertaken to dissuade persons involved in criminal activities from seeking refuge in Guernsey. When a company is incorporated, it must file its objects and the names of its promoters with the Guernsey Financial Services Commission; the information is not shared with any foreign governments and thus remains confidential. In addition, trustees must disclose the names of the beneficial owners of a trust to the commission. Guernsey also has certain information-sharing agreements with the United Kingdom and the island of Jersey.

Exchange controls: All exchange controls have been abolished in Guernsey. There are no regulations restricting the flow of capital and the repatriation of funds.

Residency and/or citizenship requirements: The Housing Authority controls immigration into Guernsey by issuing housing licences to immigrants. The supply of housing licences is meagre. With a licence, an individual can occupy a local-market property; without a licence, an individual can occupy only an open-market property. The price of local-market properties is regulated, whereas open-market properties are unregulated and thus their cost is much greater. Obtaining a housing licence, however, does not guarantee that the individual will be granted a right to work (work permit). The EU provisions on the free movement of workers apply differently to Guernsey: residents are not entitled to this free movement, but nationals of other EU countries can work there.

Company Information

Types of companies: A resident company is usually created if the company plans to undertake business on the islands; offshore investors are more likely to incorporate an exempt company or an international company. An exempt company cannot carry on business in Guernsey and cannot be beneficially owned by a resident of the bailiwick. International companies also must derive their income from non-resident sources; however, greater flexibility of the ownership structure is available. An international company would be ideal for the business of manufacturing products in Guernsey to be exported to members of the EU, for example, since the company could pay very low or no taxes and its products would not be subject to duties in the EU. Other forms of business include protected-cell companies (companies whose assets and liabilities are divided into distinct units, or cells), partnerships, and limited partnerships. Please note that the general partner in a limited partnership must maintain unlimited liability.

Fiscal policy: Resident companies are taxed on their worldwide income at the rate of 20 percent. Taxes paid to the United Kingdom or Jersey are credited up to the effective Guernsey tax rate, and taxes paid to other countries are credited up to three-quarters of the effective Guernsey tax rate. An exempt company is not liable for Guernsey taxes so long as it does not conduct business on the islands (other than collecting interest from a local bank) and continues to satisfy certain ownership restrictions. An exempt company is subject to an annual exemption fee of £500. International companies are subject to a flexible tax regime: rates vary between 0 percent and 30 percent, and are determined on a case-by-case basis for five-year terms. Capital gains are not subject to tax in Guernsey. Residents of Guernsey must withhold 20 percent from payments to non-residents for income earned on the islands; exempt companies are not subject to such withholding taxes. Guernsey has negotiated double-taxation treaties with the United Kingdom and Jersey, but only resident companies are entitled to the benefits of these agreements. Guernsey is fiscally independent from the EU.

Directors and officers: All companies are required to have a corporate secretary and a minimum of one director. Directors can be natural persons or corporate bodies, may be of any nationality, and may reside outside Guernsey. Companies must register the names of their directors and officers with the Greffe (public registry).

Shareholdings and types of shares: Shares of a Guernsey corporation must be registered — that is, bearer shares are not permitted. Shares with no par value also are prohibited. Shares may be denominated in any currency, and the company must have at least two subscribers (shareholders). Redeemable shares and shares with or without voting rights are allowed.

Capitalization requirements: There are no capitalization requirements in Guernsey and no minimum debt-to-equity ratios. Newly formed companies must pay a stamp duty equal to 0.5 percent of the authorized share capital. The minimum stamp duty is £350 (£310,000 authorized share capital) and the maximum is £5,000. At least two shares must be subscribed.

Meetings and local office: There are no restrictions on the location of board meetings, but at least one meeting must be held each year. Exempt companies can hold board meetings in Guernsey without affecting their tax status. Exempt companies must maintain a registered office in Guernsey, but they need not retain the services of a registered agent.

Annual filing requirements: All companies, including exempt companies, are subject to statutory filing requirements. Failure to file an annual return will result in the imposition of fines, the striking of the company from the register of companies, and even the confiscation of assets by the Crown. All companies are required to maintain accounting records, but only exempt companies are free from filing those returns; exempt companies can also forego an annual audit. An annual return filing fee of £100 applies to all companies.

Typical time to incorporate: Between five and seven days are required to incorporate a company in Guernsey. An advocate (Guernsey lawyer) must prepare and present statutory documents to the court for approval. Companies can be incorporated in Guernsey only by the assent of the royal court.

Availability of shelf companies: Shelf companies generally are not available; however, certain organizations have been given the right to hold such companies.

Estimated Minimum Corporate Fees

Fees are billed in Guernsey pounds, but here have been converted to U.S. dollars for comparison with other jurisdictions. The amounts below are estimates only, since billings are based on time spent rather than flat fees. The amounts given are for exempt companies.

Ongoing Fees	
Annual licence fees	US$825.00
Directors' fees	500.00
Office and agency fees	1325.00
Accounting fees	1500.00
Audit fees	Nil
Annual return filing fees	125.00
Banking fees	300.00
Communication costs	107.00
Total Ongoing Fees	**US$4682.00**

Non-Recurring Fees	
Costs of incorporation (including legal fees)	US$1500.00
Costs of establishing an international bank account	Nil
Local duty	Nil
Provision of corporate VISA card	750.00
Total Non-Recurring Fees	**US$2250.00**

Trust Information

Types of trusts: Guernsey can accommodate most types of trusts, including discretionary, non-discretionary, spendthrift, and asset-protection trusts. A trust will be subject to taxes on its Guernsey-source income only if the settlor and the beneficiaries are non-residents. The settlor can retain certain rights and powers, including rights as a beneficiary.

Effectiveness of the asset-protection trust: Combining a Guernsey exempt company and a trust can extend the protection of assets offered by the use of a trust alone. No local legislation reverses the rule against fraudulent dispositions by the settlor or the rule prohibiting the insolvency of the settlor: either event could void transfers of assets into the trust.

Disclosure and registration: There is no requirement to register the trust deed with a public body. Also, neither the trust accounts nor the names of beneficiaries and settlors need be disclosed. Trustees are required to uphold confidentiality.

Letter of wishes: A letter of wishes is common in Guernsey. If the trustee does not receive such a letter, he or she will normally consult the settlor (if the settlor is still alive) on the desired direction of trust management.

Applicable legislation: The trust laws are primarily founded on case law and on the Hague Convention on the law applicable to trusts. The Trusts (Guernsey) Law of 1988 bestows certain powers on Guernsey courts, recognizes trusts settled in foreign jurisdictions, and codifies the responsibilities and obligations of the trustees. The Trusts (Amendment) (Guernsey) Law of 1990 renders certain trusts valid, even if the settlement was in conflict with the forced-heirship laws of the settlor's home nation.

Protector: A protector may be appointed. Trustees may be required to consult the protector before exercising some of their more important powers.

Geographic location	Hong Kong is located on the southeast coast of China. It consists of 235 islands and a mainland, and has a total surface area of approximately 1,025 square kilometres.
Climate	The summers are hot and wet, and autumn and winter are cool and dry. The typhoon season runs from July to September, but strong typhoons are rare.
Estimated population	6.5 million
Capital city	Victoria, on Hong Kong Island
Currency	The Hong Kong dollar is tied to the U.S. dollar at the rate of HK$7.80:US$1.00.
Time zone	GMT plus eight hours
Official languages	English and Cantonese Chinese
Form of government	Prior to July 1, 1997, Queen Elizabeth II was the head of state and was represented on the island by a governor, whom Her Majesty appointed. With the reversion to Chinese rule (see Political Climate, below), a governor is appointed by the Chinese government. In addition to the governor, the Hong Kong government consists of two councils: the executive council and the legislative council. Members of the executive council are appointed by the governor and include five ex-officio members, one official member, and nine unofficial members. The legislative council includes sixty elected members, four ex-officio members, and ten official representatives of government departments. Prior to 1991, the governor appointed the sixty members who are now elected. Members of the legislative council serve for four years.
Legal system	The legal system is based on English common law, but it is increasingly modified by local statute.

Business Infrastructure			
Economic stability	★★★★½	Secrecy	★★
Available services	★★★★½	Cost of entry	★★★½
Political stability	★★★½	Other	★★★★

Political climate: Hong Kong was ceded to Great Britain under the Treaty of Nanking in 1842; it became a British crown colony. In 1898, Great Britain leased Hong Kong from China for a period of ninety-nine years. In 1984 the British and Chinese governments signed the joint declaration that provided for Hong Kong's reversion to Chinese rule on July 1, 1997. Under the joint declaration, Hong Kong became a special administrative region of China, and China agreed to retain Hong Kong's existing political, social, commercial, and legal systems for at least fifty years following July 1, 1997. Although many Hong Kong residents feared the transition to Chinese rule, it appears that the capitalist structure has since gone unchanged. Hong Kong remains a separate participating member of the General Agreement on Tariffs and Trade (GATT) and other international bodies.

Economic climate: Hong Kong is the eighth-largest trading economy in the world. It is a major trading centre with well-established links to most Asian countries. This heavy reliance on trade is what distinguishes Hong Kong from most other offshore jurisdictions. Hong Kong's per capita GDP was more than US$21,500 in 1994, which placed it second in Asia behind Japan, and ahead of Great Britain, Australia, and New Zealand. Companies operate in a laissez-faire economy that is remarkably free of government intervention and regulation. Heavy industry is in constant decline, as Hong Kong's economy becomes increasingly service-based. The textile and garment industries are still important, but the real-estate sector now dominates the local economy. Because of its limited natural resources, Hong Kong must import most of its food and raw materials. The estimated unemployment rate was 3.1 percent in 1996.

Financial and professional services: Hong Kong is the world's third-largest financial centre, after New York and London. There is a large community of international banks, insurance companies, merchant banks, mutual-fund companies, and venture capitalists in Hong Kong. There are approximately 170 licensed banks and another 195 restricted deposit-taking companies. All major accounting firms have offices in Hong Kong, as do many law firms from the United Kingdom, Australia, Canada, and the United States. There is, however, a noticeable absence of trust companies in Hong Kong, as is further explained below.

Communications services: The telecommunications infrastructure makes extensive use of fibre optics and is both efficient and inexpensive. Air travel and courier services are readily available, and a new airport has made air travel much easier and safer. The previous Hong Kong airport was one of the most dangerous in the world.

Secrecy: The level of confidentiality is good. The names of shareholders must be disclosed to the registrar of companies, but only the names of nominee shareholders need be disclosed if a simple declaration of trust is used. Increasingly cumbersome legislation against money-laundering activities has been introduced in Hong Kong, and this legislation requires banks to know the beneficial owners of companies. This information, however, is held in the strictest of confidence. Banks are not required to report cash transactions to government authorities.

Exchange controls: Hong Kong does not maintain any currency-exchange controls, but only a few banks offer U.S.-dollar accounts. The costs of these foreign-currency accounts are high and their efficiency is poor.

Residency and/or citizenship requirements: As a general rule, travellers to Hong Kong must obtain a visa for the purpose of pursuing education or taking up employment, training, or residence. The Hong Kong immigration department welcomes professionals and businesspersons who want to work and invest in the local economy; however, other policies prevent the entry of undesirable persons. Visa applications must be submitted to the Chinese embassy or consulate general in the country of residence of the applicant. Applicants must be sponsored by a Hong Kong resident to obtain an entry visa, and visas generally take between four and six weeks to process. A small processing fee is charged.

Company Information

Types of companies: Business activities are generally pursued through private companies limited by shares. This form of enterprise can engage in most business activities, including trading, re-invoicing (acting as intermediary between shipper and customer), investment holding, and administrative undertakings. Some restrictions exist on banks, insurance, and finance companies, as well as other organizations that sell investments to the general public. These private companies have limited liability and are established under the Hong Kong Companies Ordinance.

Fiscal policy: Corporations pay tax on assessable profits at the rate of 16.5 percent. Assessable profit includes income only from Hong Kong sources. Income earned outside Hong Kong is not taxed in Hong Kong, even if central management and control of the corporation is located there. There is a stamp duty of 0.3 percent on the authorized share capital of newly formed companies, as well as an annual business registration fee (BRF) of HK$2,250 and filing fee of HK$95 (total of US$300). There are no withholding taxes on dividends and interest, and capital gains are not subject to tax. Hong Kong companies cannot offset profits with losses from related or associated companies. Individuals are taxed at a fixed rate of 15 percent. Also, there are no taxes on dividends received from subsidiaries located outside Hong Kong. Hong Kong has negotiated a double-taxation agreement with the U.S., but this agreement is limited to certain shipping activities. Hong Kong is not a party to any exchange-of-information agreements with other countries. It does maintain some progressive estate duties for local property valued at more than HK$5.5M (US$0.7M). Banks, finance companies, insurance companies, and personal-service companies are subject to additional tax rules.

Directors and officers: Companies must appoint at least two directors and a corporate secretary. Natural persons or bodies incorporate can act as directors or as a secretary. The directors need not be residents of Hong Kong, but the corporate secretary must be. The directors' responsibilities and liabilities are laid down in the Hong Kong Companies Ordinance and in each company's memorandum and articles of association.

Shareholdings and types of shares: Each company must have a minimum of two shareholders; these shareholders can be individuals or other corporations. Shares may be denominated in any currency and are usually registered shares, with or without voting rights. Bearer shares are possible in only very limited instances and thus are quite uncommon. Anonymity may be achieved through the use of a simple declaration of trust, for which only the names of the nominee shareholders and the directors need be filed with the registrar of companies.

Capitalization requirements: The standard authorized share capital is HK$10,000 (US$1,280), which triggers a stamp duty of 0.3 percent, or HK$30 (US$4). Increases in authorized share capital are subject to a stamp duty of 0.6 percent. No minimum paid-in capital requirements are enforced in Hong Kong.

Meetings and local office: Companies must maintain an office in Hong Kong, as well as a local agent. At least one general meeting must be held every twelve months, but it may be held anywhere and by any reasonable means (such as by telephone).

Annual filing requirements: Hong Kong companies must keep proper accounts and records. Every year, companies must file audited accounts with the registrar of companies and a tax return with the Inland Revenue Department. Accounts of private companies are kept confidential. The requirement for a local audit is laid down in the Hong Kong Audit Ordinance but may be dispensed with if the company is not earning any income subject to tax in Hong Kong and if all shareholders agree. The names of shareholders and directors must also be filed annually.

Typical time to incorporate: Two weeks

Availability of shelf companies: Shelf companies are readily available and can operate under a different trading name.

Estimated Minimum Corporate Fees

Ongoing Fees	
Annual licence fees	US$288.00
Directors' fees	1000.00
Office and agency fees	900.00
Accounting fees	1000.00
Audit fees	Nil
Annual return filing fees	13.00
Banking fees	300.00
Communication costs	122.00
Total Ongoing Fees	**US$3623.00**

Non-Recurring Fees	
Costs of incorporation (including legal fees)	US$750.00
Costs of establishing an international bank account	250.00
Local duty	4.00
Provision of corporate VISA card	750.00
Total Non-Recurring Fees	**US$1754.00**

Trust Information

Trusts remain relatively unpopular in Hong Kong, possibly owing to the absence of trust legislation. Most local financial-service providers prefer establishing trusts in jurisdictions other than Hong Kong. Consequently, we will not explore Hong Kong trusts further in this section.

Geographic location	Ireland is an 83,279-square-kilometre island in the Atlantic Ocean, sixty kilometres west of Britain.
Climate	Temperate maritime
Estimated population	3.5 million
Capital city	Dublin
Currency	The Irish pound, which is equivalent to US$1.50
Time zone	GMT, or daylight savings plus five hours
Official language	English is the official language of trade and commerce.
Form of government	Republic
Legal system	Common law

Business Infrastructure

Economic stability	★★★★	Secrecy	★★★½
Available services	★★★★½	Cost of entry	★★★½
Political stability	★★★½	Other	★★★½

Political climate: Politically, the Republic of Ireland is relatively stable. The country acquired its independence from Britain in 1921, after a three-year struggle. A parliamentary democracy with a president as head of state, Ireland has a constitution that allows its president to hold only two consecutive seven-year terms. Ireland is a member of both the EU and the Organization for Economic Co-operation and Development (OECD).

Economic climate: Trade-dependent Ireland has a well-trained labour force, especially in the area of high technology. Since 1980, inflation rates have fallen and deficits have turned to surpluses. Unemployment still remains high. Ireland is a particularly welcoming environment for creative artists, who pay no taxes on the revenue earned from their creations.

Financial and professional services: Ireland has many banks, as well as financial, legal, corporate, and tax services. Many international banks have branches in Ireland, and Irish banks have branches in the United States, Britain, and Europe.

Communications services: Ireland's digital-telecommunication facilities offer direct dialling to 160 countries. The country also has efficient postal and courier services, as well as forty airports with regular flights to all major European cities and roll-on roll-off freight and ferry service to Britain and France. Ireland has radio and television stations and nine ports.

Secrecy: The Finance Act of 1994 requires companies to disclose their beneficial owners. No bearer shares are permitted. No specific legislation ensures bank secrecy, but revenue-inspection powers have to get court approval before investigating accounts. Ireland will exchange information with tax-treaty countries. In 1994, provisions were introduced to counter money-laundering activities; these provisions require financial institutions to report knowledge or suspicion of laundering.

Exchange controls: None. Foreign currencies are permitted for deposit in bank accounts.

Residency and/or citizenship requirements: Company directors and secretaries do not have to be residents, nor do trustees.

Tax treaties: Ireland has extensive tax treaties with Canada, Britain, Australia, and the United States.

Company Information

Types of companies: Ireland allows limited, unlimited, and non-resident companies. Activity is regulated by the Companies Acts of 1963 to 1990. Non-resident companies cannot trade in Ireland, and must be managed and controlled outside the country. They cannot solicit funds or sell shares to the public. Hereinafter all information pertains to non-resident companies.

Fiscal policy: If a company is managed and controlled outside Ireland, it pays no taxes.

Directors and officers: The minimum number of directors required is two; neither one can be a corporate entity. Directors need not be residents and can be of any nationality. A secretary, who need not be a resident, is required; the secretary may be a corporate entity.

Shareholdings and types of shares: Non-resident companies require one shareholder and shelf companies require two. Only registered shares are allowed, and these may be preferred, redeemable, or with or without voting rights.

Capitalization requirements: There is no minimum share capital.

Meetings and local office: Companies are required to have a registered office in Ireland, but they do not have to hold their annual meetings there.

Annual filing requirements: Companies have to file annual returns with an abridged audited account, but they don't have to file accounts with revenue authorities. These authorities reserve the right to call for accounts if they wish. Accounts have to be audited by an independent firm of public accountants, which must verify that the company's financial statement gives an accurate view of its accounts.

Typical time to incorporate: Ten to fifteen working days. A company must submit a memorandum and articles of association with a Form 1 describing the first director, secretary, and situation of the registered office.

Availability of shelf companies: Shelf companies are available.

Estimated Minimum Corporate Fees

Ongoing Fees	
Annual licence fees	N/A
Directors' fees	N/A
Office and agency fees	US$413.00
Accounting fees	N/A
Audit fees	N/A
Annual return filing fees	225.00
Banking fees	N/A
Communication costs	N/A
Total Ongoing Fees	**US$638.00**

Non-Recurring Fees	
Costs of incorporation (including legal fees)	US$1500.00
Costs of establishing an international bank account	N/A
Local duty	N/A
Provision of corporate VISA card	N/A
Total Non-Recurring Fees	**US$1500.00**

Trust Information

Types of trusts: The most common type of trust in Ireland is the express trust, which comes in four types: the bare trust, the trust creating a life interest, the discretionary trust, and the purpose trust. Discretionary trusts have a 6 percent initial tax charge and an annual charge of one percent of the value of the assets in the trust. This last charge doesn't arise until the settlor dies and all the beneficiaries reach the age of twenty-one.

Disclosure and registration: No registration or public disclosure of trusts is required. Trustees are, however, required to file income-tax returns and may be asked to name all beneficiaries (as well as to identify where they live and how much income they receive).

Letter of wishes: N/A

Applicable legislation: Authorized Investment Act of 1958

Protector: A protector may be appointed.

Geographic location	The Isle of Man is located in the middle of the Irish Sea, equal distance between England, Ireland, Scotland, and Wales. The approximate surface area of the island is 588 square kilometres.
Climate	The winters are mild and the summers cool. The island is humid and often overcast.
Estimated population	72,000
Capital city	Douglas
Currency	The Manx pound is set at par with the U.K. pound sterling. The exchange rate with the U.S. dollar is approximately US$1.00:Sgt£0.60.
Time zone	GMT, with daylight savings between March and October
Official language	English
Form of government	Domestic legislation is enacted by a two-tier Parliament named the Tynwald. The House of Keys is composed of twenty-four elected and independent members. The legislative council is formed with ten members, eight of whom are named by the House of Keys. Elections are held every five years. Queen Elizabeth II is the chief of state and is represented on the legislative council by a lieutenant-governor.
Legal system	English common law and local statute

Business Infrastructure			
Economic stability	★★★★	Secrecy	★★
Available services	★★★★½	Cost of entry	★★★★½
Political stability	★★★★½	Other	★★½

Political climate: The Isle of Man boasts one of the oldest parliaments in the world; it was established by the early Vikings more than one thousand years ago. The island does not form part of the United Kingdom, and it also is not a member of the European Union (EU); however, it enjoys a beneficial relationship by virtue of Protocol 3 of the Act of Accession (by which the United Kingdom joined the EU). Trade between the Isle of Man and the member countries of the EU escapes custom duties, but the island remains absolved from EU directives, including fiscal harmonization. The Isle of Man is a British crown dependency, but it is effectively independent from the U.K. with respect to domestic policy. The British government assumes responsibility for military defence and foreign affairs. The absence of political parties has not disturbed the political stability of the island. The Manx government must budget a surplus every year, and the quality of public services is high.

Economic climate: The local government and business community maintain a strong relationship via the Financial Supervision Commission. The commission has ensured proper regulation of the finance industry since a few important scandals broke in the 1970s and 1980s. Today, the financial-services sector constitutes approximately 50 percent of the island's national income, although agriculture, fishing, and tourism continue to play important roles in the domestic economy. The Manx government offers an industrial-aid-and-incentive program, with large capital grants for new buildings, machinery, and marketing, in addition to substantial training subsidies.

Financial and professional services: The available professional services are numerous and diversified. The island hosts more than sixty banks and many leading insurance companies, as well as all large accounting firms, fund-management companies, legal firms, and many other support services.

Communications services: The communications infrastructure in the Isle of Man is excellent. Mainland newspapers, television, and radio are available, as is Internet service. The island may be reached by ferry or by regular flight to and from most domestic airports in the United Kingdom. International courier services are also available.

Secrecy: The need for confidentiality is recognized, but so is the need to discourage illegal activity. Reporting requirements are not extensive: the names of a company's directors and corporate secretary must be disclosed annually. There is a government register of the names of shareholders and directors, but there is no requirement to disclose the names of the beneficial owners of the shares in the case of bare nominees (i.e., those established by simple declaration of trust). The exchange-of-information provisions contained in the tax treaty between the Isle of Man and the U.K. require disclosure of information only with respect to U.K. residents.

Exchange controls: There are no exchange controls. Funds may be held in any currency and are freely transferable.

Residency and/or citizenship requirements: The Isle of Man maintains strict immigration requirements for former U.K. residents. The island differs from Jersey and Guernsey in that immigrants from countries other than the U.K. are not required to obtain residency licences and there are many relatively inexpensive properties available.

Company Information

Types of companies: Offshore investors generally form one of three types of companies: resident exempt companies, non-resident companies, and international companies. A resident company may apply for tax-exempt status under the Income Tax (Exempt Companies) Act of 1984 if two conditions are met: first, the company must not be beneficially owned by a resident of the island; and second, all of the company's income must be earned outside the island, with the exception of bank-deposit interest. Resident exempt companies are popular for investment holding and for triangular trading activities with member countries of the EU. A non-resident company is one that is incorporated in the Isle of Man but is owned, managed, and controlled by persons and directors resident in jurisdictions other than the Isle of Man. Non-resident companies are often used for international trade and investment activities. Finally, resident companies may apply for international status (as international companies) and may pursue a wide range of undertakings. Foreign companies that export product to EU countries can avoid problems with value-added tax (VAT) by registering in the Isle of Man.

Fiscal policy: Individuals are taxed at progressive rates of between

15 percent and 20 percent. There are no death duties; wealth, gift, or succession taxes; or any taxes on capital gains or transfers. Resident companies must pay tax on their worldwide income at a rate of 20 percent. Resident exempt companies are not liable for local taxes, but they are required to pay an annual exempt duty of £400. Non-resident companies also are not subject to tax in the island but must pay a duty of £750 per year. International companies may choose their own tax rate, between one percent and 35 percent, but generally must pay a minimum of £300 in taxes each year. In addition, companies must pay an annual filing fee of £45. The Isle of Man has negotiated a double-taxation agreement with the U.K., but this treaty is quite limited in scope. Payments to non-resident persons by resident exempt companies and non-resident companies are excluded from any withholding taxes. Interest and dividend payments to non-residents by international companies are also excluded from withholding taxes.

Directors and officers: All companies must have a minimum of two directors. Resident companies, whether they carry exempt or international status, must have at least one resident director and a resident professionally qualified secretary. Non-resident companies are not required to have a resident director or a local corporate secretary. Directors may be corporate persons.

Shareholdings and types of shares: Non-resident companies may issue bearer shares, but resident companies, including those with exempt or international status, cannot. Shares may be expressed in any currency. Registered shares, preferred shares, and shares with or without voting rights are also permitted. Note that if bearer shares are issued, they must be allotted in registered form and then transferred. The names of those persons who ultimately hold the shares need not be disclosed.

Capitalization requirements: There is no minimum authorized capital in the Isle of Man, but the standard authorized capital is £2,000. Each company must have at least one shareholder.

Meetings and local office: All companies registered in the Isle of Man must maintain a local office on the island. Directors' meetings may be held anywhere in the world, including the Isle of Man, without affecting a company's tax status.

Annual filing requirements: All companies must maintain proper accounts, but only non-exempt resident companies need file these accounts. There are no audit requirements. A non-resident company must file a declaration that the company has satisfied the non-residency criteria. The assessor of income tax has the right to demand the accounts of any company, whether exempt or non-resident.

Typical time to incorporate: Approximately three days are needed to incorporate a company.

Availability of shelf companies: Shelf companies are readily available.

Estimated Minimum Corporate Fees

Ongoing Fees	
Annual licence fees	US$1250.00
Directors' fees	1300.00
Office and agency fees	500.00
Accounting fees	500.00
Audit fees	Nil
Annual return filing fees	75.00
Banking fees	300.00
Communication costs	107.00
Total Ongoing Fees	**US$4032.00**

Non-Recurring Fees	
Costs of incorporation (including legal fees)	US$1250.00
Costs of establishing an international bank account	600.00
Local duty	Nil
Provision of corporate VISA card	750.00
Total Non-Recurring Fees	**US$2600.00**

Trust Information

Types of trusts: A Manx trust is not subject to tax in the Isle of Man if it meets two criteria: first, the trust must have only non-resident beneficiaries; and second, all of the trust's income must be derived from outside sources or must be approved bank interest. Discretionary, purpose, and non-discretionary trusts (the latter are often called strict trusts in the Isle of Man) are permitted. An asset-protection trust may be created from these existing vehicles.

Effectiveness of the asset-protection trust: The Manx asset-protection trust is not reinforced by any particular legislation. As a result, settlors are subject to the common-law rules relating to fraudulent dispositions and bankruptcies.

Disclosure and registration: Trusts are considered private affairs and thus remain completely confidential. No trust deed need be filed with a public body, and there is no register of Manx trusts.

Letter of wishes: A letter of wishes is not legally binding but is normally issued for discretionary trusts. The letter often outlines the intentions of the settlor or the beneficiaries with respect to the eventual distribution of trust assets.

Applicable legislation: Manx trust laws are primarily based on U.K. trust legislation. The local laws applicable to trusts include the Trustees Act of 1961, the Perpetuities and Accumulations Act of 1968, the Recognition of Trust Act of 1988, the Trusts Act of 1995, and the Purpose Trust Act of 1996. The Trusts Act of 1995 helps Manx trusts resist challenges to their validity by other jurisdictions, particularly civil-law jurisdictions. The Purpose Trust Act of 1996 facilitates the establishment of trusts for commercially oriented purposes where this was not previously possible.

Protector: A protector may be appointed.

Geographic location	Jersey is the largest and southernmost of the Channel Islands. The island is located in the English Channel, approximately twenty kilometres north of France and 160 kilometres south of England. Jersey's total surface area is approximately 300 square kilometres.
Climate	The climate is temperate; winters are mild and summers cool.
Estimated population	86,000
Capital city	St. Helier
Currency	The Jersey pound is set at par with the U.K. pound sterling. The exchange rate with the U.S. dollar is approximately US$1.00:Sgt£0.60.
Time zone	GMT, with daylight savings between March and October
Official language	English is the official language, but French remains the language of the Royal Court of Jersey.
Form of government	A unicameral assembly of states composed of fifty-seven members assumes the legislative powers. Fifty-three of the seats are elected by popular suffrage — these include twelve senators, who are elected for six-year terms, twelve constables, and twenty-nine deputies. Queen Elizabeth II is the chief of state and is represented on the island by a lieutenant-governor.
Legal system	The legal system is based on Norman law; laws affecting trusts and corporations are more influenced by English common law.

Business Infrastructure			
Economic stability	★★★★	Secrecy	★★½
Available services	★★★★½	Cost of entry	★★★★½
Political stability	★★★★½	Other	★★½

Political climate: Jersey is effectively self-governing with respect to all domestic matters, including taxation. The United Kingdom assumes responsibility for defence and foreign affairs. Jersey has enjoyed long-term political stability: its unwritten constitution dates back to 1066, when William the Conqueror became king of England. Jersey also enjoys a beneficial relationship with the European Union (EU). Jersey is exempted from compliance with EU directives, including fiscal harmonization, yet exports to members of the EU are not subject to customs duties unless the product originates outside Jersey.

Economic climate: Jersey relies quite heavily on the financial-services industry, as this sector represents the main source of income on the island. Tourism, which peaks in the summer, ranks as the second most important industry, earning 40 percent of the GDP. Agriculture has declined considerably, and most foodstuffs must now be imported.

Financial and professional services: A strong financial infrastructure exists in Jersey. Banking, trust, insurance, and management companies are well regulated, and all offer high-quality professional services. The strong tradition of quality service distinguishes Jersey from many other jurisdictions.

Communications services: Jersey is part of the United Kingdom's digital network, which provides secure, reliable telecommunications. There are daily flights to London and other European cities such as Paris and Amsterdam. Courier and postal services are readily available. Travelling to Jersey by sea is also quite popular.

Secrecy: Jersey does not maintain a degree of confidentiality commensurate with that of other jurisdictions. There exists a public register of shareholders and a public register of directors. Also, in creating a company, one must disclose the names, occupations, and residential addresses of the beneficial owners of the shares. No external access is given to this information, except under exceptional circumstances.

Exchange controls: There are no exchange controls in Jersey and funds can be freely repatriated.

Residency and/or citizenship requirements: Jersey imposes severe immigration restrictions on those seeking residency status. The Housing

Jersey Law of 1949 provides for the control of sales and leases of land. Prospective residents are required to purchase properties valued well in excess of properties reserved for natives of Jersey.

Company Information

Types of companies: Foreign investment in Jersey is typically conducted through exempt companies and IBCs. A resident of Jersey cannot beneficially own either type of company, and exempt companies cannot engage in local trade. IBCs are popular for conducting international trade, holding investments, and carrying on captive insurance activities. For domestic operations, resident companies and limited partnerships are typically used.

Fiscal policy: The individual and corporate tax rates are both 20 percent in Jersey. Exempt companies are not subject to local taxes but must pay an exempt company fee, or licence fee, of Sgt£500, as well as a filing fee of Sgt£110 per year. IBCs are subject to 20 percent tax on income earned in Jersey, including bank-deposit interest, but need pay income tax of only 0.5 percent to 2 percent on foreign-source income (2 percent for the first Sgt£3 million, 1.5 percent for the next Sgt£1.5 million, 1 percent for the next Sgt£5.5 million, and 0.5 percent thereafter). IBCs must pay in advance a minimum tax of Sgt£1,200 (US$2,000) per year. Jersey has negotiated bilateral tax treaties with the United Kingdom, Guernsey, and France (this last treaty is extremely limited), but these treaties do not apply to exempt companies. Please also note that IBCs can negotiate higher tax rates if they so desire. Capital gains are not taxed, and withholding taxes do not apply to exempt companies and IBCs.

Directors and officers: Companies are required to have at least one director and a corporate secretary. A corporate body cannot fill either position. Non-residents may assume these responsibilities. The tax status of exempt companies and IBCs is unaffected by the appointment of a local director.

Shareholdings and types of shares: Shares must be registered (bearer shares are not permitted) and must have a par value. A company may issue shares with different rights and privileges, including redeemable shares and shares with or without voting rights. A company must have at least two shareholders unless it is a wholly owned subsidiary, in which case one shareholder will suffice.

Capitalization requirements: Companies are typically incorporated with an authorized share capital of Sgt£10,000, which provides for the minimum annual duty. The minimum issued capital is Sgt£2.00. There are no thin capitalization rules (i.e., covering extensive capital financing through external debt).

Meetings and local office: Companies must maintain a local office in Jersey. Exempt companies are expected to retain a local authorized agent.

Annual filing requirements: Exempt companies must maintain proper accounts and file with the financial services department an annual return that excludes these accounts. There is no audit requirement.

Typical time to incorporate: Typically, three to five days are required to incorporate a company; however, under certain conditions, a company may be formed within two hours.

Availability of shelf companies: Shelf companies generally are not available because of the requirement to disclose the beneficial ownership of the shares, as well as the nature of the company's trading activities.

Estimated Minimum Corporate Fees

Fees have been converted from Jersey pounds and may vary according to actual time spent.

Ongoing Fees	
Annual licence fees	US$500.00
Directors' fees	500.00
Office and agency fees	400.00
Accounting fees	1000.00
Audit fees	Nil
Minimum taxes	750.00
Annual return filing fees	110.00
Banking fees	300.00
Communication costs	107.00
Total Ongoing Fees	**US$3667.00**

Non-Recurring Fees	
Costs of incorporation (including legal fees)	US$1000.00
Costs of establishing an international bank account	500.00
Local duty	Nil
Provision of corporate VISA card	750.00
Total Non-Recurring Fees	**US$2250.00**

Trust Information

Types of trusts: Trusts are not as popular in Jersey as in the other Channel Islands. Four types of trusts are typically created in Jersey: the discretionary settlement (trustee has discretion in management and distribution of assets), the life-interest settlement (trustee is bound to the terms of the trust deed), the accumulation and maintenance settlement (for the maintenance and education of children), and the asset-protection trust. These latter trusts are generally governed by foreign laws and have non-resident trustees. Private trusts are exempt from tax in Jersey.

Effectiveness of the asset-protection trust: Asset-protection trusts are subject to the common-law rules that relate to fraudulent dispositions. Consequently, transfers of assets that prejudice a creditor may be voided.

Disclosure and registration: Trusts are private arrangements in Jersey and the trust documents need not be registered.

Letter of wishes: Settlors often provide trustees with a letter of wishes for discretionary trusts. The letter is not binding but may suggest the manner in which the trust is to be administered and distributions effected.

Applicable legislation: Trust law is governed by English common law.

Protector: A protector may be appointed.

Geographic location	Liechtenstein is a 36-by-10-kilometre strip of land in Central Europe between Austria and Switzerland.
Climate	Continental
Estimated population	30,000
Capital city	Vaduz
Currency	Swiss franc
Time zone	GMT plus one hour, or daylight savings plus six hours
Official languages	German is the official language, but English is also used for trade and commerce.
Form of government	Hereditary constitutional monarchy
Legal system	Civil law

Business Infrastructure

Economic stability	★★★★	Secrecy	★★★★½
Available services	★★★★½	Cost of entry	★★½
Political stability	★★★★½	Other	★★★★

Political climate: Liechtenstein is governed by a prince, who acts as head of state, and a diet (parliament) of twenty-five elected members. The country has a currency union with Switzerland and has agreed in principle to join the European Union, though with no fiscal implications.

Economic climate: Liechtenstein has a high per capita GDP. It is highly industrialized and participates in the free-trade agreement between Switzerland and the EU. The government is working to harmonize the country's economic policies with those of the EU, but it is not prepared to budge on its bank-secrecy provisions.

Financial and professional services: Liechtenstein has an excellent financial infrastructure that includes major banks, as well as legal, tax, and financial-planning services.

Communications services: The telecommunications system, which is linked to the Swiss one, has good telephone, telex, and fax services. The country has no airports and no port, but it does have an efficient railway. It has one radio station and television stations linked to Switzerland.

Secrecy: Liechtenstein has an excellent tradition of secrecy — some say better than that of Switzerland. Secrecy is maintained by law, and courts are prohibited from providing assistance to foreign authorities in cases involving political taxation and exchange controls. There are also no public-disclosure rules for deposited trusteeships. However, Liechtenstein does have strict anti-money-laundering legislation.

Exchange controls: There are no exchange controls and all currencies are accepted for deposit in bank accounts.

Residency and/or citizenship requirements: In the *Anstalt,* at least one representative and one trustee must be residents.

Tax treaties: There is one with Austria.

Company Information

Types of companies: Companies are governed by the Persons and Companies Law of 1926. There are four types of companies: companies limited by shares, private limited companies without shares, *Anstalts,* and foundations. The *Anstalt* is the most popular vehicle for foreign investment, and hereinafter all the information will pertain to this type of structure. The *Anstalt* has no member participants or shareholders. It is a hybrid of a company limited by shares and a foundation. It is popular because it can be adapted to various types of activities. It cannot bank, insure, re-insure, assure, manage funds, or engage in collective investment, but it can own property.

Fiscal policy: There is no special legislation for offshore ventures. Capital and revenue tax are levied, but holding and domiciliary companies, as well as *Anstalts* that resemble these, are exempt. *Anstalts* pay 0.1 percent to 0.2 percent capital tax, earning tax of 7 percent to 15 percent, withholding tax of 4 percent, and a stamp tax of 2 percent.

Directors and officers: The *Anstalt* requires at least one director. As long as one director is a resident, other directors can be corporate entities and of any nationality. Secretaries are not required.

Shareholdings and types of shares: An *Anstalt* doesn't have shares.

Capitalization requirements: The minimum capital requirement is Sfr30,000.

Meetings and local office: A registered office is required, but a local meeting is not.

Annual filing requirements: A commercial *Anstalt* must submit an audited financial statement to the Liechtenstein tax administration; a non-commercial *Anstalt* does not have to submit such a statement. Both have to keep proper records at their local offices.

Typical time to incorporate: Barring any hitches, incorporation takes about fifteen days. Incorporation is by notarial deed (statutes and by-laws signed by subscriber or agent), which then must be submitted to the public registry. Following civil-law practice, incorporation occurs by submitting to the public registry the following information: (1) the deed containing the statutes and by-laws signed by the subscriber or agent; (2) the entity's proposed name; (3) the division of share capital; (4) a declaration of the minimum paid capital; (5) names, addresses, and nationalities of the directors and the shareholders; (6) confirmation that a Liechtenstein representative has been appointed.

Availability of shelf companies: Shelf companies are not widely available.

Estimated Minimum Corporate Fees

Ongoing Fees	
Annual licence fees	N/A
Directors' fees	N/A
Office and agency fees	N/A
Accounting fees	N/A
Audit fees	N/A
Annual return filing fees	N/A
Banking fees	N/A
Communication costs	N/A
Total Ongoing Fees	**N/A**

Non-Recurring Fees	
Costs of incorporation (including legal fees)	N/A
Costs of establishing an international bank account	N/A
Local duty	N/A
Provision of corporate VISA card	N/A
Total Non-Recurring Fees	**N/A**

Trust Information

Types of trusts: Registered trust or trust enterprise. Trusts can be of unlimited duration but must have at least one resident trustee.

Disclosure and registration: A trust exceeding twelve months in life must be registered by the Liechtenstein trustee in the public trust register or the trust deed deposited with the court of the principality. The beneficial interests of the trust must be named.

Applicable legislation: The Law on Registered Trusts applies. Trusts are not prohibited from accumulating income, and there are no rules against perpetuities. Trusts with an unlimited duration can be created.

Geographic location	Luxembourg is a Western European country of 2,400 square kilometres. It is located between France, Germany, and Belgium.
Climate	Continental
Estimated population	400,000
Capital city	Luxembourg
Currency	Luxembourg franc (Flux1.00=US$0.03)
Time zone	GMT plus one hour, or daylight savings plus six hours
Official languages	German, French (languages of legislation), and Luxemburgish are the official languages. English is also spoken.
Form of government	Constitutional monarchy
Legal system	Civil law

Business Infrastructure			
Economic stability	★★★★	Secrecy	★★★★
Available services	★★★★½	Cost of entry	★★½
Political stability	★★★★½	Other	★★★½

Political climate: Since gaining its independence from Germany in 1867, Luxembourg has been a grand duchy, with the legislative power vested in a democratically elected senate and the executive power vested in the grand duke. The country is a member of the European Union.

Economic climate: Luxembourg has a strong economy, with a high per capita GDP, low inflation, and low unemployment. The country encourages foreign investment and 42 percent of its business comes from banking.

Financial and professional services: As is to be expected, Luxembourg has a very good financial and business infrastructure.

Communications services: Luxembourg has a modern communications system with well-developed telephone, telex, and fax services.

There are two airports and one port (Mertert). Luxembourg has an AM radio station and a television station.

Secrecy: Luxembourg enforces its strong bank-secrecy legislation. Information about deposits cannot be given without violating the law, and the punishment for that is a fine or imprisonment. Depositors are not permitted to waive bank secrecy. Bearer shares are permitted.

Exchange controls: Luxembourg does not have exchange controls; banks accept deposits in any currency.

Residency and/or citizenship requirements: Directors need not be residents, but a company must have at least one representative who is a Luxembourger.

Tax treaties: Luxembourg has tax treaties with the United States, Canada, the United Kingdom.

Company Information

Types of companies: Company activity is governed by the Commercial Companies Act of 1915. There are three types of companies available: *société anonyme* holding companies; *société à responsabilité limitée* holding companies; and *société de participation financière* trading and holding companies (SOPARFI). Holding companies cannot bank, insure, assure, re-insure, own property, engage in industrial or commercial activities, or manage assets. SOPARFI can trade but cannot bank, insure, assure, re-insure, or manage funds.

Fiscal policy: Holding companies are exempt from local tax but pay 0.2 percent per year on their share capital. SOPARFI are taxed at the normal rate of 39 percent.

Directors and officers: The minimum number of directors is three. These can be bodies corporate and of any nationality. No secretary is required.

Shareholdings and types of shares: A company must have at least two shareholders. The shares can be registered, bearer (paid in full), or preferred shares, or shares with or without voting rights.

Capitalization requirements: Minimum of Flux1.25 million

Meetings and local office: A local registered office is required, but local meetings are not.

Annual filing requirements: Annual audits are required.

Typical time to incorporate: Generally, a company may incorporate in a day. To do so, it must prepare its articles of incorporation in the form of a deed, as well as obtain a certificate of name acceptability from the trade registry and a certificate of blockage from the company's Luxembourg bankers (this confirms that its paid capital has been deposited with the bank). The deed must be presented before a notary public. Once the deed has been notarized, the articles of incorporation and the by-laws have to be lodged with the department of registration and the trade registry. The articles are then published in the official gazette.

Availability of shelf companies: Shelf companies are not available.

Estimated Minimum Corporate Fees

Ongoing Fees (depending on capital)	
Accounting	US$780.00
Dissolution	1590.00–3480.00
Transfer file	630.00
Trading permit	960.00
Tax returns	1590.00
Total Ongoing Fees	**US$5550.00–$7444.00**

Non-Recurring Fees	
Costs of incorporation (including legal fees)	N/A
Costs of establishing an international bank account	N/A
Local duty	N/A
Provision of corporate VISA card	N/A
Total Non-Recurring Fees	**N/A**

Trust Information

Luxembourg law does not recognize the trust.

Geographic location	Madeira is a four-island archipelago covering 770 square kilometres in the Atlantic Ocean. The islands — Madeira, Porto Santo, Deserta, Selvageno — are 1,000 kilometres from Portugal and 700 kilometres north of Africa.
Climate	Mediterranean
Estimated population	300,000
Capital city	Funchal, on Madeira
Currency	Portuguese escudo (US$1.00=155 escudos)
Time zone	GMT, or daylight savings plus five hours
Official languages	The official language is Portuguese, but English is used in trade and commerce.
Form of government	Parliamentary democracy
Legal system	Civil law

Business Infrastructure

Economic stability	★★★★	Secrecy	★★★½
Available services	★★★★½	Cost of entry	★★★★
Political stability	★★★★½	Other	★★

Political climate: Madeira is an autonomous region of Portugal; it has its own government and legislative assembly. The only restriction on this assembly is that it cannot override decisions of the central government in Lisbon or political unity with Portugal.

Economic climate: Madeira's main sources of income are tourism, the wine industry, and agriculture. It has attempted to attract foreign investment by developing itself as an international offshore centre. It has also created, with the European Union's support, a free-trade zone in which no taxes will be paid until December 31, 2011.

Financial and professional services: Those interested in doing business in Madeira have a great number of professional and financial services at their disposal, both on the island and in Portugal.

Communications services: Madeira offers direct dialling to anywhere in the world. Funchal airport is a ninety-minute flight from Lisbon. The airport also provides five flights a week to London and other international cities.

Secrecy: Madeira has special legislation governing bank secrecy, with civil and criminal penalties for violators. Courts, however, can order information to be disclosed by banks and other financial institutions if they believe a client is involved in criminal proceedings or if the client is suspected of drug trafficking. The names of settlors and beneficiaries are subject to secrecy regulation and can be divulged only through a court order. Stock corporations (SAs) allow bearer shares.

Exchange controls: There are no exchange controls, and banks accept deposits in any currency.

Residency and/or citizenship requirements: Directors and shareholders need not be residents, but at least one representative must be. Settlors and beneficiaries cannot be residents.

Tax treaties: Madeira's tax treaties are the same as Portugal's: they are with the United States, Canada, the United Kingdom, Australia, and New Zealand.

Company Information

Types of companies: Companies are regulated by the Portuguese Companies Code. Companies can't bank, insure, re-insure, assure, or manage funds or assets without a prior licence. They can own property. The various types of companies are private limited liability (LDA), stock corporations (SAs), general partnerships, limited partnerships, and sole traders. The first two are used for offshore ventures.

Fiscal policy: Companies in the free-trade zone pay no corporate taxes; capital gains, property, or transfer taxes; investment income taxes; stamp duties; withholding taxes on dividends or interest; import duties into the free-trade zone; or inheritance taxes. Payments made to shareholders are exempt from tax unless profits are derived from activity in Madeira.

Directors and officers: The minimum number of directors required for an LDA is one and for an SA is two. No corporate directors are permitted and no secretary is required.

Shareholdings and types of shares: An LDA requires a minimum of two shareholders and an SA requires five. There is no maximum for either type of company. LDAs issue quotas, not shares; these must be recorded at the commercial register in Madeira. SAs allow registered or bearer shares, with or without voting rights.

Capitalization requirements: LDAs require 400,000 escudos divided into quotas of no less than 20,000 escudos. SAs require 5 million escudos divided into shares of 1,000 escudos.

Meetings and local office: A registered office is required for both types of companies, and an annual meeting must be held within three months of the end of a company's accounting year. At this meeting, the previous year's accounts must be approved. The meetings usually occur at the head office.

Annual filing requirements: Books of accounts have to be kept at the company's office in Madeira. These books have to be approved by tax authorities and accounts must be prepared annually to suit the Portuguese official accounting plan. These both have to be presented to tax authorities with an annual corporate tax return. An LDA doesn't have to submit accounts to audit unless: (1) its assets exceed 350 million escudos; (2) it employs more than fifty people; or (3) its net sales exceed 600 million escudos.

Typical time to incorporate: About thirty working days. The company must obtain name approval and a licence to operate in the Madeira free-trade zone. To incorporate, an entity must have its public deed executed before a notary public and registered at the commercial registry of Madeira.

Availability of shelf companies: Shelf companies are available for LDAs, but not for SAs.

Estimated Minimum Corporate Fees

Ongoing Fees	
Annual licence fees	US$1000.00
Managers' fees	1000.00
Office and agency fees	1350.00
Secretarial and statutory book-managing fees	1000.00
Banking fees	N/A
Communication costs	N/A
Total Ongoing Fees	**US$4350.00**

Non-Recurring Fees	
Licence	US$5000.00
Setting up	3500.00
Total Non-Recurring Fees	**US$8500.00**

Trust Information

Types of trusts: Generally speaking, trusts are not recognized by Portuguese law. In the free-trade zone, however, a trust can be established at a cost of US$600 and used to plan estates, reduce property taxes, make future gifts, and carry on business and investment activities. For the trust to be considered an offshore one (1) the settlor must indicate which law will govern the trust; (2) the settlor and the beneficiaries must be deemed non-residents; (3) the trustee must be a company authorized to pursue this activity in the free-trade zone; (4) the income allocated to the trust cannot be derived from local funds; (5) the trust and the beneficiaries shall not be paid with local income; and (6) the trust cannot include immovable property in Portugal. In addition, the trust deed must: (1) name and fully identify the trust; (2) provide full identification of the settlor, the trustee, and the beneficiaries; (3) identify the property allocated to the trust; (4) classify and distribute the trust assets; (5) express the will to set up a trust; and (6) identify the law governing the trust.

Disclosure and registration: If the trust is intended to last for more than a year, the trust deed must be registered in the commercial registry of the Madeira free-trade zone within six months of its formation. The names of the settlor and the beneficiaries are protected by confidentiality laws, but they can be disclosed with a court order.

Geographic location	Malta is a three-island archipelago in the middle of the Mediterranean Sea, one hundred kilometres south of Italy.
Climate	Mediterranean
Estimated population	370,000
Capital city	Valletta
Currency	Maltese lira (1 lira = US$2.65)
Time zone	GMT plus one hour, or daylight savings plus six hours
Official language	Maltese, but trade and commerce can be conducted in English
Form of government	Parliamentary democracy
Legal system	Civil law

Business Infrastructure

Economic stability	★★★★	Secrecy	★★★
Available services	★★★★½	Cost of entry	★★★½
Political stability	★★★★½	Other	★★

Political climate: Politically stable, Malta received its independence from Britain in 1964. Ten years later it amended its constitution to become a republic, and thirteen years after that, in 1987, it incorporated neutrality into its constitution. Malta has applied for full European Union membership and has harmonized its economic, social, and fiscal laws to suit EU directives.

Economic climate: A country with cheap labour, stable politics, good labour relations, and excellent ports and port services, Malta is an attractive location to do business. The country depends on trade, industry (textile and electronics), and tourism. It has a low GDP for a European nation. The Industrial Development Act of 1988 provided incentives to encourage foreign investment. Malta established a free port in 1989 and is now recognized as one of the Mediterranean's leading trans-shipment hubs.

Financial and professional services: Malta is well equipped to receive offshore business. It has a number of banking, financial, and legal facilities.

Communications services: Malta has an advanced telecommunications system, with full satellite direct dialling to most of the world. It has AM and FM radio stations, as well as television stations. It has two ports and one airport, which supports direct flights to major European cities.

Secrecy: Malta does not permit bearer shares and requires disclosure of beneficial owners of companies to authorities; these authorities are bound by professional secrecy regulations. The Professional Secrecy Act allows for penal sanctions for government officials and employees who breach secrecy. The Prevention of Money Laundering Act uses the EU's definition of money laundering and makes it a crime to help anyone engage in such an activity.

Exchange controls: Malta has begun to relax its exchange controls, which do not apply to offshore companies. Bank deposits can be made in any currency approved by the central bank.

Residency and/or citizenship requirements: Company directors do not have to be residents, but if they are not, the company must appoint a secretary who is. Settlors and beneficiaries need not be residents at the time the trust is created.

Tax treaties: Malta has tax treaties with Canada, the United States, the United Kingdom, and Australia.

Company Information

Types of companies: Business activity is regulated by the Commercial Partnerships Ordinance of 1962, the Maltese Financial Services Act of 1988, and the Companies Act of 1995. Since it is no longer possible to incorporate offshore companies in Malta, people interested in carrying out these types of activities must create either an international holding company or an international trading company. These entities cannot bank, insure, re-insure, assure, manage funds or assets, or act as trust companies without special licences. The best bet is to set up a trading company: these types of vehicles receive a preferential tax rate and their goods enter the EU duty-free. Malta also offers employment cost subsidies, as well as capital for equipment and factories.

Fiscal policy: International holding companies pay no tax and trading companies pay only 5 percent. Shareholders are not subject to tax on dividends, interest, royalties, distribution on liquidation, or any other income.

Directors and officers: Malta requires a minimum of one director; this person cannot be a corporate entity but can be of any nationality. If the director is not a Maltese resident, then the secretary must be a licensed Maltese nominee company.

Shareholdings and types of shares: The minimum number of shareholders used to be two, but as of January 1, 1996, single member companies can be incorporated. The maximum number of shareholders is fifty. Shares must be registered and may be preferred or redeemable, with or without voting rights.

Capitalization requirements: Minimum 500 Maltese lira

Meetings and local office: Annual meetings are required, but they need not take place in Malta. A registered office is required.

Annual filing requirements: Companies are required to maintain and submit annual financial statements to the Malta Financial Services Centre (MFSC).

Typical time to incorporate: Fifteen working days. To incorporate, a company must submit its proposed memorandum and articles of association, as well as a government fee, a business plan (for general trading companies), and an original bank reference relating to the beneficial owner, to the MFSC.

Availability of shelf companies: Shelf companies are not available.

Estimated Minimum Corporate Fees

Ongoing Fees	
Management, preparing and submitting the company's and its shareholders' annual tax returns, applying to the International Tax Unit of the Malta Financial Services Centre for a refund on taxes, use of the registered office, director and secretary fees, judicial representation and acquiring employment licence from the Prime Minister's Office	
Total Ongoing Fees	**US$2120.00**

Non-Recurring Fees **(depends on a company's authorized capital)**	
Costs of incorporation (including legal fees) and costs of establishing an international bank account	
Total Non-Recurring Fees	**US$2120.00**

Trust Information

Types of trusts: Trusts may be set up for a variety of purposes, provided that the settlor and the beneficiaries are not residents and that the trust does not hold immovable property in Malta. A nominee company must be appointed as a trustee. This company is accountable only to the MFSC. The life span of a trust is one hundred years unless it is a charitable trust. The settlor's identity does not have to be revealed to the MFSC. Since Malta has adopted most of the Hague Convention on Trusts of 1984, a locally registered trust may function under a foreign law.

Disclosure and registration: A trust must be registered with the MFSC.

Letter of wishes: Letters of wishes are permitted.

Applicable legislation: The Offshore Trusts Act of 1988

Geographic location	Monaco is located on the south coast of France, near the Italian border.
Climate	Mediterranean
Estimated population	30,000
Capital city	Monaco
Currency	French franc
Time zone	GMT plus one hour, or daylight savings plus six hours
Official language	The official language is French, but English and Italian are also spoken.
Form of government	Constitutional monarchy
Legal system	Civil law

Business Infrastructure

Economic stability	★★★★	Secrecy	★★
Available services	★★★★½	Cost of entry	★★★½
Political stability	★★★★½	Other	★★

Political climate: The second smallest independent state (after Vatican City), Monaco obtained its independence in 1489, a status that was reaffirmed by the League of Nations in the 1919 Treaty of Versailles. Monaco is governed by a sovereign prince and a council elected by Monegasque citizens. The country has a close relationship to France, which involves itself in the executive, legislative, and judicial affairs of the country.

Economic climate: A wealthy country, Monaco derives its income from tourism and high-value-added non-polluting industries. It levies no personal income tax but does not want to become a tax haven. Although not a member of the EU, Monaco has a customs union with France that means that the country is subject to the EU's sixth directive and other customs rules.

Financial and professional services: Monaco's business infrastructure is limited; in an attempt to help Monegasque professionals, the country has been reluctant to grant authorization to lawyers, accountants, and other specialists. Those interested in business ventures must use the services of an administration company in Monaco or an adviser outside. There are at least fifty banks in the country. In 1993, Monaco introduced strict controls on banks and other financial institutions to counter money-laundering activities.

Communications services: All telecommunications systems in Monaco are connected through France; direct dialling is available to most countries. The country has AM and FM radio stations and television stations. It has one port and is linked to the airport in Nice. The courier and postal service is linked to, but independent from, that of France.

Secrecy: Monaco has a low level of secrecy compared with other countries. It is situated in the French franc zone, which gives France extensive control over Monegasque banking. The police have wide powers of investigation and seizure. Bearer shares are permitted.

Exchange controls: French foreign-exchange controls are still in place.

Residency and/or citizenship requirements: At least one director must be a resident, and the government can require that a certain percentage of shareholders also be citizens.

Tax treaties: None

Company Information

Types of companies: The company law in Monaco is similar to that of France. The types of companies permitted are companies limited by shares, partnerships limited by shares, limited partnerships, and general partnerships. For foreign investors, companies limited by shares are recommended, but these still have to pay tax at a rate of 35 percent. There is no separate regime for offshore entities, but the most profitable type of company to set up is the offshore trading company, provided the complete cycle of trading doesn't take place in Monaco. Banking, insurance, and financial-management activities require special licences. All in all, it is probably a better idea to look elsewhere to set up a company.

Fiscal policy: For exports and imports, Monaco has full customs integration with France, which collects and rebates Monegasque trade duties. Although Monaco does not levy any income tax, any entity carrying out commercial or industrial activity in the country is taxed at 35 percent.

Directors and officers: The minimum number of directors is two, one of whom must be a resident of Monaco.

Shareholdings and types of shares: At least two shareholders are required. Shares may be registered or bearer shares.

Capitalization requirements: Although officially there is no minimum, in practice the government is unlikely to authorize anything under one million French francs, especially for international businesses.

Meetings and local office: Companies must have proper premises; sharing with other companies is not permitted.

Annual filing requirements: Companies must prepare annual accounts in keeping with prescribed form. These must be audited by two auditors appointed from the roll of Monaco accountants. These accountants must monitor the company.

Typical time to incorporate: It takes six to twelve months to incorporate because of the need for prior government authorization of the articles of incorporation. Companies are formed by notarial deed.

Availability of shelf companies: Shelf companies are not available.

Estimated Minimum Corporate Fees

Ongoing Fees	
Annual licence fees	N/A
Directors' fees	N/A
Office and agency fees	N/A
Accounting fees	N/A
Audit fees	N/A
Annual return filing fees	N/A
Banking fees	N/A
Communication costs	N/A
Total Ongoing Fees	**N/A**

Non-Recurring Fees	
Costs of incorporation (including legal fees)	N/A
Costs of establishing an international bank account	N/A
Local duty	N/A
Provision of corporate VISA card	N/A
Total Non-Recurring Fees	**N/A**

Trust Information

Types of trusts: As a civil-law jurisdiction, Monaco doesn't have a body of law that deals with the trust. The place where a trust is formed will determine how it is governed. The country recognizes two types of trusts: (1) the foreign trust registered but not formed under Monegasque law (high fees and tax to be registered); and (2) the foreign trust administered but not registered in Monaco (no tax).

Geographic location	Located in the Eastern Caribbean, just north of Venezuela, the Netherlands Antilles consists of five islands: Curaçao (main island), Bonaire, St. Maarten, St. Eustatius, and Saba.
Climate	Tropical
Estimated population	200,000
Capital city	Willemstad, on Curaçao
Currency	The Netherlands Antilles guilder, which is linked to the U.S. dollar (US$1= NAFL1.78)
Time zone	GMT minus four hours, or daylight savings plus one hour
Official language	The official language is Dutch, but people also speak English.
Form of government	Parliamentary democracy
Legal system	Civil law

Business Infrastructure			
Economic stability	★★★★	Secrecy	★★
Available services	★★★★½	Cost of entry	★★★★½
Political stability	★★★★½	Other	★★★

Political climate: Having obtained control over its internal affairs from the Netherlands in 1954, the Netherlands Antilles is one of the most stable countries in the Caribbean. The country is still a member of the kingdom of the Netherlands, and it has an associate status with the European Union.

Economic climate: The Netherlands Antilles derives its income from oil refining, its free-trade zone, and the financial industry in Curaçao. Since the 1940s, the government has been dedicated to creating a favourable climate for offshore business and has signed double-taxation treaties with many countries. The country imports all of its consumer and capital goods and still receives financial aid from the Netherlands.

Financial and professional services: Curaçao is one of the most developed islands in the Caribbean; it has a good business infra-structure that includes banks as well as financial, legal, corporate, and tax advisers. Recently implemented regulations on the liability of managing directors has pushed many incorporation companies to ask for (1) the names, nationalities, home and business addresses, and occupations of all beneficial owners of a company, as well as legible photocopies of their passports; (2) a letter of reference from a reputable law firm or bank; (3) information on company activity; and (4) an affidavit from foreign nationals saying they will obey the local fiscal laws.

Communications services: The Netherlands Antilles has an adequate telecommunications system that includes telephone, fax, and telex services. The country has AM and FM radio stations and television stations. It has three ports (Kralendijk, Philisburg, and Willemstad) and four airports, which offer daily flights to Europe and North and South America.

Secrecy: The Netherlands Antilles has no specific legislation governing bank secrecy, but the criminal code provides for fines and jail sentences for breaches of confidentiality. There is no requirement to disclose beneficial owners of companies, and there are no treaties for exchange controls. The National Ordinance on Penalization of Money Laundering of 1993, the National Ordinance for the Reporting of Unusual Transactions of 1996, and the National Ordinance for Identification When Rendering Financial Services of 1997 have been passed to better regulate illegal activity.

Exchange controls: The Netherlands Antilles imposes exchange controls, but offshore companies may be exempted from these. Bank deposits can be made in any currency.

Residency and/or citizenship requirements: At least one director must be a resident.

Tax treaties: There are treaties with Canada, the United States, and the United Kingdom.

Company Information

Types of companies: Business is regulated by the commercial code of the Netherlands Antilles. Offshore companies cannot bank, insure, solicit funds, or trade within the country. They also cannot undertake any investment business other than managing their own assets. Companies available to foreigners are offshore companies.

Fiscal policy: Offshore companies that derive all their income from outside the Netherlands Antilles are taxed at 2.4 percent to 6 percent, depending on their activities. The country does not impose withholding tax on dividends, interest, royalties, or capital gains.

Directors and officers: A minimum of one director is required, but this person must be a resident and cannot be a corporation. No secretary is required.

Shareholdings and types of shares: The minimum number of shareholders required is one. Shares can be registered or bearer (these must be paid in full), preferred shares, redeemable shares, or shares with or without voting rights.

Capitalization requirements: US$30,000 is the minimum capital required, but the minister of justice can refuse to issue a so-called declaration of no objection if he or she considers the capital too low for the purpose of the company.

Meetings and local office: No local meeting is required, but a registered office is. Offices can be located at a licensed trust and management company, a law firm, or an accounting firm.

Annual filing requirements: There is no requirement to file audited accounts with the registry, but each company must present a tax return, a profit-and-loss statement, and a balance sheet to the country's tax inspector.

Typical time to incorporate: Five to eight working days. To incorporate, a company must obtain approval for its draft articles of incorporation from the ministry of justice. A deed of incorporation must then be executed before a notary public. The company must also obtain a business licence, a managing director's licence, and a foreign-exchange exemption licence.

Availability of shelf companies: Shelf companies are available.

Estimated Minimum Corporate Fees

Ongoing Fees	
Annual tax or licence fees	US$60.00
Domiciliation and management fees	1200.00
Chamber-of-commerce fee	40.00
Accounting fees	950.00
Audit fees	N/A
Annual return filing fees	N/A
Banking fees	N/A
Communication costs	N/A
Total Ongoing Fees	**US$2250.00**

Non-Recurring Fees	
Costs of incorporation (including legal fees)	
	US$1500.00–2500.00
Costs of establishing an international bank account	N/A
Local duty	N/A
Provision of corporate VISA card	N/A
Total Non-Recurring Fees	**US$1500.00–2500.00**

Trust Information

Trusts are not recognized in the Netherlands Antilles.

Geographic location	Nevis is small circular island covering ninety-two square kilometres; it is approximately 400 kilometres southeast of Puerto Rico. The island hosts an extinct volcano that rises nearly a thousand metres.
Climate	Nevis enjoys a subtropical climate. The rainy season spans the months of May and November.
Estimated population	9,000
Capital city	Basseterre (capital city of the Federation of Saint Kitts and Nevis)
Currency	The Eastern Caribbean dollar ($EC) is at a fixed rate of exchange ($US1.00:$EC2.70). This rate has remained unchanged for more than twenty years.
Time zone	GMT minus four hours
Official language	English
Form of government	Nevis is governed by a locally elected assembly and by the house of assembly of the government of the Federation of Saint Kitts and Nevis. The federal house of assembly consists of fourteen members, and the premier of Nevis holds an executive position in the federal government.
Legal system	The legal system is based on English common law; the British privy council remains the final court of appeal.

Business Infrastructure			
Economic stability	★★★★	Secrecy	★★★★½
Available services	★★½	Cost of entry	★★★★½
Political stability	★★★★½	Other	★★★★

Political climate: Nevis is a conservative democracy; historically, it has been praised as one of the most free nations in the world. The country gained its independence from the United Kingdom in 1983, at which time it joined the Federation of Saint Kitts and Nevis. Queen Elizabeth II remains the head of state and is represented by a governor general.

Economic climate: The Nevisian economy is highly dependent on the sugar-cane industry. Depressed world sugar prices have substantially hurt the Nevisian economy, since much of the arable land is dedicated to the growth of sugar cane and most other food must be imported. Also, unlike many other Caribbean countries, Nevis earns only a small proportion of its GDP from tourism.

Financial and professional services: The Nevisian financial sector is not as highly developed as that of other countries. Currently, there are only three international banks (including the Bank of Nova Scotia and the Royal Bank of Canada), three trust companies, and one management company. Growth of the financial-services industry is expected.

Communications services: Nevis possesses a state-of-the-art telecommunications infrastructure. At its heart is a cable and wireless fibre-optic digital system. Nevis uses a U.S. area code (809), and it may be reached by direct dialling. Most flights to Nevis are indirect, and Nevisian postal services are mediocre.

Secrecy: Nevis affords a high level of secrecy to companies incorporated under the Nevis Business Corporation Ordinance (NBCO) of 1984. This secrecy is a result, in part, of the fact that no specific anti-money-laundering legislation has been enacted. Individuals with illegitimate business purposes are deterred by existing legislation, which provides for the revocation of a entity's articles of incorporation if there is reasonable proof that the company has undertaken criminal activity. Any unauthorized disclosure of information to foreign authorities is a punishable crime.

Exchange controls: There are no exchange controls or any requirements to report currency transfers. Bank accounts may be kept in U.S. dollars.

Residency and/or citizenship requirements: No migration restrictions were found.

Company Information

Types of companies: Companies established under the NBCO are best suited for foreign-investment activities. Such corporations cannot engage in banking, insurance, fund management, and related activities. NBCO-established companies cannot conduct business in Nevis, nor can they own domestic real property. As an alternative to NBCO-established corporations, foreign investors can also create limited liability companies (LLCs). LLCs have a limited life, but they permit greater flexibility in the types of activities that can be undertaken and do not require representation by a local agent.

Fiscal policy: A company established under the NBCO does not pay any Nevisian taxes. It is immaterial whether it draws its income from capital gains, dividends, interest, or other means. In addition, Nevisian local companies are not taxed on income earned in a foreign jurisdiction. A double-taxation treaty exists between the Federation of Saint Kitts and Nevis and the United Kingdom.

Directors and officers: Only one director is required for companies established under the NBCO; that director need not be a resident of Nevis, and corporate directors are permitted. There are no registration requirements for directors. LLCs may designate managers within or outside the company as directors. There are no requirements to report changes in directorship.

Shareholdings and types of shares: Nevis allows complete flexibility in the types of shares that NBCO-established companies may issue. Bearer shares, preferred shares, and shares with or without par value are permitted. The minimum number of shareholders is one. The names of beneficial owners of a trust need not be registered with a public body; however, the beneficial owners must be identifiable or ascertainable from the circumstances.

Capitalization requirements: The company must issue at least one share of par value or one share of no par value.

Meetings and local office: There are no meeting requirements. NBCO-established companies and LLCs must maintain a local registered agent. Currently, there is only one registered agent in Nevis. No local office is required.

Annual filing requirements: NBCO-established companies and LLCs are not required to maintain financial records, to have audited accounts, or to file annual returns.

Typical time to incorporate: The incorporation process may take a couple hours or a couple of days. It can add a week to the incorporation process to send the documentation from Nevis. To incorporate, a company must file articles of incorporation, appoint a registered agent, and pay the capitalization tax. Trusts are also relatively easy to create.

Availability of shelf companies: Shelf companies are available.

Estimated Minimum Corporate Fees

Ongoing Fees	
Annual licence fees	US$200.00
Directors' fees	500.00
Office and agency fees	700.00
Accounting fees	500.00
Audit fees	Nil
Annual return filing fees	65.00
Banking fees	300.00
Communication costs	146.00
Total Ongoing Fees	**US$2411.00**

Non-Recurring Fees	
Costs of incorporation (including legal fees)	US$625.00
Costs of establishing an international bank account	250.00
Local duty	Nil
Provision of corporate VISA card	400.00
Total Non-Recurring Fees	**US$1275.00**

Trust Information

Types of trusts: Nevis allows the formation of trusts for a broad range of purposes, including estate planning and asset protection.

Effectiveness of the asset-protection trust: It is extremely difficult to dismantle or circumvent an asset-protection trust in Nevis. The creditor must establish beyond a reasonable doubt (not on a preponderance of the evidence) that the settlor intended to defraud the creditor. In addition, any legal challenge must be raised within one year of the formation of the trust.

Disclosure and registration: Every international trust must register its name, as well as the names and addresses of its trustee and its registered office. No trust deed need be filed with the registrar.

Letter of wishes: No prohibition to letters of wishes was uncovered.

Applicable legislation: The principal legislation relating to international trusts is the Nevis International Exempt Trust Ordinance of 1994.

Protector: Nevisian trust legislation does permit the use of a protector.

Geographic location	Niue is an island in the South Pacific, roughly 1,500 kilometres northeast of New Zealand (between the Cook Islands to the west and Samoa and Tonga to the east).
Climate	Tropical
Estimated population	Less than 2,000
Capital city	Alofi
Currency	New Zealand dollar
Time zone	GMT minus eleven hours, or daylight savings minus six
Official languages	English (for commerce) and Niuean (a Polynesian dialect)
Form of government	Parliamentary democracy
Legal system	English common law

Business Infrastructure

Economic stability	★★½	Secrecy	★★★
Available services	★★★	Cost of entry	★★★½
Political stability	★★★	Other	★★★

Political climate: Despite the relative lack of information about the island, it can be gleaned that Niue gained its independence from New Zealand in 1974. It is a British-style democracy whose external affairs and defence are still controlled by New Zealand.

Economic climate: Niue is a poor country whose economy is still underdeveloped. The island relies on fishing and tourism, as well as on financial aid from New Zealand. Industry and agriculture are barely developed. Recent cuts to the public sector and a push to provide financial services suggest, however, that this economy may well become more productive. It is certainly worth keeping an eye on — especially since the government has instituted various incentives to encourage foreign investment.

Financial and professional services: Although Niue has an underdeveloped financial and business infrastructure, it is estimated that the island's corporate services will increase. The International Business Companies Act of 1994 regulates business in Niue.

Communications services: The island has telephone, telex, and facsimile systems, with direct dialling from most countries. It has one airport and no harbours or ports. There are no television stations and no short-wave radio stations. There is one AM and one FM radio station.

Secrecy: Various laws in Niue ensure a high level of confidentiality. Banking is protected by the Niue Bank Act of 1994 and by the Off-Shore Bank Act of 1994. Trust confidentiality is protected by the Trusts Act of 1994, as is the confidentiality of companies incorporated under the International Business Companies Act of 1994. Bearer shares are allowed, as are fixed or discretionary trusts. The trustee can be given full discretion to appoint beneficiaries, who have to be identifiable by name or by affiliation (i.e., son, niece, etc.).

Exchange controls: Niue has no exchange controls.

Residency or citizenship requirements: There are no residency or citizenship requirements for international business companies or trusts.

Tax treaties: IBCs don't qualify for any of Niue's double-taxation treaties.

Company Information

Types of companies: For offshore investment purposes, Niue offers the international business company. This company cannot hold property, trade, bank, insure, assure, re-insure, or manage funds or assets in Niue. It also cannot solicit funds from or offer shares to the public.

Fiscal policy: IBCs are exempt from local taxation, as well as from all other forms of taxation in Niue. Trusts established under the Trusts Act of 1994 are also exempt from taxation, but those established under the Trustee Act (New Zealand, 1956) might be liable.

Directors and officers: Niue requires only one director; this director need not be a resident and can be a corporation. No corporate secretary is required, and meetings don't have to take place in Niue. IBCs must have a registered office and an agent in Niue.

Shareholdings and types of shares: Niue imposes no restrictions on the number of shareholders a company may have, but the types of shares must be specified in the company's memorandum of incorporation. Registered and bearer shares are permitted, as are preferred shares, redeemable shares, shares with no par value, and shares with or without voting rights.

Capitalization requirement: US$10,000

Meetings and local office: No annual meetings are required, but a meeting must be held if requested by 50 percent of the shareholders. A teleconference may replace a meeting, provided that all the participants can hear. The company must maintain a local office.

Filing requirements: Niue requires no accounting or auditing of a company's books, but companies must keep financial records for their members.

Typical time to incorporate: Two days. To incorporate a company, the registered agent must submit a memorandum and articles of association to the registry.

Availability of shelf companies: Shelf companies are available.

Estimated Minimum Corporate Fees

Ongoing Fees	
Licence fees	US$150.00
Annual tax or exemption fees	N/A
Directors' fees	N/A
Office and agency fees	N/A
Audit fees	N/A
Annual return filing fees	N/A
Banking fees	N/A
Total Ongoing Fees	**US$150.00**

Non-Recurring Fees	
Costs of incorporation (including legal fees)	US$750.00
Costs of establishing an international bank account	N/A
Provision of corporate VISA card	N/A
Total Non-Recurring Fees	**US$750.00**

Trust Information

Types of trust: Niue recognizes various types of trusts, including unit, discretionary, asset-protection, and purpose trusts.

Effectiveness of the asset-protection trust: Trusts established under Niue law cannot be broken by claims against the property from other jurisdictions, not even in cases involving succession rights or rights stemming from marriage or divorce.

Disclosure and registration: Trusts must be filed with the registrar of the court. The register must contain the names of the trustees, the settlor, and the beneficiaries, as well as an indication of the trust's purpose. The register is kept secret, except if the court suspects drug trafficking, money laundering, or other criminal activity.

Letter of wishes: Either the settlor or the beneficiary may leave a letter or memorandum of wishes with the trustee.

Applicable legislation: The Trustee Act of 1956 (New Zealand) and the Trusts Act of 1994 (provides for offshore structures)

Protector: A protector may be appointed.

Geographic location	Panama is located in Central America, between Costa Rica and Colombia. The country covers approximately 78,000 square kilometres and is famous for its canal, which links the Caribbean Sea and the Pacific Ocean.
Climate	The climate is tropical, with an extended eight-month rainy season.
Estimated population	2.7 million
Capital city	Panama City
Currency	The local currency is the Panamanian balboa, which is fixed at par with the U.S. dollar. The U.S. dollar is widely used in international trade.
Time zone	GMT minus five hours
Official languages	Spanish is the official language, but English is widely spoken in international trade.
Form of government	Panama is a republic, therefore the president is the head of government and the head of state. The executive branch of government is composed of the president and his or her two vice-presidents. A seventy-two-member assembly forms the legislative branch. Both branches of government are elected for five-year periods, and the next elections are expected in May 2004.
Legal system	The legal system is based on Spanish civil law, although it's influenced by common law with respect to companies.

Business Infrastructure

Economic stability	★★	Secrecy	★★★½
Available services	★★½	Cost of entry	★★★★½
Political stability	★★½	Other	★★½

Political climate: Contrary to popular belief, the political climate in Panama has not been that turbulent. Panama was a Spanish colony annexed to Colombia prior to 1903, at which time it became an independent republic. In 1989, the United States invaded the country to help preserve Panama's most important resource: the Panama Canal. Before the invasion, Panama had adopted a protectionist attitude towards foreign trade, but it has since become more open to foreign interests.

Economic climate: Owing to some favourable tax policies, banking, insurance, construction, and free-trade zone operations now represent the key domestic industries. The Panamanian free-trade zone is one of the largest in the world, second only to that of Hong Kong. Former protectionist policies and a high level of indebtedness have negatively affected the country's economy, which over the past few years has been sluggish. The economic outlook, however, is improving, and the country has now met all the requirements for joining the World Trade Organization (WTO).

Financial and professional services: Panama currently suffers from a shortage of skilled and professional labour. While all banking, accounting, legal, and management services are available, a contracting economy has encouraged some professionals to leave or to bypass Panama to establish practices in other jurisdictions.

Communications services: Panama boasts an advanced telecommunications infrastructure. Daily flights are available from a few major U.S. cities, as are overnight courier services.

Secrecy: Trustees are bound to strict secrecy provisions. The names of shareholders are not disclosed to the registrar (though the names of directors are).

Exchange controls: Panama does not maintain any exchange controls.

Residency and/or citizenship requirements: Very little information relating to the immigration of individuals to Panama could be found. Possibly because of the shortage of specialized labour, it seems that the Panamanian government wants to attract foreign professionals to the country by providing certain tax incentives. In particular, foreigners are taxed only on income earned in Panama.

Company Information

Types of companies: Most offshore investors establish companies in Panama to take advantage of the country's free-trade zone. As a result, non-resident companies are generally incorporated under the Corporation Statute Law 32 of the 1927 Commercial Code. These companies can provide banking, trust, investment, or insurance services without a licence, but they cannot offer the services of a registered office for other companies. Limited liability companies and limited partnerships are also available, but these are much less popular.

Fiscal policy: Panama does collect corporate and individual income taxes. Income earned outside Panama is not taxable in the country. Income earned by free-trade zone companies in the re-exportation of goods to other countries is subject to progressive taxes of between 2.5 percent and 8.5 percent. Sales by free-trade zone companies to persons within Panama but outside the zone are subject to higher progressive tax rates. There are no withholding taxes for payments of dividends and royalties by free-trade zone companies to foreign companies; other payments, such as interest, commissions, and financing charges, are subject to a 6 percent withholding tax.

Directors and officers: Panamanian companies must have at least three directors. In addition, the directors must appoint a president, a treasurer, and a corporate secretary. Directors may also act as officers. The directors and officers can be of any nationality, and they need not reside in Panama; however, they must be natural persons, not corporate entities.

Shareholdings and types of shares: Many types of shares may be issued by a free-trade zone company, including shares with the following characteristics: voting, non-voting, bearer, registered, preferred, par value, and no par value. Bearer shares are permitted but only if paid in full (i.e., no subscriptions). Share capital may be denominated in any convertible currency.

Capitalization requirements: The company must have at least one shareholder. There are no minimum share-capital requirements, but the standard authorized share capital is US$10,000.

Meetings and local office: A Panamanian company must maintain a local office with a registered agent. There are no requirements to hold local meetings. Meetings by telephone, by proxy, or by other means are permitted.

Annual filing requirements: None, if a company's income is derived from non-Panamanian sources. It is not necessary to prepare or file accounts or financial statements, but directors must keep such accounts as are necessary to properly reflect the financial status of the company.

Typical time to incorporate: The incorporation process is short and usually takes only one day.

Availability of shelf companies: Shelf companies are available.

Estimated Minimum Corporate Fees

Ongoing Fees	
Annual licence (franchise) fees	US$150.00
Directors' fees (for two local directors)	1000.00
Office and agency fees	500.00
Accounting fees	500.00
Audit fees	Nil
Annual return filing fees	Nil
Banking fees	300.00
Communication costs	195.00
Total Ongoing Fees	**US$2645.00**

Non-Recurring Fees	
Costs of incorporation (including legal fees)	US$800.00
Costs of establishing an international bank account	Nil
Local duty	Nil
Provision of corporate VISA card	750.00
Total Non-Recurring Fees	**US$1550.00**

Trust Information

Types of trusts: Although Panama is a civil-law jurisdiction, it does recognize the concept of a trust. Also, Panama does not impose any limits on the types of trusts that may be created in its jurisdiction. This presents certain advantages and disadvantages. In a common-law jurisdiction, a settlor's imposition of severe restrictions on the power of a trustee so as to remove control could be viewed as repugnant to the concept of a trust and could serve to invalidate it. The same is not true in Panama: a settlor can limit the trustee's powers and can provide him or her with specific instructions on the management of the trust assets, all without piercing the trust veil. However, this increased flexibility is a double-edged sword: Panamanian trusts are not very popular with offshore investors because other jurisdictions, with their increased level of regulation, provide greater security.

Effectiveness of the asset-protection trust: The traditional common-law rules relating to trusts do not apply in Panama. No specific legislation serves to reinforce the asset-protection trust; however, the fact that trustees are bound to absolute secrecy may afford the settlor considerable protection from outside claims. One source of information claims that outside inquiries into the trust can go no further than the trustee (i.e., the settlor cannot be linked to a discretionary trust).

Disclosure and registration: The establishment of a trust in Panama is a private arrangement. No public body requires disclosure or registration of information pertaining to the trust.

Letter of wishes: A letter of wishes (more commonly referred to as a memorandum of wishes in Panama) is common with discretionary trusts. Memorandums are not legally binding, but trustees normally adhere to their instructions.

Applicable legislation: No specific legislation could be located with respect to trusts.

Protector: The absence of significant regulation suggests that a settlor would be permitted to appoint a protector to ensure proper management of the trust assets by the trustee.

Geographic location	The republic of Seychelles is a group of 118 islands in the middle of the Indian Ocean. The islands are located east of Africa and northeast of Madagascar. Their total land area is approximately 455 square kilometres. The largest island, Mahé, hosts the capital city. The country is located outside the cyclone belt.
Climate	The climate is tropical and humid. The monsoon seasons cool the temperature, but severe storms are rare.
Estimated population	72,500
Capital city	Victoria
Currency	The Seychelles rupee (SRe) has a floating exchange rate and is valued at approximately five rupees to the U.S. dollar.
Time zone	GMT plus four hours
Official languages	English and French are the official Seychelles languages. Creole is also spoken.
Form of government	A directly elected president is chief of state and head of government. The legislative branch is represented by a unicameral Parliament with thirty-three members, each of whom is elected by direct and proportional votes. Presidential and parliamentary elections are held every five years. Elections are expected in March 2003.
Legal system	The legal system is based on English common law and French civil law. Customary law also plays an important role.

Business Infrastructure

Economic stability	★★★	Secrecy	★★★½
Available services	★★★	Cost of entry	★★★★
Political stability	★★½	Other	★★½

Political climate: France first settled Seychelles in 1770. In 1814, the islands were ceded to the United Kingdom under the Treaty of Paris. The country gained its independence in 1976 and adopted a new constitution in 1993, which significantly changed the political climate: two new political parties were created and the government's involvement in day-to-day economic activities was reduced. The current president has been in power since 1977.

Economic climate: Tourism greatly contributes to the Seychelles economy: the industry represents approximately 70 percent of the country's foreign-exchange earnings and it employs nearly 30 percent of the workforce. In the past, fluctuations in the level of tourist activity had a severe effect on the economy. Since 1992, however, the Seychelles government has emphasized diversity by trying to reduce the country's reliance on tourism. Farming, fishing, small-scale manufacturing, and the offshore-services sector have been heavily supported. The financial-services sector, however, came into being only in December 1994, with the enactment of legislation dealing with offshore companies and offshore trusts. In February 1995, the Seychelles International Business Authority (SIBA) was created to administer the new offshore laws.

Financial and professional services: As stated earlier, the financial-services sector in Seychelles is still in its infancy. The number of banks, management companies, and trustee companies is continually increasing, but at the present time, a wide selection of professional services is not available. For example, there are only two licensed trustees in Seychelles.

Communications services: The main island, Mahé, boasts modern satellite communications, but most islands can be reached only by radio telecommunications. Three-day courier services are available through the larger international courier companies, and there exists regular airline services to and from many major European cities, including London, Paris, Frankfurt, and Rome.

Secrecy: It is specifically prohibited to disclose any information pertaining to international trusts, except where required by the Seychelles supreme court in an investigation of certain criminal activities, including drug trafficking and money laundering. To maintain confidentiality, civil court proceedings with respect to international business companies (IBCs) may be heard in chambers rather than in open court.

Exchange controls: The country does maintain exchange controls, but IBCs and international trusts are exempt from such controls.

Residency and/or citizenship requirements: No visas are required to enter Seychelles, but the specific requirements for gaining residency or citizenship are unknown.

Company Information

Types of companies: The Seychelles IBC is best suited to offshore investors looking for a corporate vehicle to hold title to investments and vessels. An IBC cannot carry on the business of banking, insurance, re-insurance, or fund and asset management, and cannot provide the services of a registered office in Seychelles. In addition to IBCs, investors can incorporate international trade-zone (also called free-zone) companies, which can import (and export) products destined for re-export.

Fiscal policy: With the exception of annual licence fees, IBCs are fully exempt from local taxation. An interesting feature of the country's annual licence fees for IBCs is that they remain fixed for the life of the company. For IBCs with an authorized share capital of less than US$5,000, the annual licence fee is fixed at US$100. The fee is US$300 for IBCs with authorized share capital above US$5,000 but below US$50,000; US$1,000 for IBCs with authorized share capital greater than US$50,000; and US$350 for companies with no par value shares. Seychelles is not currently a party to any double-taxation treaties, but the government is trying to negotiate some.

Directors and officers: An IBC must have a minimum of one director. This director may be a natural person or a corporate body, need not be a resident of Seychelles, and may be of any nationality.

Shareholdings and types of shares: Seychelles IBCs may issue bearer shares, registered shares, shares with or without par value, preferred shares, redeemable shares, or shares with or without voting rights.

The authorized capital can be expressed in any currency. An IBC must have at least one shareholder.

Capitalization requirements: IBCs are not subject to any minimum capitalization requirements. The standard authorized share capital is US$5,000.

Meetings and local office: IBCs must maintain an office with agents registered in Seychelles. There are no requirements that corporate meetings be held in Seychelles.

Annual filing requirements: IBCs are not required to maintain accounting records or to file accounts with the Seychelles International Business Authority (SIBA).

Typical time to incorporate: Owing to the high level of automation at SIBA, only a few hours are required to incorporate a company in Seychelles.

Availability of shelf companies: Shelf companies are available.

Estimated Minimum Corporate Fees

Ongoing Fees	
Annual licence fees	US$100.00
Directors' fees	500.00
Office and agency fees	850.00
Accounting fees	500.00
Audit fees	Nil
Annual return filing fees	Nil
Banking fees	300.00
Communication costs	256.00
Total Ongoing Fees	**US$2506.00**

Non-Recurring Fees	
Costs of incorporation (including legal fees)	US$350.00
Costs of establishing an international bank account	Nil
Local duty	Nil
Provision of corporate VISA card	750.00
Total Non-Recurring Fees	**US$1100.00**

Trust Information

Types of trusts: Seychelles international trusts are exempt from local taxation and may be used for a wide variety of purposes, with few exceptions. An international trust cannot hold real property in Seychelles, and the settlor(s) cannot be residents of the country at the time the trust is created.

Effectiveness of the asset-protection trust: Seychelles legislation does not specifically reinforce the asset-protection trust. As a result, fraudulent dispositions by the settlor or his or her insolvency could render the transfers to the trust invalid. However, Seychelles will not enforce the judgement of a foreign court with respect to forced heirship.

Disclosure and registration: In most cases, there are no requirements to disclose the names of the settlor or the beneficiaries. It is against the law to disclose any information relating to an international trust, except if the Seychelles supreme court is investigating criminal activities. A one-time fee of US$100 must be paid to register the trust with the Seychelles government.

Letter of wishes: A letter of wishes may be given to the trustee, but it does not legally bind him or her.

Applicable legislation: Legislation enacted in 1994 provides for the creation of international trusts, removes any restriction on the accumulation of income within the trust, permits trustees and settlors to be named as beneficiaries of the trust, and allows settlors to select the body of law applicable to the trust.

Protector: A protector may be appointed by the settlor or the beneficiaries to oversee their interest in the trust.

Geographic location	Located in Central Europe, Switzerland is a country of 41,293 square kilometres. It is bordered by France, Germany, Austria, Italy, and Liechtenstein.
Climate	Temperate
Estimated population	More than 7 million
Capital city	Bern
Currency	Swiss franc
Time zone	GMT plus one hour, or daylight savings plus six hours
Official languages	The three official languages are French, German, and Italian, but English is also spoken.
Form of government	Federal republic
Legal system	Civil law

Business Infrastructure			
Economic stability	★★★★	Secrecy	★★★★
Available services	★★★★½	Cost of entry	★★★
Political stability	★★★★½	Other	★★★½

Political climate: Switzerland, one of the most stable countries in the world, was founded in 1291. In 1848 it became a federal republic with one central government and twenty-six cantons. Neutrality is the basis for Swiss foreign policy.

Economic climate: Switzerland is one of the world's top financial centres. Despite having a high per capita GDP (above that of most big Western European economies), Switzerland has been experiencing some economic difficulties. In 1997 domestic consumption waned and the country was forced to rely on exports — a situation made worse by a strong franc.

Financial and professional services: Switzerland has an excellent financial infrastructure that includes banks, law and accounting firms, and tax and financial advisers.

Communications services: Switzerland has a superior telecommunications system, with direct dialling for telephone, faxes, and telexes.

It has AM and FM radio stations and television stations. It has one port and many airports, three of which (Zurich, Geneva, and Basel) offer daily flights to Europe and overseas. It also has an efficient rail system.

Secrecy: Despite recently dwindling secrecy regulations, Switzerland is still top notch for bank secrecy, except if criminal activity (i.e., activity illegal in Switzerland) is suspected. Unlike other countries, Switzerland protects banking secrecy in its criminal and administrative laws. Secrecy can't be breached by tax authorities for assessment or evasion, but banks must comply with Swiss court orders that are issued to help governments go after criminals. Bearer shares are permitted.

Exchange controls: There are no exchange controls.

Residency and/or citizenship requirements: At least one director must be a citizen.

Tax treaties: Switzerland has tax treaties with the United Kingdom, the United States, Canada, New Zealand, and Australia.

Company Information

Types of companies: Switzerland offers three types of companies: trading firms, limited liability companies, and corporations. The last is the one most recommended for foreign business activity. Companies must obtain licences for banking, insurance, and transport activities. Although companies must receive approval from the government first, they can own property.

Fiscal policy: There are no real tax breaks for companies seeking to do business in Switzerland. They must pay up to 9.8 percent federal tax, as well as cantonal and municipal taxes of between 17 percent and 35 percent. Some cantons offer tax reductions, and double-taxation treaties may further reduce a company's burden.

Directors and officers: Directors are elected by shareholders. Although the minimum number of directors is one, at least one director must be a citizen. Corporate directors are not permitted and no secretary is required. Annual meetings need not take place in Switzerland.

Shareholdings and types of shares: The minimum number of share-holders is three. Shares can be in registered or bearer form (these have to be paid in full). The par value of shares is 10SFr. Shares with different voting rights can be introduced.

Capitalization requirements: There is a minimum capitalization requirement of 100,000SFr.

Meetings and local office: A local office is mandatory, as is an annual meeting.

Annual filing requirements: Proper financial statements must be prepared within six months of the financial year-end. These must be audited and presented to shareholders at the annual meeting. The shareholders must approve these by electing one or several auditors to go over the statements. At least one auditor must have a registered or branch office in Switzerland.

Typical time to incorporate: Eight to ten days. A deed and by-laws certified by a notary public must be filed with the cantonal commercial register.

Availability of shelf companies: Shelf companies are not available.

Trust Information

As a civil-law jurisdiction, Switzerland has not introduced a counterpart to the Anglo-American concept of a trust. The Swiss court, however, will recognize a trust that has been properly formed in a foreign jurisdiction, especially if the settlor has some connection to that jurisdiction.

Geographic location	The Turks and Caicos Islands are a group of thirty islands in the North Atlantic, between Miami, Florida, and Puerto Rico. Four of the islands — Providenciales, North Caicos, Middle Caicos, and East Caicos — make up more than 90 percent of the country's surface area.
Climate	The climate is tropical and warm. Gulf waters surround the islands.
Estimated population	14,000
Capital city	Cockburn Town (note that Providenciales Island is the financial centre)
Currency	The U.S. dollar is used as currency.
Time zone	GMT minus five hours
Official language	English
Form of government	The government of the Turks and Caicos Islands is based on the traditional British parliamentary model. The legislative assembly is made up of twenty members, thirteen of whom are elected. An executive council is formed from the members of the legislative assembly. A governor is appointed by Queen Elizabeth II and presides over the executive council.
Legal system	Common law modified by a few local laws

Business Infrastructure

Economic stability	★★★★	Secrecy	★★½
Available services	★★★★½	Cost of entry	★★★★½
Political stability	★★★★½	Other	★★½

Political climate: The Turks and Caicos have been under British rule since 1766. The country was a dependency of Jamaica until 1962, and it was annexed to the Bahamas until 1973, after which it became a British crown colony. As a result, the British government is responsible for a number of matters, including military defence and foreign affairs. Only two political parties hold seats in the legislative assembly, and the next elections are expected in April 2004. The governor must submit any local statutory changes to the British government for approval.

Economic climate: Fishing dominates the local economy, but tourism is growing annually. The number of visitors to the islands reached 87,000 in 1996. In addition, the fees derived from offshore financial activities now represent a significant portion of annual government revenues. Most food must be imported, since farming is very limited.

Financial and professional services: The availability of financial and professional services on the islands is limited. However, the growth of the offshore industry should spur the development of this sector.

Communications services: The telecommunications infrastructure in the Turks and Caicos Islands is fair. There are two underwater telephone cables and one satellite earth station. The islands may be reached by a daily ninety-minute flight from Miami.

Secrecy: The Confidentiality Relationships Ordinance of 1979 renders the disclosure or misuse of confidential information a serious criminal offence. The Turks and Caicos Islands have adopted some important anti-trafficking legislation to deter money-laundering, fraud, and other illicit activities.

Exchange controls: There are no exchange controls. Most bank accounts are in U.S. dollars, since that currency is used locally.

Residency and/or citizenship requirements: The local government heavily regulates any persons authorized to operate in the financial-services sector. No other information could be found about specific barriers to becoming a resident or citizen of the islands.

Tax treaties: The Turks and Caicos Islands have not negotiated any bilateral tax treaties, and consequently are not required to divulge any information to foreign taxation or revenue authorities.

Company Information

Types of companies: A number of corporate or business structures are available in the islands, including exempt companies, international business companies (IBCs), limited partnerships, and limited liability companies (LLCs). The exempt company is best suited for international trade and investment.

Fiscal policy: The Turks and Caicos Islands are free from any taxes, including taxes arising from income, capital gains, sales, death, or gifts. Corporations are required to pay an annual registration fee, based on their authorized share capital. The minimum fee is US$300.

Directors and officers: At least two directors are required for exempt companies, but there is no obligation to disclose the names of the directors to any public authority. The directors can be corporate entities and may be of any nationality or country of residence.

Shareholdings and types of shares: All types of shares are permitted, including bearer shares, shares with or without par value, preferred shares, and non-voting shares. A company's memorandum and articles of association, which must be filed with the companies registry, do not have to disclose any specific information about shareholdings, including the names of any shareholders.

Capitalization requirements: There are no paid-in capital requirements, but the standard authorized share capital is US$5,000. There must be at least one shareholder and the company must issue a minimum of one share with par value or one share without par value.

Meetings and local office: Exempt companies are required to maintain a local office and a local registered agent. Once a company has been incorporated, it must advertise the location of its office in the local newspaper.

Annual filing requirements: In the Turks and Caicos Islands, there are no requirements to maintain proper financial accounts or to have those accounts audited. Exempt companies are not obligated to submit an annual information return to any public authority.

Typical time to incorporate: In general, two days are required to incorporate an exempt company, but this process can be accelerated for a fee.

Availability of shelf companies: Shelf companies are available.

Estimated Minimum Corporate Fees

Ongoing Fees	
Annual licence fees	US$300.00
Directors' fees	700.00
Office and agency fees	400.00
Accounting fees	500.00
Audit fees	Nil
Annual return filing fees	Nil
Banking fees	300.00
Communication costs	150.00
Total Ongoing Fees	**US$2350.00**

Non-Recurring Fees	
Costs of incorporation (including legal fees)	US$700.00
Costs of establishing an international bank account	500.00
Local duty	Nil
Provision of corporate VISA card	750.00
Total Non-Recurring Fees	**US$1950.00**

Trust Information

Types of trusts: The most common trusts are asset-protection trusts, short-term trusts (the short life is only to reduce probate fees), and perpetual trusts.

Effectiveness of the asset-protection trust: No specific legislation has been enacted to enforce asset-protection trusts. As a result, the laws governing the setting aside of these trusts are based on common law. This means that a prejudiced creditor need only demonstrate that the settlor could reasonably have known of the existence of the creditor at the time of the transfer. The rule suggests that even debts arising a short time after the transfer of assets to the trust would qualify.

Disclosure and registration: There is no requirement to register the trust deed with any public body: all trust documents remain completely confidential. Even the local government must obtain a court order to view the documents.

Letter of wishes: There does not appear to be any legislation that prevents the use of a letter of wishes. In fact, the Turks and Caicos Islands are rather open to the participation of the settlor in the administration of trust assets, which serves to reinforce our belief that letters of wishes may be used.

Applicable legislation: Local legislation in the area of trusts has been kept to a minimum: the government has enacted only the Trust Ordinance of 1990 and the Trustee Licensing Ordinance of 1992. The former statute provides trustees with guidance in the administration of assets if the settlor has failed to give any instructions. The latter statute controls and regulates which persons may act as trustees. Other legislative highlights include the abolition of the rule against perpetuities and accumulations (trusts can be of unlimited duration) and the termination of a beneficiary's interest upon the insolvency of that beneficiary.

Protector: Local legislation permits the appointment of a protector to ensure that trust assets are administered in accordance with the settlor's wishes.

Geographic location	Vanuatu consists of eighty-three small islands and is situated 2,400 kilometres northeast of Australia and 1,300 kilometres west of Fiji. Its total land surface area is approximately 12,200 square kilometres.
Climate	The climate varies; it's subtropical in the south and tropical in the north.
Estimated population	140,000
Capital city	Port Vila, on the island of Efate
Currency	The currency is the vatu, which is pegged to a basket of other foreign currencies. The approximate exchange rate is US$1:VT110.
Time zone	GMT plus eleven hours
Official languages	Bislama, English, and French are the official languages, although English remains the predominant language of trade and commerce.
Form of government	A republic, Vanuatu has a parliamentary form of government, with a president as head of state and a prime minister elected by Parliament. A single legislature, composed of fifty members, is elected by general suffrage every four years.
Legal system	Common law

Business Infrastructure			
Economic stability	★★★	Secrecy	★★★½
Available services	★★★½	Cost of entry	★★★★½
Political stability	★★	Other	★★½

Political climate: Vanuatu, formerly known as the New Hebrides, was established at the London Convention of October 20, 1906, by agreement of the British and the French. Vanuatu gained its independence in 1980, but the country has a history of political instability. Although Vanuatu has benefited from increased political balance, and is committed to becoming and remaining an important financial centre, it is noteworthy that the country underwent an attempted coup d'état in the spring of 1997.

Economic climate: Vanuatu's economy is stable and its financial policies orthodox. Agriculture and forestry account for roughly 80 percent of the country's GDP. Tourism and financial services also significantly contribute to the local economy.

Financial and professional services: There are more than one hundred banks and trust companies registered in Vanuatu, including some of the fifty largest in the world. In the country's push to become an international offshore financial centre, it has encouraged the work of a range of professionals, including lawyers, accountants, and insurance managers.

Communications services: Port Vila boasts a sophisticated telecommunications infrastructure that includes an earth satellite station. Courier services are available. Direct flights link Port Vila to Australia, New Zealand, and New Caledonia.

Secrecy: Vanuatu imposes criminal sanctions on any person who divulges or forces another person to divulge confidential information. Secrecy is strictly maintained, and the government does not require the registration of directors' and shareholders' names.

Exchange controls: Vanuatu maintains no foreign-exchange controls. Funds may come and go in whichever currency the account holder chooses.

Residency and/or citizenship requirements: Individuals must obtain a permit to become residents of Vanuatu. Skilled and wealthy individuals are usually granted permits, provided they do not have criminal records. Acquiring citizenship is a ten-year process.

Company Information

Types of companies: Vanuatu recognizes four types of companies: local companies, exempt companies, foreign companies, and international companies. Since international companies are better suited for investment activities because of the minimal disclosure and compliance requirements, the information provided below is directed towards this type of company.

Fiscal policy: Although an international company is subject to an annual minimum tax or exemption fee of US$300, no taxes are payable on its net profits. It is immaterial if the profits originate from business income, capital gains, dividends, or interest. There are no taxes on income earned abroad, and no wealth or inheritance taxes. Vanuatu is not a member of any double-taxation agreements and is not required to disclose information to foreign tax authorities.

Directors and officers: The minimum number of directors required for international companies is one. Corporate directors are permitted. The directors may be of any nationality and need not be residents of Vanuatu. International companies can hold their meetings abroad, and there is no requirement to register the names of the directors with the local government. There is no need to appoint a corporate secretary.

Shareholdings and types of shares: Vanuatu is very flexible about the types of shares issued by companies. Bearer shares are permitted. International companies are not required to disclose the names of their shareholders — or, in the case of a trust, of the beneficial owners.

Capitalization requirements: There are no minimum capitalization requirements in Vanuatu. The standard authorized share capital is US$10,000.

Meetings and local office: There is no requirement to hold meetings, annual or otherwise.

Annual filing requirements: International companies are not required to maintain records or to file annual returns.

Typical time to incorporate: Between one hour and one day

Availability of shelf companies: Shelf companies are readily available.

Estimated Minimum Corporate Fees

Ongoing Fees	
Annual licence fees	US$300.00
Directors' fees	650.00
Office and agency fees	550.00
Accounting fees	500.00
Audit fees	N/A
Annual return filing fees	N/A
Banking fees	300.00
Communication costs	247.00
Total Ongoing Fees	**US$2547.00**

Non-Recurring Fees	
Costs of incorporation (including legal fees)	US$1100.00
Costs of establishing an international bank account	325.00
Local duty	N/A
Provision of corporate VISA card	450.00
Total Non-Recurring Fees	**US$1875.00**

Trust Information

Types of trusts: Only the types of trusts permitted under common law (i.e., not legislated) are available in Vanuatu. Asset-protection trusts are not as popular in Vanuatu as they are in other jurisdictions.

Effectiveness of the asset-protection trust: Vanuatu has no specific legislation regarding asset-protection trusts yet. The common-law rules relating to fraudulent dispositions apply.

Disclosure and registration: The trust deed must be stamped, but there is no requirement to file information with the government. The trust deed and the resulting trust are considered private affairs.

Letter of wishes: A settlor can provide his or her trustee with a letter of wishes, but such letters are not legally binding. As long as the wishes do not violate any laws and do not contravene the trust deed, however, the letter will generally be followed by the trustee.

Applicable legislation: The rule against perpetuities is modified to postpone the vesting of property for at least eighty years. Income can be accumulated for up to twenty-one years. Trust legislation is still developing in Vanuatu.

Protector: A protector (often called an appointer in Vanuatu) may be appointed by the settlor to oversee the activities of the trustee. The protector has the power to remove and replace trustees.

Geographic location	Situated in the South Pacific, halfway between Hawaii and Australia, Western Samoa consists of nine islands (two large and seven small).
Climate	Tropical
Estimated population	220,000
Capital city	Apia, on the island of Upolu
Currency	Western Samoan dollar (US$1=WS$2.50)
Time zone	GMT minus eleven hours, or daylight savings minus six hours
Official languages	Samoan (official language) and English (corporate documents)
Form of government	Constitutional monarchy with a native king
Legal system	Common law

Business Infrastructure

Economic stability	★★★★	Secrecy	★★½
Available services	★★★★½	Cost of entry	★★★½
Political stability	★★★★½	Other	★★½

Political climate: Western Samoa belonged to Germany until a United Nations mandate gave the islands to New Zealand in 1914. After the Second World War, it was a UN trust territory until gaining its independence in 1962. Its constitution provides the country with a parliamentary government that combines traditional Samoan social structures and a democratic voting system. Western Samoa holds elections every three years and is very stable politically.

Economic climate: Although it's a South Pacific hub, Western Samoa is a poor country dependent on foreign aid, remittances from families living abroad, and agriculture. In 1987, the government passed extensive offshore legislation to attract business to the country. In the early 1990s, however, a series of natural disasters wiped out the country's infrastructure, as well as its major export crops. Recently, the economy has been improving and tourism developing.

Financial and professional services: Western Samoa has legal, accounting, banking, and financial advisers.

Communications services: Western Samoa has three airports, which offer direct flights to New Zealand, Australia, Hawaii, Fiji, and the Cook Islands. It also has four ports (Apia, Asau, Mulifanua, and Sadelologa). Facsimile, telex, and direct-dialling services are available from most countries. The country has one AM radio station but no television station.

Secrecy: The Western Samoan International Companies Act prevents, by threat of penal sanction, the disclosure of information by officers of an international company or a trust company. The contents of trust deeds and the beneficiaries' names can remain secret. Bearer shares are permitted.

Exchange controls: There are no exchange controls, but the central bank's approval is required for direct investment in Western Samoa.

Residency and/or citizenship requirements: Directors need not be residents, but a secretary must be and the company must be registered in Western Samoa.

Tax treaties: None

Company Information

Types of companies: Three types of companies can carry on business in Western Samoa: domestic companies (governed by the Samoa Companies Order of 1935), international companies, and foreign companies. The last two can be used for offshore ventures. International companies cannot trade with Western Samoans or own real estate in the country. They cannot bank; insure; assure; re-insure; or manage funds, collective investment schemes, trusts, or trustee companies without a private licence. The pieces of legislation governing offshore ventures are the International Companies Act of 1987, the International Trusts Act of 1987, the Offshore Banking Act of 1987, and the International Insurance Act of 1988.

Fiscal policy: International companies registered under the

International Companies Act are not liable for taxes of any kind in Western Samoa. Trusts are not taxed.

Directors and officers: Western Samoan companies require only one director; corporate directors are permitted. The director need not be a resident, but then the company must have a resident secretary or agent.

Shareholdings and types of shares: International companies require only one shareholder. Shares may be registered (in which case, they can be issued partly paid) or bearer (which must be fully paid). Shares may be par value or no par value, and can be issued in most major currencies.

Capitalization requirements: There is no minimum share capital.

Meetings and local office: Meetings may be held anywhere, and resolutions in writing signed by all directors may take the place of a meeting. Telephone meetings are also permitted. A company's office must be registered with a trustee in Western Samoa.

Annual filing requirements: Accounts must be kept either at the registered office or anywhere else the director deems suitable. The audit requirement can be waived, and there is no obligation to file an annual return.

Typical time to incorporate: One day. To incorporate, a company must submit an original and unsigned copy of its memorandum and articles of association, as well as paying a registration fee to the registrar of international and foreign companies. The registrar issues a certificate of incorporation that is renewable every year upon payment of fees.

Availability of shelf companies: Shelf companies are available.

Estimated Minimum Corporate Fees

Ongoing Fees	
Annual licence fees	US$300.00
Directors' fees	N/A
Office and agency fees	N/A
Accounting fees	N/A
Audit fees	N/A
Annual return filing fees	N/A
Banking fees	N/A
Communication costs	N/A
Total Ongoing Fees	**US$300.00**

Non-Recurring Fees	
Costs of incorporation (including legal fees)	N/A
Costs of establishing an international bank account	N/A
Local duty	N/A
Provision of corporate VISA card	N/A
Total Non-Recurring Fees	**N/A**

Trust Information

Types of trusts: Trusts may be purpose, asset-protection, or international trusts. Trustees can add or delete beneficiaries without affecting the validity of the trust.

Effectiveness of the asset-protection trust: The law punishes those who betray internal information about a trust.

Disclosure and registration: There is no requirement to register a trust.

Letter of wishes: N/A

Applicable legislation: The Trustee Companies Act of 1987

Protector: A protector may be appointed.

Notes

1. *Saunders v. Vautier* (1841), 41 Beav. 115.
2. *Sociedad Financiera Sofimeca CA and Others v. Kleinwort Benson (Jersey) Trustees Limited and Others* (13 July 1992).
   See also *Jurgen von Knieriem v. Bermuda Trust Company Limited and Grosvenor Trust Company Limited* (1994), 154 S.C.B.
3. A controlled foreign affiliate is a non-resident corporation whose shareholding structure is such that the taxpayer is a Canadian resident and owns no less than one percent of the corporation, and the taxpayer and persons with whom the taxpayer does not deal at arm's length own no less than 10 percent of the corporation. A controlled foreign affiliate is controlled by one of the following: the taxpayer; four Canadian residents other than the taxpayer; the taxpayer and four other persons resident in Canada; the taxpayer and persons related to the taxpayer; or persons related to the taxpayer.

4. A list of the types of property considered taxable Canadian property was presented in the previous chapter.

5. An adjustment is made for interest discounts and premiums on bonds.

6. Dividends paid out of the capital dividend account are tax-free when paid to Canadian residents; therefore, you should make sure to pay out the dividends from this account before emigrating from Canada.

7. Pension benefits earned while you were a non-resident and not working in Canada are exempt from tax.

8. This includes only the portion of the payment that would have been taxable had the payment been received by a Canadian resident.

9. This includes only the portion of the payment that would have been taxable had the payment been received by a Canadian resident.

10. No withholding taxes apply for copyrights of any artistic works, whether literary, dramatic, musical, or otherwise, except for motion picture films and films or tapes for television use.

11. Withholding taxes apply to the share of income attributable to non-resident beneficiaries, whether paid or credited. See our discussion on Canadian resident trusts.

Index

individual countries
bank accounts in, 150, 160
IBCs in, 23, 150, 161
protection of secrecy in, 150
U.S. government pressure in, 150, 159, 160
cash transfers, 54
Cayman Islands, 150, 160, 161, **207–13**
income taxes in, 149
purpose trusts in, 49
trusts in, 45, 162
Channel Islands, 149, 150. *See also names of individual islands*
charitable trusts. *See* trusts, purpose
cheques
certified (cashier's), 54
and transfer of funds, 53–54, 57
children
as beneficiaries of a trust, 80
dependent, and residency status, 66
transfers of property to, 101
China, People's Republic of, 111 (table)
citizenship, 62–63
civil law, 34–35
claimants. *See* creditors
common law, 33–34
courts of, 33
and residency status, 71–72, 83–85
and trusts, 33–35, 46–47, 80, 162
communications. *See also* Internet
and banks, 52, 56
industry, 29–30
and offshore investment, 164–65
in offshore jurisdictions, 148, 162
company
definition of, 19
subsidiary, 30
con artists. *See* scams
confidentiality. *See* scams; secrecy, protection of

constitutional trust scams, 144
controlled foreign affiliate, 27–28, 73, 156
Convention on Law Applicable to Trusts (1984), 35
conveyances, 46
fraudulent, 35–36, 46, 124–25
Cook Islands, 45, 152, 161, 162, **214–17**
copyright. *See* intellectual property
corporations. *See also* corporations, offshore; IBCs
control of, 71–72, 74–75
definition of, 19–21
directors of, 20–21, 25, 71
dividends from, 8, 20, 21
domestic, 22
employees of, 20–21
equity in, 74–75
exempt, 23, 160
and FAPI rules, 72–75
management of, 20–21
officers of, 20
ownership of, 20–21
and place of incorporation, 72
regular, 22
residency of, 71–72, 123
shareholders of, 20–21
small business, 98
taxation of, 20, 21, 26
withdrawals from, 56
corporations, offshore, 10, 21–23, 123, 160–61
benefits of, 21–22, 26
equity in, 74–75
fees for, 25, 160
uses of, 26–31
cottages and residency status, 85, 126
credit cards
and the Internet, 167
and offshore bank accounts, 52, 55, 57, 159
scams involving, 142
creditors
claims to assets of, 124–25

protection of assets from, 9–10, 11, 45, 46, 47–48, 53
and trusts, 36, 161 (*see also* asset-protection trusts)
crime. *See* trusts, fraud and; money laundering; scams; tax evasion
currency, 14
and bank accounts, 52
and development bonds, 153
foreign, 12, 52
in offshore jurisdictions, 148
Cyprus, 30, 45, 111 (table), 151, **218–21**

debit cards, 52, 57, 159
deductions, tax. *See* tax deductions
deemed disposition, 87–88, 90, 126
deemed residents, 64–66, 72
deferred profit-sharing plans (DPSPs), 80, 101
Denmark, 111 (table)
departure from Canada, 86, 88, 90. *See also* non-resident status
dependants
and residence status, 66, 84, 86
and tax credits, 99
deposit insurance, 159
depreciation, 102
derivative funds, 155
development bonds, 12, 148, 152–54
disclosure, 11–12, 155, 157. *See also* scams
disposition
deemed, 87–88
fraudulent, 35–36, 46, 124–25
dividends
to beneficiaries of trusts, 78–79
of Canadian corporations, 8
corporate, 21
and FAPI rules, 73
from offshore corporations, 13, 24
taxation of, 101, 157
and tax treaties, 24
divorce, 10–11, 45, 101

Dominican Republic, 111 (table)
double taxation, 30–31, 83, 94
double-taxation treaties, 24, 27, 29
DPSPs (deferred profit-sharing plans), 80, 101
dual citizenship, 63
dual residency, 83
dwelling, and residency status, 83–84, 126

e-commerce, 168–69
Egypt, 111 (table)
e-mail. *See* Internet
employment
income from, 103
losses from, 95, 96–97
rules about in offshore jurisdictions, 25
encryption, 56, 166–67
England. *See* United Kingdom
entitlement, absolute. *See* trusts, entitlement to
equitable title. *See* trusts, beneficiaries of
equity, law of, 33–34
equity investments, 5, 12–13, 16–17
equity scams, 141
estate taxes, 8–9, 101
scams to reduce, 143
Europe, 151, 159, 160, 161, 162. *See also names of individual countries*
exchange restrictions, 14, 25
exempt companies, 23, 160
exporting. *See* import/export business

factual residents, 63–64
family allowance, 85, 126
FAPI (foreign accrual property income) rules, 7, 72–75, 169
and beneficiaries of trusts, 80
and IBCs, 27–28, 122–24
purpose of, 73

Philippines, 115 (table)
planning, offshore. *See* offshore
    planning
planning, tax. *See* tax planning
Poland, 116 (table)
ponzie scams, 136
Portugal, 149
power of attorney, 71
prenuptial agreements, 10
prime bank instrument scams,
    137–38
privacy, 47–48. *See also* secrecy,
    protection of
and the Internet, 56, 166–67
property. *See also* capital gains;
    capital losses
    appreciation of, 88–89
    business, 93
    disposition of, 87–88, 92–94,
    97–98
    location of, 93–94
    resource, 93, 102
    scams for encumbering, 141
    taxable Canadian, 88–90, 92–94
property, ownership of
    and capital gains taxes, 29, 68
    through offshore companies, 29
    and residency status, 83–84
    transfer of, 79, 92–94, 101
    and trusts, 42
protector (of a trust), 40, 41,
    43–44, 78, 162
pure trust scams, 144
pyramid scams, 136

Quebec, 14
    legal system of, 34–35
    Pension Plan, 68, 99
    and property transactions, 93
    taxation in, 65, 66

rates of return
    on development bonds, 153
    on offshore investments, 12–13
registered education savings plans
    (RESPs), 101

registered pension plans (RPPs), 90
registered retirement income funds
    (RRIFs), 90, 101
registered retirement savings plans
    (RRSPs), 80, 100, 101, 128–29,
    158
registration (company), 19, 161
regulated industries, 29–30
regulation
    of banks, 57
    of currency, 14
    of gambling, 130–31
    of IBCs, 25
    of investment in offshore
    jurisdictions, 13, 153–54,
    155–56
rental income, 84, 101
    and section 216 election, 102
repatriation of funds, 24
    from intellectual property, 29
    from offshore bank accounts,
    55–56
reporting requirements
    for corporations, 25, 160
    for foreign investments, 155,
    157
    under Income Tax Act, 53
    for property transactions, 92–94
    for withdrawals from bank
    accounts, 55–56
residency rules, taxation. *See also*
    non-resident status; part-year
    residents
    for corporations, 70–71
    in offshore jurisdictions, 25, 161
    personal, 62–69
residency status
    and common law, 71–72, 83–85
    and dwelling, 83–84, 126
resource property, 93, 102
RESPs (registered education savings
    plans), 101
retirement, offshore, 128–30
retirement allowances, 101
retirement trusts, 15
Revenue Canada. *See also* Income

Tax Act; taxes; tax forms; tax
rules
and FAPI rules, 72–75
and GAAR, 75, 156–57
International Taxation Office, 86
and offshore banks, 51
publications, 104–9
and residency status, 63–69,
79–80, 83–87
validity of decisions of, 62
Web site, 105
Revenue Quebec and residency
status, 65, 66
risks, offshore, 12, 51. *See also*
security
Romania, 116 (table)
Royal Bank, 155–56
royalties. *See also* intellectual
property
and offshore holding companies,
29
taxation of, 101
and tax treaties, 24
RPPs (registered pension plans),
90
RRIFs (registered retirement
income funds), 90, 101
RRSPs. *See* registered retirement
savings plans
ruling, advanced, 86–87

Sark, 151
Saunders v. Vautier, 37–38
SBCs (small business corporations),
98
scams
advanced-fee, 136
bankroll/bank-debenture, 140
and confidentiality agreements,
140, 145
credit card, 142
living trust, 143
misuse of valid investment
instruments, 142
money-hiding, 144
Nigeria, 138–40

and non-disclosure statements,
137
passport and titles, 141
prime bank instrument, 137–38
private bank, 142
property encumberment, 141
pure trust, 144
pyramid (ponzie), 136
reasons for success of, 135–36
"secrets" tapes, books, and
seminars, 141
telemarketing, 136–37
tips for avoiding, 145–46
trust, 143–45
upgrade, 141
Web sites about, 142, 146
Scotia Bank, 155–56
Scotland, 34
secrecy, protection of, 25, 27, 45
and bank accounts, 51, 52,
53–54, 55, 148, 151
in the Caribbean, 150
in Europe, 151, 160
and IBCs, 161
laws to enforce, 10, 11, 24, 48,
58, 148, 167
and pressure from outside
governments, 148, 150, 151,
152, 159, 160
in the South Pacific, 152
and trusts, 11, 36, 47–48, 161,
162
"secrets" tapes, books, and
seminars scams, 141
security
and asset protection, 9–10
and development bonds, 153
and the Internet, 56, 166–67
separation, 84. *See also* divorce
settlor, 33, 36–37, 80. *See also*
trustees; trusts
and asset transfers, 124–25
as beneficiary, 79
powers of, 41
as protector, 44
residence of, 41

About the Authors

Dr. Sunny Handa (B.Comm., LL.B., LL.M., D.C.L.) holds a doctorate in laws from McGill University. Handa is a lawyer (a member of the Law Society of Upper Canada) and is counsel to the Canadian law firm of Fasken Martineau. He is also an adjunct professor of law at McGill University, where he specializes in high-technology and intellectual property law. In addition to being widely published in the legal field, Handa has also co-authored three books for a business audience: *Getting Canada Online: Understanding the Information Highway* (Toronto: Stoddart, 1995), *CyberLaw* (Toronto: Stoddart, 1997; Malaysia: Pelanduk Publications, 1998), and *CyberLaw: What South Africans Need to Know about Doing Business OnLine* (South Africa: Ampersand Press, 1999). He is currently working on two legal books — one on communications law and another on copyright law. As a lawyer practising primarily in the areas of international intellectual property and information technology law, he has made the use of offshore structures to benefit from regulatory differences an important focus. For Handa, writing this book was the culmination of a long-standing desire to research and publish a personal guide to offshore legal mechanisms.

Dr. Danielle Miller (B.A., M.A., Ph.D.) received her Ph.D. in comparative literature from the Université de Montréal in 1996 before entering the national program in McGill University's Faculty of Law. Miller has extensive publishing experience in both of Canada's official languages. Her work in comparative studies has led to an interest in globalization and eventually in the economic and taxation systems of various countries. Miller's interest in offshore investing began in earnest in late 1995. She spent the summer of 1996 researching the area while collaborating with a large European firm on a project concerning electronic commerce. She will be completing her articling with McCarthy Tétrault.

Richard Smith (B.Comm., C.A.) is a member of the Institute of Chartered Accountants of Ontario. He is enrolled in the Bachelor of Laws and Master of Business Administration program at the University of Toronto. Prior to returning to university, Smith worked as a chartered accountant for three years with Coopers & Lybrand (now PricewaterhouseCoopers). Throughout his time at Coopers & Lybrand, he acquired a strong knowledge of and interest in the various aspects of taxation. Smith's interest in this project stemmed from his eagerness to explore the complex tax issues surrounding offshore planning.